COASTAL
COMMAND
VS
THE U-BOAT

A complete World War II
"Coastal Command Review"

by Peter G Dancey RAF (rtd)

- Contents -

Preface

Bibliography :

Preface

Although the wartime work of Coastal Command was probably the least publicised of all the RAF's operational command's there is no doubt of the important contribution the Command made to the ultimate victory. The Battle of the Atlantic was a war that was never won, and indeed continued to be fought until the bitter end until VE Day in May 1945. The quest to maintain our supply lines open was a formidable one, the best that could be hoped for was to keep losses down to a manageable level, and there is no doubt that this was achieved by the squadrons of Coastal Command.

Submarines, like ships, are pretty vulnerable to explosives, particularly if the explosives are big enough; but unlike ships, submarines are extremely difficult to find. In the First World War, practically the only way of finding a submarine was by using a ship, not only a slow, costly and very inefficient business but also a dangerous one : the success or otherwise of the mission often depended on who found whom first ! Even as new long-range aircraft were becoming available before the Second World War, German Admiral Doenitz believed his U-Boats could only be sunk by Naval ships. He proclaimed that 'an aircraft can no more sink a submarine than a crow catch and kill a mole'. How wrong he was. Of the 784 enemy submarines sunk during WW II, 429 were due to air action. Of these, 366 were destroyed by land-based aircraft of the RAF, USAAF, US Navy and 63 by aircraft of the FAA.

The most difficult part in sinking submarines is finding them in the first place. This is where the speed and versatility of the airplane is such an important factor, since as is now well known it can search wide areas of the ocean in a comparatively short time. A submariner must live in constant fear that wherever he might be his position could be revealed by a long-range maritime patrol plane. The submarine commander must constantly be on his guard, as there are a number of ways of detecting the presence of submarines, submerged or otherwise.

How did Coastal Command find its U Boats ? Initially of course it was the Mark 1 Eyeball that was used pending the arrival of better devices and the improved 10 cm ASV III radar and Leigh Light. This entailed many monotonous hours gazing down at the sea, which could induce a trance-like condition - which at times could well prove fatal ! The best height for surfaced U-boat spotting was around 1,500-2,000 feet, but this meant a vigilant conning tower look-out might see the aircraft before it saw the U-boat, or at least simultaneously. Since a U-boat could submerge fully in 25 seconds from the sounding of the warning gong, all the aircraft was likely to see was a diving "swirl" and once it was underwater there was nothing to indicate either its depth or direction. If the surfaced U-boat was charging its batteries then it can be detected by radar, or if the airplane happened to be near enough then it could, of course, be seen by the naked eye. Unfortunately without the modern detection aids of today such as sonobouys - dropped into the water to listen for noises sent out from the submarines propellers or internal noise or MAD (Magnetic Anomaly Detectors) detecting disturbance of the earths magnetic field, then once submerged it was a "Scarecrow". Having been alerted, once submerged it was lost to its attacker, it is hardly surprising in the early days, "kills" were few and far between.

As the task became more and more critical, after a temporary lull, while the German U-boat commanders concentrated their efforts off the east coast of America, during the year ending March, 1942, Bomber Command transferred to Coastal Command seventeen squadrons (204 long-range aircraft with crews). These squadrons were supposed to be on loan, but some never ever returned. The struggle to safeguard our shipping went on from day one of the war and continued to the last.

What has often been overlooked about the Battle of the Atlantic, was it was, a constant battle of technology between the two sides, with the Germans arming their submarines heavily with AA weapons to counter the Coastal Command threat, in addition to introducing two new types of torpedo which could be aimed at a convoy from long distance, with the ability to run in and out of the lines of ships in long loops — with the almost certainty they would hit something in the process. This book recalls the constant endeavours of Coastal Command to counter these advances. The airplanes, the equipment, the squadrons, and the men along with the Commands important contribution in respect of Reconnaissance, Photographic and Meteorological Reconnaissance and Air/Sea Rescue duties

In testimony to the brave crews of Coastal Command in WW II and their close co-operation with the Royal Navy throughout, the author relates the following statement made after the war by Lt-Cdr John Bourgat RN.

" I sometimes feel that the magnificent part played by RAF Coastal Command in the late war is not given full recognition by the general public of our country. I speak as a naval officer, and during the war as an officer in cruisers engaged in heavy escort duties with convoys throughout the Atlantic and Northern Seas, and subsequently in command of my own ship, employed frequently in close escort work with convoys of all types. Apart from such effective and spectacular operations by Coastal Command in the Battle of the Bay of Biscay on 27 December, 1943, which I personally experienced as First Lieutenant of HMS *Enterprise* in company with HMS *Glasgow,* and which in my opinion has not been given to the acclaim that is its due. I am reminded of the long hours in convoy work when we depended so greatly and were so fully helped by the Sunderlands and Catalinas flying ahead and around the formation of ships, to give us advance warning of the presence of U-boats, thus enabling us to fully deploy and prepare for the attacks which were bound to come."

ACKNOWLEDGEMENTS

THANK YOU ...

I am deeply grateful to the individuals, organisations, institutions, family and friends who have helped with the research and verification of facts for this book.

Especially to my wife, Carol, for her patience and encouragement and the lend of her 'ears' for the inevitable appraisals, reappraisals and rewrites, and Tony Stiff at Galago Books for his enthusiasm and willingness to see it into print. A special thanks must go to the wartime members of RAF Coastal Command, without whom, of course, there would be no book; Milton Keynes Central Lending Library; Bletchley Park Museum; The RAF historical Branch; Naval Historical Branch; The US Navy Historical Center; Imperial War Museum; The Public Records Office, Kew; and to *Flight International,* for permission to use their copyright *Flight Colour Series.*

Pictures & Illustrations;
Front Cover: ASV I-equipped Short Sunderland flying-boat by *Wilfred Hardy GAvA*
Back Cover: Vickers Warwick ASR Mk I with Mk IA lifeboat under fuselage. Vickers Aircraft Ltd.
Other: Short sunderland on 'moonlight' patrol from original painting by Gp Capt Norman Hoad AFC
Coastal Command B-17 Flying Fortress artwork by *Pete West*

Chapter 1   The (Coastal) Command is Born

In May, 1936, the RAF was completely re-organised giving rise to Training Command under Air Marshal Sir Charles S. Burnett, and on the 14 July, Bomber Command (Air Chief Marshal Sir John M. Steel), Fighter Command (Air Chief Marshal Sir Hugh C. T. Dowding) and Coastal Command (Air Chief Marshal Sir Arthur M. Longmore). AM Longmore had a rather short tenure as AOC-in-C Coastal Command handing over to Air Marshal Philip B. Joubert de la Ferté on 1 September, 1936.

Elevated to Command status from the previous RAF Coastal Area, ADGB (Air Defence Great Britain) organisation set up in 1925, Coastal Command operations patrolling the English Channel started in 1938, using obsolete flying boats. While the 'Battle of the Atlantic' had no real start date, it continued throughout the whole of the war and the only end that can be put to it, is the day Admiral Doenitz ordered his U-boats to surrender on 4 May, 1945. Even then only eight U-boat commanders surrendered immediately, many refused to follow British Admiralty instructions issued on the 8 May, and 221 declined to fly the black flag of surrender and were scuttled in defiance, instead.

Coastal Command established its headquarters at Northwood, near Watford, set up by Air Marshal Sir Frederick W. Bowhill, who also set up the Command Operations Rooms at the same time. Later on promotion to ACM, Sir Frederick Bowhill himself assumed command from Joubert on 18 August 1937. It was to ACM Bowhill that the task fell to take a rather poorly equipped organisation into the Second World War. Although it must be said that by the time of his handover to ACM Joubert who assumed command for a second time on 14 June 1941, that the shrewd and technically astutue Bowhill, had firmly laid the foundations on which Joubert could build for the future. At the start of hostilities there were only three operational Groups and one Training Group :

No. 15 with its H. Q. at Plymouth, Devon, with three and a half squadrons
No. 16 with its H. Q. at Chatham, Kent, with five squadrons
No. 17 with its H. Q. at Lee-on-Solent, a Training Group
No. 18 at Rosyth, Scotland, with nine and half squadrons.

Each Group H. Q. was manned by a joint naval and air staff, sharing the same operations room where contrary to the myth, all worked well together, with no discord between any of the personnel of the two services.

Total Coastal Command strength amounted to 19 squadrons (171 aircraft), of which 10 operated Avro Anson twin-engined light reconnaissance bombers with a maximum speed 178 mph and range of around 250 miles; three with the newly introduced Short Sunderland flying-boats with a maximum speed of 213 mph with an endurance of 12 hours and 2,000-lb payload, two with Supermarine Stranraers, two were equipped with Vickers Vildebeest biplane torpedo-bombers long past their prime, and there was one obsolescent SARO London unit. The most up-to-date type being one squadron of American Lockheed Hudsons with a top speed of 246 mph and a patrol endurance of six hours.

Coastal Command Group - Area's of Responsibility

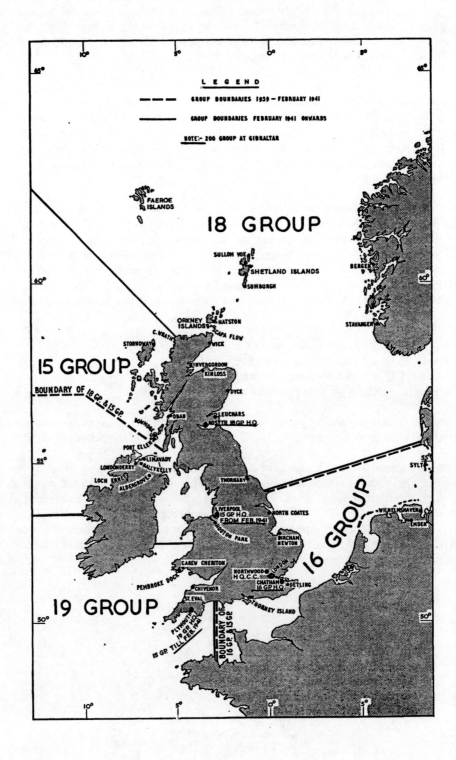

An indication of the weakness of the new Command at this time, is highlighted by the fact that more than half the units operated the ubiquitous Avro Anson, which although it served the air force well in numerous roles for almost a quarter of a century; it was less than suitable for Coastal Command's needs in 1939. Indeed, when its military career began on 6 March, 1936, with No. 48 Squadron; six days later the Air Ministry issued Air Ministry Order (AMO A53), warning :

1. The Anson is a civil* type of aircraft adapted for service purposes and is therefore restricted to the type of flying allowed within the normal civil category.
   * (Avro 652 six-passenger airliner)

2. The following instructions are therefore to be observed in flying the Anson :
   (i) the aircraft must not be subjected to violent manoeuvres at any speed...
   (ii) An air speed indicator reading of 170 knots must not be exceeded in any condition of flight.
   (iii) No attempt to spin the aircraft is permitted.
   (iv) The engine speed for continuous cruising must not exceed 2,100 rpm...

In addition with an armament of only one .303-in machine gun and another in a turret behind, it was not armed for combat. Its bomb-load of just four 100-pounders, rendered it almost totally useless for U-boat attacks. But even worse was its limited range which prevented it spanning the North Sea which it was to patrol; leaving a gap of about 50 miles between the extreme limit of its range and the Norwegian coast.

Note : The Avro Anson was the first airplane to attack a U-boat on 5 September, 1939.

In reality these aircraft enabled the Command to do little more than provide coastal patrols and air cover to the deep-sea convoys within range of the UK bases. Indeed in these early days often anything available that could fly was pressed into service with the Command, including D.H. Tiger Moths and Hornet Moths that were employed on coastal patrols off the east coast. Some additional resources were afforded by way of four squadrons of Bristol Blenheim F.I fighters for patrols over the North Sea, and personnel of No.10 Squadron RAAF, which was working up in Britain on RAF Sunderlands, who on the outbreak of war, on receipt of their own aircraft on 11 September, 1939, were promptly transferred to Coastal Command. Later Boeing B-17 Flying Fortresses and Consolidated B-24 Liberators were received to operate alongside the Lockheed Hudsons in protecting the convoys.

The weapons with which the aircraft were at first equipped were totally inadequate for the task of destroying U-boats. The Ansons could only carry 100-lb bombs, which with the aircraft lacking a proper bomb-sight, if they flew low in an attempt to hit their elusive targets were as dangerous to themselves as the enemy. At least one Anson and two FAA Sea Skuas were destroyed by their own bombs in September, 1939, alone. Nevertheless on 5 September, 1939, the first airplane to attack a U-boat was an Avro Anson. The inadequacy of the anti-submarine weapons available was uncomfortably demonstrated on 3 December, 1939, when a 100-lb Mk III anti-submarine bomb was dropped in error by one of the Ansons on a British submarine, HMS *Snapper,* and although the weapon struck the boat at the base of its conning tower the pressure hull was undamaged. Between September 1939 and May 1940, only one attack resulted in a sinking. This occurred on 30 January 1940, when *U-55* having been attacked by a surface convoy of escorts, having exhausted her batteries, was eventually helped on her way to the bottom by a Short Sunderland flying-boat of No. 228 Squadron dropping her 250-lb bombs, after the U-boats captain had given the order to scuttle and abandon her. A shared Naval and Coastal Command "kill", with a little help from the U-boat crew.

The 250-lb and 500-lb Mk III bombs carried by the Sunderlands were equally ineffective unless they exploded within six to eight feet of the U-boats pressure hull, this degree of accuracy virtually impossible in the absence of a good low-level bomb sight. Even the Lockheed Hudson which had entered Coastal Command service in 1939, the only maritime aircraft with a bomb-release that could lay a stick of bombs, depended for aiming on the Mk IX bomb sight, which required a steady run in on the target, at a height not below 3,000 feet. At this time this type of attack posed little threat to a manoeuvring U-boat and it was only later when the depth-charges were modified for air-drop did they prove more effective.

The first actual U-boat "kill" *(U-31)* by a British aircraft was made by a Bristol Blenheim of No. 82 Squadron Bomber Command, on 11 March, 1940. Coastal Command itself having to wait until the 3 July, to make its first "kill", when a Short Sunderland of No.10 (RAAF) Squadron sank *U-26.* This in part due to the German Navy having only a dozen or so of its 57 U-boats of modern design at sea in 1939, with 32, and 14 of its older types too small for operations in the Atlantic. Albeit another 79 were being built or on order. In reality many of the 'modern' designs were plagued with teething troubles, which kept them in dock for long periods, as an adequate labour force had not been allocated for U-boat repair. This meant rather fortuitously for Coastal Command and its inadequate resources, rarely more than six or eight U-boats were in their designated areas of operations at the same time, in fact at times there were only between three and five, and sometimes even fewer. Even so, on the day war was declared, there were seven or eight U-boats already on station to the west of the British Isles - their first "kill" the British liner *Athenia* sunk the same day.

Already in 1939, Britain had lost 221 ships, 53 in September, 46 in October, 50 in November and 72 in December, of which 114 were sunk by U-boats or mines laid by U-boats. In the same period the German Fleet lost nine U-boats, six sunk by the Royal Navy. The losses although not disastrous were the cause of some concern to Admiral Doenitz, Commander of the U-boat Fleet as at this time until mid-1940 U-boat production averaged only two per month. Until mid-1940 some twenty-seven U-boats were lost, with only twenty new replacements received. From this point of view it can be considered that initial operations against the U-boat were successful.

The first concerted operations involving the U-boat fleet came with the German invasion of Norway on 9 April, 1940. Thirty-one U-boats were available for operations at this time, and they made over thirty attacks on Allied shipping including battleships and troop transports. Luckily the gods were on the side of the Allies, for the Germans the attacks were an unmitigated disaster. Nearly all the torpedos fired failed to explode on their targets or ran underneath them. It appeared the magnetic fuses were disabled by the geophysics in northern territorial waters, but also the mechanical fuses were faulty as were the depth-charge devices on a variety of weapons. So serious were these problems that on 17 April, all the U-boats were withdrawn from the campaign.

Meanwhile the UK had problems of its own, in particular Coastal Command, who had just received the Saro Lerwick twin-engined monoplane flying-boat in June 1939, and the Blackburn Botha strike plane, which was intended to replace the Anson. Both types were complete failures, the Lerwick in particular had some unpleasant handling characteristics, which were never cured, and several of the twenty-one built were lost in accidents. The Botha was seriously underpowered and indeed saw service with only one front-line squadron No. 608, completing only 308 sorties when all were subsequently redeployed on training duties. These failures were indeed far reaching, involving Shorts in resurrecting its Sunderland flying-boat production lines, when it should have been producing Stirling bombers. The Botha maritime strike plane having been banished to training duties was declared obsolete in August, 1943, and withdrawn from use completely in 1944.

Even more serious was the Battle of France and that countries capitulation, which meant the Germans were able to operate with impunity all down the Atlantic coast from Norway to Spain. Ultimately this saved the U-boats a considerable amount of time on transiting to their designated operating areas in the Atlantic and therefore they were able to spend much longer periods on patrol. This in itself represented an effective 22% increase in U-boat strength as well as affording the Germans such excellent facilities in French ship yards to maintain the U-boat fleet, the first of which arrived at Lorient on 7 July, 1940.

The table below, from Sir Maurice Dean's *The RAF and Two World War's* summarises the number of U-Boats deemed operational in the period September, 1939 to May, 1945. Figures from other sources purport to disagree, although the basic ratios remain very similar. The figures include all six types of U-boats used throughout this period.

Month/Year	1939	1940	1941	1942	1943	1944	1945
January		33	23	89	214	170	155
February		34	22	101	221	167	156
March		31	30	111	231	164	156
April		31	30	119	237	161	150
May		23	40	128	239	157	126
June		26	47	130	218	181	
July		29	60	140	209	180	
August		28	60	152	178	151	
September	42	31	74	169	167	146	
October	49	26	75	192	177	139	
November	38	25	81	205	163	148	
December	38	22	86	203	163	152	

Meanwhile, the total inadequacy of the ordnance available to Coastal Command and the total lack of operational success, made the powers that be realise a far more potent weapon was needed, to counter the threat to Allied shipping. As is usual, lessons learnt in WW I, when it was generally concluded to sink a submarine would need a bomb with 300-lb of H.E. giving an all-up weight of around 550-lb and a impact or delay fuse to detonate the weapon around 40 feet below the sea surface, were overlooked. Nevertheless, operational weapons research scientists had observed that more U-boats were destroyed while diving and that a kind of depth-charge was needed. Fortunately, an Air Commodore Huskinson was on the Ordnance Board, and although he had been blinded by a bomb explosion during the 1940/41 Blitz, he and some naval colleagues produced the Torpex-filled depth charge with a shallow 'pistol'. It was to prove to be a much more practical weapon than the Amatol-filled depth charge set to explode at a depth of at least 50 feet then in use.

The difficulties of aiming any sort of weapon at a crash diving submarine in the rough waters and weather encountered in the North Atlantic were realised, and cameras were fitted to the tail of ASW aircraft to take pictures of the dropping depth charges as they straddled the target U-boat, and through Operational Research studies, data was made available, that led to the design of a low-level bomb-sight. The cameras also revealed that the weapons dropped, being generally cylindrical in shape, often bounced along the wave tops before sinking. The solution to that problem involved fitting concave noses and spoilers to the charge and a tail that would act like a rudder, and throw the weapon sideways on hitting the water. This also overcame the problem where a number of the older type depth charges were breaking up on hitting the water unless dropped from below 300 feet. With the inherent inaccuracies of radio altimeters of the day, meaning a night depth-charge attack often created a real risk of the airplane flying into the sea.

By the end of May 1940, fourteen U-boats had been destroyed by the Royal Navy, five had been lost due to other causes, one had been sunk by the FAA and one, as already mentioned was claimed by Coastal Command. The inadequacies of Coastal Commands inventory both in range and offensive armament, were quite debilitating with the best it could hope for, was to force surfaced U-boats to dive. The new bases available to the Germans on the French coast meant a ever rising toll of Allied shipping was lost in the Western Approaches and 153 vessels were lost in the period July to September for the loss of only five U-boats. Although this was only the first of a number of low points the Allies would experience in the Battle of the Atlantic.

At this time most of the U-boats had a maximum speed of around 8 knots when submerged, but this reduced to only 4 knots if the boat was to achieve its maximum submerged range of 80 miles. For this reason they spent a good deal of time on the surface. By day of course this exposed them to discovery by reconnaissance aircraft ; but at night they were reasonably safe, because without airborne surveillance radars that became available later, the chances of detection at night by the few patrols flown, were slim. In addition, asdic, which the Royal Navy had invested heavily in, during the inter-war years was unable to detect surfaced U-boats. For these reasons they normally operated at night and made their attacks on the surface. At this time it was a losing battle for Coastal Command. The range of the airplanes in use was totally inadequate, the flares used for illumination were inadequate and their was no others means available of illuminating a target for an attack to be made.

As the Operational Research Unit set up by AM Bowhill, strove to find technical solutions to many of these problems the sinkings continued to rise and by October, 1940, ships were lost at the rate of two per day. Particular heavy losses were experienced at the end of the month, when 38 merchant vessels were lost in three days and two nights. This was made even worse when the liner SS *Empress of Britain,* sailing from the Middle East to Liverpool in the north-west of England, was damaged by a Focke-Wulf Fw 200C-1 Condor reconnaissance-bomber and then sunk by a U-boat.

Ex-WW I U-boat commander, forty-nine year old Admiral Karl Doenitz, *Fuhrer der U-boote,* later Grand Admiral and Commander-in-Chief of Naval Forces was a dedicated naval officer, he was determined and ruthless, at the same time he was also highly professional and flexible in the use of the resources available to him. It was not long before Focke Wulf Fw 200 Condor long-range reconnaissance planes with an operational radius of 1,000 miles began to fly reconnaissance sorties from their bases in western France.

Although available in only small numbers (280 of all variants built), the four-engined Focke-Wulf Fw 200C-1 recce-bomber had a range of 2,150 miles and could carry a bomb-load of over 2,750-lbs, and posed a considerable threat at this time. The first military variants had become available to the Luftwaffe in early 1940, with Groups 1 and 3 of KG 40 based in Bordeaux-Merignac and Trondheim-Vaernes. Later operating from other newly occupied bases in Norway, Denmark and France. The Condors were able to make sweeps deep into the Atlantic, where they could launch their own attacks on shipping and/or direct U-boats on to designated targets. In May, 1940, Condors claimed 48 ships sunk, three times as many as were sunk by U-boats during the same month. In the months of August and September, they sank 90,000 tons of Allied shipping and between 1 August, 1940 and 9 February, 1941, a total of 363,000 tons. The C-1 was later supplemented by the Fw 200C-3 in the summer of 1941, with a strengthened fuselage, the armament was increased and uprated engines increased its bomb-load to over 4,000 lb. Another important variant, the FW 200C-4, introduced early in 1942, carried a variety of radar detection equipment with the antenna in the nose. A few of the later models carried two radio-controlled Henschel Hs 293 missiles, along with a Fw 200C-8 which saw very little service. The Condor became less effective in 1943, as convoy anti-aircraft defences improved and Bristol Beaufighter long-range fighter patrols intensified, and by 1944, they began to be withdrawn from maritime operations and were re-assigned to transport duties.

In November, 1940, shipping losses to U-boats fell to 32 and remained at that level for the next three months. There were four main reasons for the drop, which of course at the time the British were unaware. First, following the intense operations at the end of October, most of the U-boat fleet returned to port to rearm and in some cases for refit. Second, a number of U-boats were withdrawn from operational service to be used to train new crews for the new submarines expected from the German shipyards in the Spring of 1941. Third during September, 1940, 29 U-boats were transferred from the Atlantic to the Mediterranean, with the Germans increased concern with regards to operations in this theatre. Eighteen of those transferred actually arrived. Five were sunk en-route and another six were so badly damaged they abandoned the attempt. The fourth reason was due, at last to increased patrol activity by maritime patrol airplanes of Coastal Command. In addition this increase in maritime patrol activity forced a change in U-boat patrol patterns which had the effect of reducing the time they spent in their operational areas.

Luftwaffe Focke-Wulf Fw 200 Condor Recce-bomber

At the same time the U-boats began to employ new tactics devised by Doenitz. While it has already been said it is difficult to say exactly when the Battle of the Atlantic began, already in 1940, by June, sinkings of British, Allied and neutral ships amounted to 140 vessels — 585,496 gross tons. Of this already frightening total, aircraft accounted for 105,193 tons, and U-boats for 284,113 tons. In July the total was 386,913 tons equivalent to 105 ships. The slight fall in U-boat enemy shipping sinkings, on 17 August, 1940, convinced Hitler, it was time to implement the "Doenitz system" or "wolf-pack" tactics.

The "Doenitz system", consisted of three distinct component parts :
1. Intelligence; knowledge of convoy movements and positions, sometimes derived from air reconnaissance (Fw 200 Condors), but usually by *B-Dienst* (German Intelligence) and the penetration of the British and Allied Mechanical Ship (BAMS) Code,where intercepted information supplied to U-boat H.Q. was relayed immediately to the relevant U-boats.

2. To shadow the discovered convoy by one or more U-boats on the surface in daylight — in good visibility it was possible to see a convoy's smoke 30 to 40 miles away; in bad visibility a U-boats hydrophones could pick up a convoy's sound up to 20 miles away

3. On instructions from German Naval H.Q., - but *only* on receipt of such instructions - a combined night attack by the whole "pack" of U-boats in the vicinity should be made, either a submerged or surface attack, according to the prevailing circumstances.

It was this system that was used with minor variations for attacking shipping convoy's until 1944. Its nerve centre was at first situated at Lorient, France, but moved to Paris in March, 1942. Its weak point was the volume of wireless telegraphy (W/T) traffic passing between the U-boats or reconnaissance aircraft and the shore-based Command in Paris. It was realised should the day come that British Intelligence was able to read the U-boat ciphers as the *B-Dienst* was reading the BAMS Code, then the tables would turn. Which eventually thanks to the "Y" Service at Bletchley Park, Bucks, it did.

The change in *modus operandi* by the Germans and their submarines in February, 1940, led to a re-organisation in Coastal Command. As now it was the Western Approaches that were of prime concern rather than the North Sea. No 15 Group headquarters moved up from Plymouth to Liverpool, to carry on the battle, while No. 19 Group was formed at Plymouth facing the South-Western Approaches and the Bay of Biscay, where most of the U-boat activity would occur in 1943. No. 19 Group was co-located with the Headquarters of the RN C-in-C Western Approaches, an arrangement that would prove fortuitous, when the crucial battles began. But still, up to September, 1941, Coastal Command aircraft following 245 U-boat attacks could claim only 1 "kill" , 1 surrender, and three destroyed in collaboration with the Royal Navy, and a possible 12 damaged. Nevertheless in spite of Admiral Doenitz initiatives the last four months of 1941, had shown a shift in favour of the Allies in the War at Sea. Which, apart from the greater involvement of the U.S. Navy in convoy escort duties could be attributed to four main reasons; - first from June, 1941, onwards German U-boat W/T was increasingly intercepted and de-ciphered by Bletchley Park, with a result convoys could be routed away from areas of high U-boat activity. Second, H.F. radio detection equipment was becoming more readily available for use at sea and on land, making it possible to get accurate "fixes" on the position of the submarines radio transmission, even if extremely brief. Third, ASV radar equipment was improving and at the same time maritime radars for shipping was being introduced. The fourth reason that sometimes gave rise to over optimistic views on the success of the U-boat campaign was a further change in German U-boat dispositions. This was implemented in June 1941, when coincident with the attack on Russia, Hitler required U-boats be deployed to the Arctic and to the Baltic, leaving at one stage only 8 to 12 U-boats on station in the Atlantic. Then, during August 1941, 10 U-boats were sent to the Mediterranean in an effort to secure German lines of communication to North Africa, and 15 more were deployed to a point of high Allied shipping activity off Gibraltar. The net result was that for a time U-boat activity in the North Atlantic all but ceased, just when unbeknown to the Germans of course, there was grave concern in Britain how long the serious losses in the Atlantic could be absorbed without seriously damaging the nations means to continue to fight the war against the Axis Powers. Coming as it did, soon after Hitler's decision to postpone his plans to invade Britain (Operation *Sea Lion*), probably the second tactical blunder by the German High Command in two consecutive years.

This was tempered to some degree, by the Allies, Britain in particular, failure to bomb the re-enforced concrete pens for the U-boat fleet being constructed in the French ports. Had attacks been mounted at this time it is possible more damage might have been inflicted on the boats themselves as well as the structures, which from the end of 1941 onwards were almost impenetrable.

In the meantime the Doenitz system had been all to effective, and the success of the 'wolf-packs' whereby the U-boats often attacked at night on the surface, being intimately linked by W/T communication between the submarines and their base commanders, who supported by the *B-Dienst* in penetrating British naval and merchant shipping codes, for a while gave the German Navy a high degree of tactical long-range battle control unparalleled in the history of war. Sinkings of ships rose steadily and alarmingly (over one million tons in March and April 1941) so that Churchill felt obliged on 6 March, 1941, to issue a Battle of the Atlantic directive requiring the RAF to concentrate on objectives related to this battle.

The directive was long and comprehensive but included the following main points:
1. We must take the offensive against the U-boat and Focke-Wulf wherever we can and whenever we can. The U-boat at sea must be hunted, the U-boat in the building yard or in dock must be bombed. The Focke-Wulf and other bombers employed against our shipping must be attacked in the air and in their nests...

3. All the measures approved and now in train for the concentration of the main strength of Coastal Com mand upon the North-Western Approaches, and their assistance on the East Coast by Fighter and bomber Commands, will be pressed forward...

6. The Admiralty will have the first claim on all short-range AA guns and other weapons that they can mount upon suitable merchant ships plying in the danger zone...

7. We must be ready to meet concentrated air attacks on the ports on which we specially rely (Mersey, Clyde and Bristol Channel). They must therefore be provided with a maximum defence...

Coastal Command were faced with a number of problems, not least the operational short-comings of the Saro Lerwick which it had hoped would serve in large numbers and lessen the burden on the limited number of Short Sunderlands available at the time, and the inability to arrange for increased orders and advanced delivery of Consolidated Catalina's from the United States. At one time, it looked as though Coastal Command might be absorbed into the Royal Navy and run as a separate Naval Air Service. This, as a result on 4 November, 1940, of the First Lord of the Admiralty, A. V. Alexander, writing a memorandum detailing Coastal Command's need for, "1,000 airplanes in operation at the earliest possible moment". In his estimation a minimum of 826 shore-based naval co-operation airplanes were needed in home waters — which, with the Command now having twenty-eight squadrons with 461 aircraft, this left a shortfall of about 400 and an additional overseas deficiency of about 480. Of the 26 Coastal Command squadrons only around 281 aircraft were available on any given day. The two attached FAA squadrons, with an establishment of just 18 aircraft only seven were usually available. Total Coastal Command operational strength at any time amounted to no more than 305 aircraft, which in addition to the U-boat offensive, was called on for surveillance on enemy shipping, reconnaissance for the RN, an offensive against German coastal shipping, support for the Arctic convoys carrying supplies to Russia, photo reconnaissance and ASR. At the same time in November, 1942, RAF Gibraltar came into existence placed directly under the control of Coastal Command.

At a meeting of the Defence Committee, chaired by Winston Churchill and with the Minister of Aircraft Production, Lord Beaverbrook present, it was Beaverbrook who proposed the Navy should absorb Coastal Command to the dismay of Alexander, who was merely trying to obtain more resources for a part of the RAF which, as he saw it, were not getting all the help they might, from members of the Air Staff. Churchill quite properly tendered a word of caution, adding that, "it would be a poor economy to duplicate training grounds or set up competition between the services in the market for aircraft. This said, with the First Sea Lord Admiral of the Fleet, Sir Dudley Pound, reminding the meeting of its original business : the need to strengthen Coastal Command and following a Defence Committee enquiry, that reminded there should be no repeat of the First World War, when the RNAS expanded at the expense of the RFC, and further interjection by Churchill, the proposal was dropped. The final conclusions published in a joint report on 9 March, 1941, gave rise to what became known as Coastal Command's "Charter". The main point being, the change in the provision of men and machines would not lead to a net increase in resources, in fact unbeknown at the time, it was eventually to be improved technology that would have the greatest influence on the situation.

In the interim, short and mid-term programmes were agreed by the two services. In the short term Coastal Command was to receive a squadron of Vickers Wellington fitted with "long-range (12 miles) ASV II" radar, a squadron of Bristol Beaufort torpedo-bombers were to replace the Vildebeests, and a long-range squadron of Bristol Beaufighters, with the establishment of the long-range fighter units to be increased from 16 to 20 airplanes. This representing an increase of one and half squadrons to the battle order. Furthermore the anticipated arrival of 57 of the American Consolidated PBY-5 Catalina flying-boats, with their increased range (4,000 miles) and endurance (17.6 hours) promised to add another four squadrons in 1941, with a total increase of 15 squadrons by June, 1941.

Even with the acquisition of 50 WW I-vintage American destroyers in September, 1940, naval convoy escort was totally inadequate, with rarely more than three vessels in attendance. Air escort provided by Coastal Command was a help but was of no avail at night, when except for a palliative patrol on a moonlit night, they were not normally flown. The Command used its tactic designed to combat submerged attack by day, consisting of patrolling a "box" 15 miles wide ahead of the convoy, and 15 miles across either side of its bow. This form of escort with the merchant ships well in view, was considered essential in maintaining the morale of the merchant seamen, but the shortage of aircraft meant that no long-range cover could be deployed.

From the outset it was the aerial mine that became an important weapon for the Command, when it joined with Bomber Command in its quest to lay an average of 1,000 mines a month. The mining operations delayed and damaged or sank a number of submarines. They were a great nuisance when laid in the Baltic, where they caused constant delays and difficulties for the Germans, with regards to submarines sea trials and crew training. Mines laid by Coastal Command aircraft were also effective in slowing up ships carrying vital supplies of iron ore for Germany from Scandinavia and Spain. And German troop transports in the Baltic were also delayed and hindered by British aerial mines. The most important single achievement was probably the damaging of the German battleship *Gneisenau* when she escaped with the *Scharnhorst* from Brest up the English Channel in February, 1942.

In Europe, as in the Pacific, there are no valid statistics available of the damage inflicted on enemy ships by aerial mines. However, ACM Harris, claimed that "during the whole period of the war one vessel is known to have been sunk or damaged for every fifty mines that were laid". As an approximation this statement may be true although it cannot be substantiated by official documentation. Nevertheless it has been estimated that in the last year of the war, over one-third of all men in the German Navy were employed in mine-sweeping and escort duties. In September, 1944, the Naval Liaison Officer of the Luftwaffe Operations Division in the Baltic is quoted as saying", "Without training in the Baltic and safe escort through coastal waters and the routes to and from operations in mid-ocean, there can be no U-boat war. Without freedom of movement in the Baltic we cannot use transport in coastal waters. We no longer command the sea routes within our own sphere of influence, as is shown by the day- and week-long blocking of shipping routes in the Baltic Approaches".

The introduction of twelve ASV radar equipped Lockheed Hudsons that were replacing the Ansons did little to alleviate the Command's problems as the range of the radar was only three miles, but it did pose a threat when used at night against a surfaced submarine tracking a convoy under the cover of darkness. The main drawback of this equipment (apart from its size and weight) was the volume of short-range signals which it picked up from the sea's surface - commonly known as "surface clutter" - especially in choppy sea conditions. Only by flying very low at around 200 feet, could a real target be distinguished from the "clutter", with a maximum range of three and half miles detection, down to half a mile. The equipment was always unreliable and there was no means of illuminating the target. Nevertheless better things were to come and in the spring of 1940, an order was placed for 4,000 improved centimetric ASV III sets. The ASV III bringing a more powerful transmitter and more sensitive receiver, promising an improved detection range. More importantly perhaps having been designed and engineered from the outset for mass production; it was much more robust and reliable than its predecessor. But this was the future, for now, Coastal Command were forced to "soldier on" with its ASV I sets, too few depth-charges, too few aircraft and too few trained crews. A degree of success was achieved with what resources were available by aircraft flying from Iceland, Scotland and Northern Ireland leading to the U-boats moving farther south, to the west coast of Africa. This move soon countered by basing Short Sunderland flying-boats and Lockheed Hudsons at Freetown, Sierra Leone. The Fw 200 Condor threat lessened as long-range Bristol Beaufighters began to enter service, and Hawker Sea Hurricanes were used as catapult fighters on convoy merchant ships to drive them off. The fighter could be launched when a Condor was picked up on radar and at the end of the sortie the pilot could take to his parachute and wait to be picked up by the convoy.

Early catapult fighters were manned by FAA crew, but in May, 1941 the RAF formed the Merchant Ship Fighter Unit at Speke, Liverpool. The first mission flown on 3 August 1941, by Lt R. Everett, from a naval catapult ship brought a Fw 200 Condor down. The catapult-armed merchantmen (CAM-ships) continued in use until July 1943, when they were superseded by merchant aircraft carriers (MAC-ships). Although the number of operational launches from CAM-ships were few, most resulted in a "kill", and although hazardous, were an expedient means of convoy protection at a time when carriers were not available.

By the end of 1940, it had become clear Britain was losing the war in the Atlantic, with 1,281 British, Allied and neutral ships, amounting to 4,745,033 gross tons of shipping lost of which the U-boats had accounted for 585 ships (2,607,314 tons). For the loss of only 32 U-boats in sixteen months, two a month ! Statisticians of the *Kreigsmarine* estimated that taking account of the speed at which the Allies were building ships, U-boats would need to sink more than 700,000 tons per month. In the same period Coastal Command had lost 323 aircraft, although 40 per cent had been lost on long-range reconnaissance missions of German naval ports and units. Its inventory now included maritime Vickers Wellingtons, A.W. Whitleys, Bristol Beauforts and Northrop N3PB seaplanes, in addition to most of the basic types already mentioned. Personnel, air and ground crew totalled around 28,000.

Following the debacle in April, 1940, when the German forces attacked Norway and Denmark at the same time, with the FAA struggling to provide air cover for the British and Norwegian forces, with its Blackburn Sea Skua, Gloster Sea Gladiator and Fairey Swordfish biplanes, in the second half of 1940, and the early months of 1941, Air Marshal Bowhill, decided to meet the problems head-on. He decided it would be necessary to do something effective with regards to the "Atlantic Gap" and as such No. 30 Wing in Iceland with Battles, Sunderlands and Hudsons was formed, to be joined later by the highly effective No. 330 Norwegian Squadron with its Northrop Seaplanes. This move did help to narrow this critical U-boat hunting-ground to some extent.

It is of interest to examine No. 330 Squadrons operations at this time, in their endeavours to close the "Gap". The squadron formed at Corbett Camp, Fossvaegur, Reykjavik, Iceland, as the first Norwegian unit in the RAF battle order on 25 April 1941, from Norwegian naval personnel under C.O. Cdr H. A. Bugge, Royal Norwegian Navy. On 19 May 1941, the freighter *Fjordheim* arrived from Canada, with eighteen Northrop N-3PB three-seat single-engined patrol bombers which had been offered to Britain by Norway for maritime patrol duties. Following assembly of the aircraft and work-up the units first patrol as No.330 Squadron Coastal Command occurred on 23 June, when Lt Stanserg and crew flew a night convoy escort. Having been declared operational the C-in-C Coastal Command inspected the squadron on 11 July 1941,and on the 20 July, a detachment of three aircraft ("B" Flight) was based at Akureyri on the north coast. By August 1941, the squadron was flying over 40 patrols a month, with the first contact with the enemy made on 27 August, when Quartermaster Helgesen in GS-A depth-charged a U-boat, although with little effect, and the following day Quartermaster Holdo attacked *U-570* with similar results as it was under escort to Iceland, having surrendered two days earlier to a No. 269 Squadron Lockheed Hudson. On 11 September "C" Flight was established at Budareyri, on the east coast.

All three flights continued patrols throughout the winter but not without loss. The losses in the main, due to the atrocious winter weather. In 1942, operations were scaled up in support of the North Atlantic and Arctic convoys, and on 25 April the C.O. and his crew were lost whilst on patrol in Northrop GS-A. Three days later the squadrons first aerial engagement came when Quartermaster Buer of "B" Flight engaged a Focke Wulf Fw 200 Condor reconnaissance type which was attacked and destroyed. As new C.O. Cdr Brinch assumed control the squadron was now flying more than 100 sorties a month, and in June the first two of six Consolidated Catalina G.R.3 flying-boats arrived to supplement the hard-pressed Northrops. The new aircraft immediately increasing the squadrons operational capabilities, with the first Catalina patrol flown by Lt Abildsoe and his crew on 21 July,in FP526, although ironically it was "B" Flights Northrops that had contact with a further two long-range reconnaissance Fw 200 Condors in the month.

The squadron continued its patrols throughout the summer albeit little was seen of the enemy until the 9 October, when Lt Bulekin of "C"Flight attacked and damaged a three-engined six-seat Blohm und Voss "Flying Clog" BV138 reconnaissance flying-boat with the aircraft left to continue on its way with an engine ablaze. By this time the squadrons inventory of 18 Northrop N-3PB had been reduced to just eight serviceable aircraft, the others having been lost or cannibalised for spares with a number of Catalinas also lost. But it had already been decided to withdraw the squadron to Oban, Scotland, where it arrived on 28 January to re-equip with Short Sunderland G.R.3 flying boats under C.O. Cdr T. Deisen. "C" Flight having remained at Budareyri to maintain patrols with the few remaining Northrops.

Photo - Short Sunderland GR. 5 WH-A
No. 330 (Norwegian) Squadron

The development of U.S. bases in Newfoundland, Nova Scotia, and later Greenland was another step in narrowing the "Gap", but it remained, and it was there that some of the bitterest battles were fought, until 1943. The significance of this and the introduction of the badly needed new aircraft can be appreciated when it is considered the Lockheed Hudson could operate nearly 500 miles from base, and the Wellingtons and Whitleys could spend two hours on station at that distance, the Sunderland could spend two hours at 600 miles and the Catalina the same amount of time at 800 miles. But the Consolidated B-24 Liberator, with its maximum fuel load of 2,500 gallons, could spend three hours patrolling over 1,100 miles from base. Of the early types the "DWI" Wellington was of great importance. The early threats to shipping came more from magnetic mines than submarines and the Wellington with its large magnetic coil suspended underneath, played a major part in detonating these when the menace reached its peak in 1939. Between November 1939 and May 1940, one-eighth of the magnetic mines swept or detonated were dealt with by the 'DWI-equipped' Wellingtons of Coastal Command. It is of interest that the only really 'modern' type available was the American-built Lockheed Hudson which like the Anson before it, was a military version of a civil airliner, the Lockheed 14 Super Electra. Initial versions were poorly armed, lacking a rear turret,and regarded by crews as difficult to fly. Nevertheless it was a No. 224 Squadron Hudson I (N7217) of Coastal Command, from RAF Leuchars, Scotland, flown by Flt Lt. A. Womersley that destroyed a Dornier 18 flying-boat during a patrol over Jutland on 8 October, 1939, the first aerial "kill" of WW II.

In July, 1940, still in its infancy and heavily reliant on reconnaissance during the period of possible invasion after the Battle of Britain, RAF Coastal Command assumed responsibility for the Photographic Reconnaissance Unit (PRU) (formerly Photographic Development Unit), at Hendon and the Photographic Interpretation Unit (formerly the semi-civilian Interpretation Unit) at Wembley, both of which now came under the auspices of the RAF. The founder of the PRU was Wing Commander F. S. Cotton (with Group Captain F. W. Winterbotham), but with the formalisation of the unit to serve all RAF Command's needs, as well as the Royal Navy, Cotton lost his command, to his deputy, regular officer Wing Commander G. W. Tuttle DFC. None the less, the Air Council did pay tribute to "the great gifts of imagination and inventive thought which Cotton had brought to bear on the technique of photography in the RAF". Bomber Command's special needs were well recognised by the new organisation and as such it enjoyed a "privileged position in relation to the other users." Although from mid-August in the midst of the Battle of Britain, low-flying Coastal Command Hudsons supported RAF Benson PRU Spitfires in monitoring the enemies ports for any signs of a possible launch of an invasion fleet. Keeping the enemy under constant surveillance, valuable information was passed to Fighter Command between July and October 1940, for the loss of only seven PRU Spitfires in 650 sorties...

By 1941, Coastal Commands equipment had improved beyond all recognition and the original nineteen squadrons of 1939, had grown to forty. In addition the American Mk 24 acoustic torpedo became available, as did the 600-lb anti-submarine bomb. The average range of the aircraft operated had doubled, effective and efficient Bristol Beaufort torpedo-bombers and long-range Beaufighter fighters - although still all too few - had taken their place in the battle order. More than half the aircraft had been fitted with the improved ASV II radar. Experiments with regards to effective camouflaging of the Commands airplanes was underway as were experiments of an airborne searchlight (Leigh Light). And it was at this time Air Marshal Sir Philip Joubert assumed command (for the second time). Previously he had been AOC Coastal Command, from 1 September, 1936 to 18 August, 1937.

Unfortunately Joubert's second tenor of office, which was to last from June 1941 to February, 1943, was to coincide with the lull of the 'false dawn', while the *Kreigsmarine* were concentrating their efforts elsewhere. In particular in the disastrous year of 1942, when the stranglehold on British, Allied and neutral shipping with nearly 8,000,000 tons lost in the year, threatened the war would be lost outright very soon. Shipping, wrote Churchill, "was at once the stranglehold and sole foundation of our war strategy". Nevertheless it was Joubert's realisation that the Battle of the Atlantic was a technical one, that was to lay the basis for the Command to eventually gain the ascendence on the U-boat menace.

In reference to the 'false dawn', shipping losses in June 1941, amounted to 109 ships, 432,025 tons of which U-boats accounted for over 70% - some 310,143 tons. The most significant reduction occurred in July and August with 120,975 tons and 130,699 tons respectively. It was these two months that saw the U-boat operations sink to their lowest level, and it looked for a while as if the Allies were in control of the situation. In truth the Allies were puzzled, there had been no fall in the number of operational U-boats - in fact there had been a slight rise from 47 in June to 60 in July and August with a steady increase until the end of the year with 86 operational in December. Some historians accredit the 'false dawn' to Operation *Barbarossa*, but as early as the 6 March, 1941, Grand Admiral Raeder issued a directive stating : "The main target for the Navy during the Eastern Campaign still remains Britain". One factor that can be attributed to the fall, is the extension of the American "Security Zone", which with still neutral U.S. destroyers in the Atlantic almost indistinguishable from those lent to the British Royal Navy, Admiral Doenitz issued his own statement in June, "to forbid any action against destroyers except in self-defence". The other most important single factor was that of the code-breaking advantage that U-boat headquarters had enjoyed was on the waiver, and of course Bletchley Park were availed of the short-signal code books taken from *U-110*. From May onwards all the *Kurzsignale,*the short signals in which the U-boats transmitted their sighting reports and weather information were read and later all "officer-only" signals. By August, all *Heimisch* (Home Waters) settings of the German naval Enigma machines were readable with a maximum delay of 72 hours or often the information made available in only a few hours.

The fact that the false dawn was due more to the Germans own actions was even more frustrating for Coastal Command who were unable to take advantage of the changes without better arms and equipment, including airplanes. AM Joubert, made continual representations to the Air Ministry for allocation of H.P. Halifaxes to fill his need for a long-range airplane. But these fell on deaf ears; leaving Joubert wondering whether the enemies of Coastal Command were abroad or at home. The solitary, Consolidated Liberator squadron (No.120 formed at Nutts Corner, Northern Ireland on 2 June, 1941), was plagued with teething problems which took a considerable time to sort out. Of the 67 Consolidated Catalina flying-boats delivered by September, 1941, nine had been written off, three were under repair and only twenty-six were operational in the UK, with nine more in Gibraltar and nine in the Far East; with only 18 deliveries expected by the end of the year. Deliveries of Short Sunderland flying boats were also virtually at a standstill due to labour troubles at Shorts in Belfast, and the preference by the company given to the production of Short Stirling bombers. The fact that six Stirling bombers could be built in the time it took to build three Sunderlands, was also significant, with Winston Churchill suggesting to the First Sea Lord of the Admiralty that in view of the false dawn and that bombers were needed for the strategic bombing offensive on Germany, production of Stirlings should take prominence. Churchill went further in suggesting, that it would be desirable to transfer even the few squadrons of Whitleys and Wellingtons to Bomber Command. But with AM Joubert with only sixty useful airplanes at the time Churchill was persuaded to defer decision on this matter until January, 1942. In addition to the AOC-in-C Bomber Commands refusal to release even small numbers of aircraft to Coastal Command there was also the question of Bomber Commands role in the Sea War.

In a letter to the Chief of Air Staff (CAS) dated 4 July, AM Joubert, proposed greater co-operation between the three Commands in the Sea War. He suggested that Bomber Command should take each U-boat base in turn and reduce it to the same condition that Plymouth was now in, following five days of bombing by the Luftwaffe. AM Joubert had sent a copy of his letter to the AOC-in-C Bomber Command who replied that he was firmly convinced his scant resources would be better employed on attacking objectives in Germany, and, though he realised that his bombing effort must be deflected from their primary role in order to attack the major naval units at Brest, he could not agree to include the U-boat Biscay bases. Views which found the support of the CAS.

Joubert realised there was little to be gained in pressing his argument further, but at the same time was greatly concerned that the false dawn should have led people to believe the Battle of the Atlantic had been won; "as a number of official pronouncements and newspaper articles had indicted". He perceived there was a new threat to his efforts to build-up the Command to meet the threat which he was convinced was only a matter of time, would be renewed with increased intensity. Support from ACM Portal did not exactly instil him with confidence. In a further letter dated 5 September, he presented his concerns to the Air Ministry, stressing that the U-boat Fleet was growing rapidly and, if no drastic steps was taken, we should reckon by the summer of 1942 of up to 150 U-boats operating at sea. (It is of interest to examine the actual figures)

He reiterated while a certain amount of harrying was inflicted on them at some points in their sea cruises, they

	Total Fleet	Operational	Atlantic Area	Med Area	Norway Area
May	296	128	89	20	19
June	313	130	90	19	21
July	331	140	101	16	23
August	342	152	113	16	23

could count on complete quiet and rest in harbour. He again strongly recommended that these bases be bombed frequently (not necessarily with large numbers of aircraft) so that at least some interference could be made to the smooth working of the Biscay port facilities. The Air Ministry replied that, while fully appreciating the value of harassing attacks on U-boat bases, such attacks would constitute a very considerable and unwarranted diversion from the present planned operations as approved by His Majesty's Government. Not content with this rather curt reply, the Air Council informed the CAS that it considered that the AOC-in-C, Coastal Command, in common with the Admiralty, had overlooked the long-term indirect contribution which the bomber offensive had made and was still making to our security at sea by attacks, not only on the main German ports but on the German industrial effort as a whole. This industrial effort supported their navy, just as much as their military or other war effort. The Air Ministry had accepted that Bomber Command should support the naval strategy more directly when the Battle of the Atlantic was in its earlier and critical stage but it saw no justification whatever for a return to this defensive strategy now when conditions at sea had so much improved and we were beginning to develop fully the air offensive to which we must look for winning as opposed to losing the war.

The work on the U-boat "pens" which concerned Joubert greatly, had become evident as early as January, 1941, and continued to be clearly shown month by month as a result of the Commands photographic reconnaissance flights. Construction of these massive bomb-proof pens had started at Brest and continued through to August at Lorient, St Nazaire and La Pallice. Two distinct opportunities were afforded to bomb the preparatory work of laying the foundations, done behind caissons which kept the sea water out, obviously highly vulnerable to blast bombing and the subsequent erection process was highly susceptible to attack until the massive roof was put in place, after which bombing became useless. In July, 1941, few roofs were in position and much of the foundation work was still in a vulnerable situation. But by January, 1942, the pens at Brest and Lorient and the majority at the other ports were pass the stage where bombing would have any effect. The missed opportunity of 1941, was to come back to haunt the Air Ministry. By the end of 1942, the U-boat activity had intensified dramatically and on 23 December, Bomber Command were ordered by the War Cabinet to bomb the U-boat bases. In five weeks from the middle of January Bomber Command's night attacks on Lorient and St Nazaire alone consumed 50% of its total bombing effort; they destroyed almost everything, except the pens.

Chapter 2   The end of the "False Dawn"

The first indication that the "false dawn" was over, came in September, 1941, when sinkings suddenly increased again to 285,942 tons, over 70% by U-boats. However, a fall to 218,289 tons in October, and then to the very low figure of 104,640 tons in November, again served to convince some in authority that the September increase was just a blip. This was not the view of the Admiralty or Coastal Command who had the good sense to take a number of special circumstances into account. Without doubt the low November figure, reflected the severe Atlantic autumn gales. But those who had made close studies of the U-boat war to date were well aware, from reduced W/T activity, that their had been, for some un-explained reason a sharp drop in the number of U-boats operating in the Atlantic, which was difficult to link to any Allied actions. W/T intercepts revealed the September sinkings had been achieved by around 20 U-boats. On 1 November, 1941, there were 10 in the Atlantic and six more off Gibraltar; on 8 December, there were only 12 in the whole Atlantic, all off Gibraltar, and by 1 January, 1942, there were only six. These continuing reductions in U-boat activity lead the Admiralty Operational Intelligence Centre, to comment; - the primary object seems, at least temporarily, to be no longer the destruction of merchant shipping.

However, for Admiral Doenitz, the ultimate and decisive criterion for the use of the U-boat was as a weapon to sink as quickly as possible the maximum amount of tonnage of enemy shipping and tonnage of potential use to the enemy. He realised that the U-boat was an essential weapon in the Sea War, that with the increasing American involvement - was becoming a race between Allied shipbuilding capacity and U-boat availability. His aim was for 300 operational boats (never achieved), and the 81 of November and the 86 of December were well short of this. He knew that those boats available should be used economically and deployed in areas where they could find and destroy the largest numbers of ships in the shortest possible time. However, not all German naval staff were of the same mind, a number were in favour of using the U-boat on other tasks if necessary; such as to create a strategic diversion, for reconnaissance purposes, to protect blockade runners, and to help in other critical situations. It was on this basis that Hitler himself ordered the withdrawal of at least 33% of the fleet from the Atlantic to guard against a possible British invasion of Norway. A decision which Doenitz regarded as as a useless waste of U-boats on a task not their own, detracting from the U-boats front-line operations, namely the supply war where they were the only effective weapon. Soon, with the attack on Pearl Harbour by the Japanese on 7 December, 1941, and America's entry into the war, in February, 1942, Doenitz's U-boats were back in force, to begin what Winston Churchill called "the terrible massacre of shipping along the American coast".

In his first term of office AM Joubert had made his presence felt as the main advocate as to the maritime uses of radar; in his second on the same theme he championed the further development of the rather disappointing airborne ASV Mark I - giving rise to the improved ASV II and the much improved ASV III. One of the primary tasks of the Coastal Command Development Unit (CCDU) formed on 30 December, 1940 at Carew Cheriton, in Wales, was to solve some of the Commands technical problems, and to further the development of the highly secret ASV radar. Initial equipment was a single D.H. 87 Hornet Moth, an Anson and a Bristol Beaufort but these were soon supplemented with an A. W. Whitley, Lockheed Hudsons and Vickers Wellingtons.

Experiments of a primitive airborne search radar system fitted to a Handley Page Heyford bomber began in March 1937, resulting in useful returns being received from transmitted pulses that had "bounced" back off of shipping, in the harbour at Harwich. The AOC Coastal Command was quick to recognise the potential of these findings with regard to detection and attacks of enemy shipping. ASV (Air to Surface Vessel) evolved in two main mode configurations, the first was the homing mode in which the radar was aimed ahead of the aircraft with two overlapping beams, and the other, the search mode, with two narrow beams radiated sideways from the aircraft and in this mode there was the two added advantages, that the maximum detection range was increased as a result of the narrowed beam and the greater area covered in a single sweep. In practice the aircraft would search with its sideways looking aerials then having found its target turn through 90° and home in, with its forward looking array. Initial trials in the UK were carried out with Avro Anson K8758, with the antenna array fitted on the port side only. The six-element transmitter Yagi array was fitted on the tailplane with the transmitter itself fitted close by in the rear fuselage. The receiving array was a similar Yagi carried on a 4 x 2-in piece of wood protruding out of one of the centre fuselage windows. Tests over the sea at Bawdsey gave a maximum range of up to 20 miles on medium-sized vessels and 30 miles near to the coastline. It was about this time that the real value of sideways looking radar in respect to ground-mapping was realised when on the 9 May 1938, in association with a hastily assembled photographic recorder the first crude pictures of the aircraft carrier *Courageous* and surrounding coastline were received at a range of 8 miles. Unfortunately it was to be another twenty years before the true potential of this initial research could be reached.

It was at this time that the Fleet Air Arm also became interested in ASV and several demonstration flights were made at Lee-on-Solent for some senior officers who were adamant for FAA purposes they would need an equipment with a 360° search area, to track shipping ahead of and behind the aircraft. There was no PPI at this time but a crude demonstration of the requirement was achieved by a single rotating dipole, where minimal interruption of the signal reception indicated the direction of the target. Although it should be said at this stage a number of rotating antenna systems had appeared on both the Martlesham Heath operated Ansons, and that satisfactory results were never really achieved with the maximum detection range more than halved, and so it was, the idea was eventually abandoned in favour of the original overlapping beams.

Almost immediately the A.I (airborne intercept) equipment fitted in Anson (K6260) was modified to search, mainly downwards. As a result of these trials within a few weeks work began on ASV Mk.1 radar and preparations were made for fitment of the equipment to an RAF Hudson, a Fairey Swordfish and Supermarine Walrus of the Fleet Air Arm. It should be noted that when fitted with ASV, the Fairey Swordfish could not carry a torpedo, so the type flew in support of each other, one for the search and the others for the attack. Coincident with aircraft arrivals a RAF St Athan MU, ASV sets were arriving from the manufacturer and it was not long before equipments were being fitted to aircraft of No.220, 233 and 224 Squadrons Coastal Command. By this time No.220 Squadron who had supplied the original Avro Anson trials aircraft had moved north to Scotland at RAF Leuchars equipped with American Lockheed Hudson aircraft for sea-search and escort duties. The ASV equipment was found to be easier to install than the A.I. particularly in the Hudson as it was a much roomier aircraft than the Bristol Blenhiem or Beaufighter. In general as ASV sets became available, Hudson's were flown in from the squadrons and by the early part of 1940 approximately 2-3 a week were being converted. As work continued the installation team were joined by two new members, John Pringle and Alan Hodgkin. Both studied at Cambridge and Hodgkin, an extremely talented individual who after the War was a recipient of the Nobel Prize, was the main man behind the introduction of centimetric-wave interception radars in Britain.

It was about this time that a team was sent to the Pembroke Dock Coastal Command base to investigate fitment of ASV to the No.10 Squadron (RAAF), Sunderland flying boats which were flying patrols over the Bay of Biscay and the Atlantic approaches. John Pringle took charge of the Sunderland installations and it was not long before the whole was completed and work started on the Consolidated Catalinas also at the base. However, the ASV Mk.1 was soon superseded by the longer range 150cm ASV Mk II which was almost ready for productionisation before war started in 1939. RAF Coastal Command Lockheed Hudson crews soon realised that the ASV.1 was hardly likely to win the war for them. It was soon discovered that the "target returns" from the fairly bulky equipment fitted to their aircraft were covered in a massive array of short-range signals or "surface clutter" - especially in high or choppy seas and only by flying at dangerously low levels (less than 200 ft) could a recognisable target be obtained at a maximum range of 3.5 miles with minimum target observation down to half a mile. The ASV 1 equipment was very unreliable and even when it did work there was no means of illuminating the located target. Against this background it was therefore truly amazing that the ASV II should have been put into full-scale production as early as the spring of 1940, with an order for 4,000 sets.

The man responsible for the success of ASV II was Dr A. G. Touch, with the equipment becoming one of the most versatile radars ever built. It was produced in Great Britain, the USA, Canada and Australia, and used in every theatre of war. It also gave rise to the Coastal Defence radar and later the Home Chain Low (CHL) and GCI radars. Later the Army used the ASV II as the basis for its Search Light Director (SLC), with parts of the design also used in the wartime OBOE blind-bombing system, as used by the Pathfinder squadrons of Bomber Command. After the experience with ASV 1 the new 1.5-metre set was amazingly trouble free with many of the early deliveries fitted to aircraft such as the Hudson, Whitley, Wellington, Beaufort, Warwick ASR.IA, Liberator I, and Short Sunderland flying boats. It is interesting to note that in a number of instances the addition of the ASV antenna arrays drastically changed the standard recognition profile of the aircraft, many of which carried both forward and sideways looking arrays. These types were followed by the Swordfish, Albacores and Catalinas operated by the FAA.

By the summer of 1941, more than 100 RAF Coastal Command aircraft were equipped with ASV II. The Hudsons patrolled the North Sea, the Armstrong Whitworth Whitleys the north-western approaches, with the Short Sunderlands and Vickers Wellingtons covering the Bay of Biscay and nearer reaches of the Atlantic. As crews became more familiar with the equipment and experience and confidence in its operation grew, attacks on submarines increased and Allied shipping losses dropped dramatically. Dr Bowen continued to work on improving the ASV's performance. He made a number of changes to the transmitter and its output and also to the sensitivity of the receiver giving improved detection range. Equipment reliability was improved by the introduction of mass production engineering techniques the equipment having been designed with this in mind from the outset. Unfortunately many factors slowed production at this critical stage not least of course the demands of the Battle of Britain but within the year of the four hundred aircraft engaged on anti-submarine duties 75% were fitted with ASV II. This meant at any one time some 8-10 radar-equipped aircraft would be involved in the search for each individual operational German U-boat.

The first successful attack was on the night of 30 November 1941, when a Armstrong Whitley 'B' of No.502 Squadron equipped with ASV II located and sank *U-206* in the Bay of Biscay. A few weeks later a Fairey Swordfish of No.812 Squadron FAA operating out of the "Rock" had a dramatic run of success against at least five submarines attempting to pass through the Straits of Gibraltar into the Mediterranean. All of which were severely damaged and forced to return to their bases for repair. The first FAA "kill" was made on 21 December, 1941, when Sub-Lieutenant Wilkinson, flying Swordfish 'A' of 812 NAS attacked and sank *U-451*. A number of other successes followed until the beginning of 1942, when for a number of reasons events took a reversal, not least due to the fact that the Germans had discovered that British airborne radars operated on 200 MHz and had subsequently fitted their submarines with a listening device "Metox" (so called after the French firms that made them under orders), that gave them warning of a radar equipped search aircraft.

British radar secrets were also revealed to the Germans when Rommel captured a serviceable Vickers Wellington aircraft with ASV II fitted in Tunisia, and began using it to detect Allied shipping in the Mediterranean. When the German High Command discovered what was happening they ordered the aircraft to Berlin, where after extensive examination they were so impressed by the ASV equipments performance they immediately started work on a version of their own.

Luckily in the summer of 1940, thanks to Sir Robert Watson-Watt the resonant cavity "magnetron" became available and the development of the centimetric ASV III with its ability to detect an aircraft at six miles and a submarine conning tower at four miles was now a reality. As with the A.I. sets the difference the magnetron made was quite incredible, and it was to this end that a Bristol Blenheim took off from Christchurch near Bournemouth in the south of England, fitted with an A.I. Mk VIII, to which a modification to its front end and scanner had been carried out so as to produce a very narrow beam pointing obliquely down, so that, with the scanner rotated about a vertical axis at 30 rpm a picture of the surface ahead of and below the aircraft was displayed giving a clear indication of rivers and lakes, towns (and below 5,000 ft), individual large buildings such as hangars etc.

Over the next two years, work on the centimetric radar gave rise to the development of the new improved ASV III and its corresponding land variant the H2S. By the end of 1942 performance of the ASV III had improved beyond all expectations. The equipment was now capable of detecting convoys at up to 40 miles range and surfaced submarines at 12 miles, with great clarity. Problems did, however remain at this time with production and scheduling of deliveries. In an effort to alleviate the situation it was decided to fit some of the Bomber Command H2S radars with a "Klystron" valve transmitter instead of a magnetron. However, it soon became obvious that whilst a Klystron H2S was possible it would require major development work to produce an equipment to give similar results to those sets fitted with magnetrons. Progress on the Klystron H2S was severely affected when half of the development team including EMIs Dr.Blumlein were killed on the 16 April 1942 in a Halifax (V9977) trials aircraft crash. Soon after this incident it was decided to use the magnetron in H2S radars but with the Battle of the Atlantic reaching a critical peak the Air Staff decreed that 40 H2S sets should be modified to ASV III sets and that the Americans, who, following Sir Henry Tizard's exchange of technology mission to America, had the Radiation Laboratory of MIT (Massachusetts Institute of Technology, Cambridge, Massachusetts) build an airborne radar set which was produced by Western Electric by the summer of 1943. It also developed a parallel ASV III equipment, the SCR 517, and agreed to fit this to all Consolidated B-24 Liberators destined for Coastal Command. Whilst development work continued and other critical decisions had to be made in the light that it was inevitable that sooner or later either a Bomber or Coastal Command aircraft would inevitably be shot down with the possibility that within hours the Germans would have a captured equipment to examine. After a protracted period of discussion it was decided that Bomber Command should be the first to take the equipment to war.

However, in March 1943, No 172 Squadron Coastal Command, Leigh Light Wellingtons were fitted with ASV Mk III radar to guide them into a position where their searchlights could expose and reveal U-boats. The technique soon producing positive results. With *U-488* attacked by Wellington 'G' on the 20 March 1943, although she escaped unscathed. In hindsight this proved to be the best decision as it gave Coastal Command almost eight months operational use before the Germans produced an effective countermeasure. By which time the inevitable had already happened when on 2 February 1943, a Short Stirling bomber fitted with an H2S radar set was shot down near Rotterdam. Immediately work began on the development of a countermeasures system although as it was to be discovered the Germans at that time had a lot of catching up to do in the field of centimetric radars, thus permitting Coastal Command its eight month honeymoon with its new radar equipped aircraft.

Wartime H2S sets also pioneered air-to-ground radars used for navigation, such as Gee II and Gee III and DME Similar radars were developed by the Soviets, France and Sweden etc and lead to the development by the Americans of an IFF (Identification Friend or Foe) radar to distinguish between friendly and enemy aircraft. In the event it was No 502 Squadron which was to pioneer the use of ASV II radar and it has the distinction of being the first to locate and destroy a German submarine using the equipment, sinking *U-206* in the Bay of Biscay on 30 November 1941. One of the first squadrons to use ASV III to great effect was No.172 Squadron with its general reconnaissance Vickers Wellingtons which it used to great effect to expose German U-boats in the Western Approaches and the Bay of Biscay. On average, the squadron recorded one radar contact every four sorties.

Among the first ASV centimetric radars to become available in the United States around the same time as the breakthrough with the SCR 720 (A.I. Mark X) was the SCR 717 produced by the Western Electric Company, which was similar in design to the SCR 720, but had a range-azimuth or B-scan feature. Several other brands, such as the Philco DMS 1000, were built with a Plan Position Indicator (PPI) display. (Providing full 360° scan- search). This Philco design was later developed into the APS and APQ series for the US Navy and Air Corp respectively. The equipments were fitted to Consolidated B 24 Liberators and many other types of aircraft which were used extensively in the Atlantic and the European theatres. It is without doubt that it was these airplanes that finally decided the Battle of the Atlantic in the Allies favour. Finally allaying the U-boat menace for good. Centimetric radar systems also played their part in defeat of the Japanese in the Pacific, but in an entirely different way. As Japan too had to a great extent relied on its Merchant Shipping Fleet to sustain the homeland and supply its forces spread all over the Pacific, the fleet first became prey to US submarines and then to ASV radar-equipped aircraft.

Again it was the Consolidated B 24 Liberator that was the major protagonist, when equipped with the Western Electric SCR 717 sets it ranged over the south-west Pacific and China Seas. Instead of carrying Leigh Light equipment as in Europe, the aircraft were equipped with a radar blind-bombing attachment designed at the Radiation Laboratory at MIT, called LAB, or Low-Altitude Bombing attachment. This allowed for completely blind bombing attacks to be made on ships at sea and as the Japanese had latterly made a decision to move most of their supplies by night, the LAB equipped bombers soon had a devastating effect on the Japanese sea-going supply lines. Between them US submarines,and radar equipped bombers virtually destroyed the entire Japanese Merchant Fleet. The definitive WW II ASV equipment was the ASV Mark X..

The realisation of the importance and difficulties associated with the war against the U-boats, led AM Joubert to work unceasingly and imaginatively to ensure that Coastal Command should benefit from all relevant scientific and technical advances. The process had been started by AM Sir Frederick Bowhill who was equally technically astute. Three months before relinquishing his command Bowhill had appointed Professor P. M. S. Blackett as his scientific adviser, a position which Joubert was only too willing to continue. With his backing, Blackett set up an Operational Research Unit which in due course was to consist of five prominent members of the Fellows of the Royal Society : including Blackett himself, Sir John Kendrew, Professor E. J. Williams, Professor C. H. Waddington and Professor J. M. Robertson. The primary function of the group was both collectively and individually to subject every aspect of Coastal Command's work to scientific scrutiny, to determine where any new developments available might be applied in the U-boat war. At the same time the senior naval liaison officer at Coastal Command Headquarters, Commander Peyton-Ward began recording comprehensive details of all individual sightings and attacks on U-boats as they took place and by the end of 1941, in his own words, "he had become specialised in all aspects of Coastal Command's war against the U-boat. Holding this key position for the remainder of the war, he worked closely with the Admiralty Submarine Tracking Room.

Professor Blacketts Operational Research Unit studied every aspect of operations against the U-boat, including : angles of attack, depth charge settings, aircraft colours, etc. It was important to make the Commands aircraft inconspicuous to the U-boat conning tower look-outs for as long as possible. In the northern hemisphere, plain white paint on all sides and under surfaces were found to confer a "remarkable degree of invisibility". This gave rise in the summer of 1941, to the "White Crow's of Coastal Command." By 25 July, 1941, the Operational Research Unit had issued Tactical Instruction (No. 15) :

 (i)   The attacking approach was to be made by the shortest path and at maximum speed.
 (ii) The actual attack could be made from any direction relative to the U-boat.
 (iii) The depth setting of all depth-charges was to be 50 feet, the spacing of depth-charges in a stick was to be 60 feet and all depth-charges carried are to be released in one stick.
 (iv) The idea was to attack while the U-boat or some part of it was still visible.
       Data was included, however, to enable pilots to estimate quickly how far ahead of the point of final disappearance where their stick should be placed if the U-boat got under just before release was possible.
 (v)   It was pointed out that if the U-boat had submerged for more than 30 seconds, that success was unlikely owing to the progressive uncertainty as to its position in either plane (plan or depth)
 (vi) The height of release of depth-charges must not be greater than 100 feet until an aiming sight was provided
       but the restriction against aircraft carrying depth charges at night was modified.
       (although by January, 1942, it was recognised for low-level operations at night in bad weather there was a basic requirement for a radio altimeter ; - it was a long time before Coastal Command received approved aiming sights or radio altimeters.
 (vii) Great stress was laid on the need for training and constant exercises so as to attain a high standard of attack and aiming accuracy.

It was emphasised, sighting a U-boat and killing a U-boat were two different things, but it was now recognised that the connection between the two was very intimate indeed; it was not just that without a sighting there would not be a kill, it was that there would only be a certain kill while the U-boat was in sight. This problem remained throughout the war and whilst it was realised the U-boats travelled to locate their targets mainly at night on the surface, in 1940, AM Bowhill gave permission for Squadron Leader H. de V. Leigh, an ex-WW I pilot with experience of anti-submarine work, employed on personnel duties at Coastal Command Headquarters to try out an idea he had for an airborne searchlight. Leigh proposed the searchlight be linked to the ASV radar and by March, 1941, work began in fitting a Royal Navy 22/24-in searchlight into the under turret of a Vickers Wellington, as well as devising a successful means of carrying away the asphyxiating fumes from the carbon arc lamp.

The prototype Leigh Light Wellington, (P9223) was a DWI (Direct Wireless Installation) airplane, fitted with the massive 48 ft underfuselage hoop for exploding magnetic mines. The searchlight was installed in the retractable "dustbin" turret. The controls for this turret were positioned in a transparent nose which replaced the front gun turret. The "handlebar" grips were similar to those used by air gunners, giving the narrow 4° beam of the light some sideways and vertical movement, permitting a degree of compensation for drift on the approach. Two dials indicated the direction of the beam to port or starboard, permitting it to be pre-set before being switched on. The electrical supply required was provided by a Ford V 8 engine already used in the DWI equipped Wellingtons. Fitted in the centre fuselage the engine ran a dynamo, which itself weighed 784-lbs. Eventually on 24 April, 1941, P9223 was flown to Limavady, Londonderry, Northern Ireland, for initial trials and after some initial disappointments on 4 May, with Squadron Leader Leigh operating the light himself a full trial was held against a submarine of the Royal Navy. A RN Officer witnessing the test made the following report.

The aircraft was not heard by the submarine until it [the submarine] had been illuminated, and was able to dive, and an attack down the beam for 27 seconds was made before pulling out at 500 feet. The effort was most impressive,and there seems no doubt that, given an efficient aircraft crew and good team work, this weapon would be invaluable in attacking U-boats on the surface at night and in low visibility.

The Leigh Light concept had been proven and with a few refinements proposed by Leigh was ready for use operationally. Bowhill immediately wrote to Joubert then in a desk job at the Air Ministry to suggest that Squadron Leader Leigh should be officially entrusted with the task of introducing searchlight ASV-equipped aircraft into operational service. But Joubert at this stage favoured the Helmore/GEC "Turbinlite" system adopted earlier by Fighter Command for its night fighter Havoc's (converted Douglas Boston bombers). The "Turbinlite" had been the brain-child of Group Captain W. Helmore, and Joubert instead transferred responsibility for further development of Coastal Command's searchlight to him. Shortly afterwards Joubert succeeded Bowhill as AOC-in-C Coastal Command and in a short time he reversed his decision in favour of the Leigh Light, admitting his initial decision made at the Air Ministry was wrong. In his own words, he was reported to have said :

When I took over at Coastal Command having so closely associated with the Helmore Light I thought it might be given a general application by being used against U-boats as well. I thought that its wide beam and great illuminating power would be valuable. I therefore gave instructions that Squadron Leader Leigh was to return to his duties as Assistant Personnel Officer. After some two months I found, as I do not mind admitting, that I had made a mistake. I found out that the Helmore light was unnecessarily brilliant for use against U-boats and otherwise unsuitable. I then came to the conclusion that Leigh's Light was preferable for use against U-boats, and decided to drop the Helmore and concentrate on the Leigh Light.

In the meantime Squadron Leader Leigh and the CCDU had continued their trials with the Leigh Light Wellington, which was flown to Carew Cheriton on 6 May, 1941. As the trials continued using the Govan Light Vessel as a target, it was found the optimum height to make an approach was 250 feet, with the searchlight able to traverse about 10° to port and starboard. At the same time the heavy generating system was replaced by seven 12 volt batteries fitted in the centre bomb-bay, the batteries charged by the aircrafts engines. Unfortunately the space taken by the batteries and 140 gallon overload fuel tanks fitted, reduced the bomb-load to four depth-charges instead of the normal six. The batteries could maintain the light for about 6 minutes before it extinguished, but otherwise would remain fully charged if the light was not switched on for more than three half-minute periods per hour. With a full war load, no front turret and the Leigh Light fitted aft the Wellington became tail-heavy, as well as being somewhat under-powered with its two 1,000 hp Bristol Pegasus XVIII radial engines, making take-offs rather hazardous. In addition the propellers were non-feathering, so the airplane could not remain airborne on one engine, it was soon evident that precise flying and co-ordination would be necessary for the successful operation of the Leigh Light Wellingtons. CCDU trials were completed in December, 1941, the unit moving to Ballykelly, Northern Ireland, on 6 December, 1941. Later the Air Ministry approved the installation of the Leigh Light and ASV II in six Wellingtons (Mark I L4319, IA P9223, IC R1231, VIII Z8721, XII MP636, XIII MF 636), to be redesignated as Mark VIIIs, with another 30 to be converted if the first proved successful on operations.

None the less even with Joubert's complete support, it took nearly another year before the Leigh Light was given official approval when five Vickers Wellingtons of No.172 Squadron fitted with the Light, undertook their first operational night patrol. Initially the cupola housing the light was raised and lowered by means of block and tackle through the former ventral defensive position, but later this crude method was replaced by hand-pumped hydraulic power.

No. 172 Squadron had formed at RAF Chivenor, North Devon, on 4 April, 1942, from No.1417 (Leigh Light) Flight which itself had formed on 18 January, 1942, at Chivenor, to trial the Leigh Light equipped Wellingtons under Squadron Leader J. H. Greswell. The first of No.1417's modified Wellingtons arrived around two weeks later, and eventually the flight had six aircraft, although on 13 April, one crashed into a cliff near Hartland Point on the north coast of Devon following the loss of a propeller. Although AM Joubert had requested another 20 Leigh Light Wellingtons to form No. 172 Squadron under Wing Commander J. B. Russell, these airplanes did not arrive. Nevertheless training continued and by June, they were ready for operational work. Joubert realised that if the system was to be adopted these airplanes must prove the viability of the idea once and for all. On 3/4 June, he gave orders four of them should be sent out to patrol the Bay of Biscay, the fifth airplane having previously had its wing damaged by a petrol bowser. Witnessed by AVM G. R. Bromet, the AOC No. 19 Group the aircraft took off in succession between 20.33 hrs and 20.45 hrs, under the captaincies of Flt. Lt. A. W. Southall, Plt Off. F. Blackmore, Wing Commander J. B. Russell and Squadron Leader J. H. Greswell. They set course for the Scilly Isles and swept the Bay of Biscay at about 2,000 feet, on fan-shaped patrols, as far as the north coast of Spain.

Each crew consisted of two pilots, a navigator and three wireless operator/air gunners. The latter manned the ASV radar, the wireless and tail-turret, changing places every 20 minutes to ensure that concentration on the ASV radar returns was as high as possible. It was a pitched dark night with no moon. The first three airplanes landed back at Chivenor between 05.11 hrs and 05.20 hrs, having found nothing, other than a few fishing vessels and a single merchant vessel. But, Wellington ES986 'F' flown by Squadron Leader Greswell had located the same U-boat twice. Shortly after 02.00 hrs, when about 60 nautical miles north-west of Cape Penas on the north coast of Spain, the radar operator, using the forward aerials reported a contact 5 miles to port. Squadron Leader Greswell called action stations, turned to port and began to descend. Immediately the navigator Plt Off. S. J. Pooley, lowered the Leigh Light. The second pilot, Plt Off. Alan W. R.Triggs (RAAF), moved into the nose to operate the controls of the light. The radar operator continually relayed positional information and directions to Greswell over the intercom. On his first run, he failed due to a false setting of the pressure altimeter, originally set at Chivenor, placing the aircraft about 100 feet too high for the attack causing the beam to overshoot the target.

The submarine that Greswell had located was an Italian boat *Luigi Torelli*, and amazed that an aircraft which had made contact carrying a bright light had not attacked them, they decided it must have been German and fired recognition flares... This gave Greswell their exact position, quickly confirmed by his ASV radar, and with a reset of his altimeter, he was now able to come in at the prescribed height of 250 feet and P/O Triggs switched on the light at a distance of three quarters of a mile - and there exactly where it should have been the *Luigi Torelli* was illuminated for the Leigh Light attack. Squadron Leader Greswell, dropped four Mk 8 250-lb Torpex depth-charges from a height of only 50 feet at 35 feet intervals across the submarine. The U-boat was so badly damaged that she immediately made for St Jean de Luz for emergency repairs - but instead came close to being interned in the Spanish port of Aviles. Eventually, following a second attack on 7 June, by two Short Sunderlands 'X' and 'A' of No.10 Squadron (RAAF) piloted by P/O T. A. Egerton and Flt. Lt. E. Yeomans respectively; having escaped from Santander, she served with the Japanese in the Pacific, until finally being captured by the Americans at the end of the Pacific War, having been sent to Kobe to have her engines overhauled, she was finally scuttled by the Japanese in August, 1946.

On the return flight home, ES986 made a second surfaced contact, with another Italian vessel the *Morosini*, that unbeknown to Greswell of course, had left Bordeaux on 25 May, along with the *Luigi Torelli* he had just attacked. However, with no depth-charges left the crew opened fire with their machine guns. Greswell circled the submarine permitting the crew two such attacks, before heading home to land at Chivenor at 05.57 hrs, seven hours after taking off. There was much jubilation at No. 172 Squadron's headquarters as all the training and trials work of No.1417 Flight had been vindicated and of course at the time the crew believed it had sunk its first U-boat with a possible second damaged. One particular jubilant member of the crew was Plt Off. Pooley, who was the young scientist that had invented Torpex, the explosive used in the depth-charge used operationally for the first time. It being 30% more powerful than the Amatol used previously. At one time the Air Ministry had considered that Pooley was too valuable to risk his life on operational flying, but he had insisted on a posting to an operational Coastal Command squadron. Following the mission the future of the Leigh Light seemed assured and AM Joubert made the following statement :

"The result was highly gratifying. Three of the Wellingtons found no U-boats, but the ease with which they illuminated ASV contacts which turned out to be fishing vessels left little doubt of the merits of Leigh's invention. The fourth aircraft gave further witness in the best possible way. It contacted, "homed" on to, and successfully illuminated two enemy submarines".

Photo :   Photo :

Squadron Leader Humphrey de   Wing Commander
Verde "Sammy" Leigh. inventor   Jeaffreson H. Greswell
of Leigh Light.

On 6 July, 1942, another No.172 Squadron Wellington 'H' scored the units first Leigh Light "kill" *U-502* and in August, seven aircraft were detached to Wick in the north-east of Scotland for Leigh Light patrols over the North Sea. On 14 September, 1942, these aircraft formed the basis of a second Wellington Leigh Light Squadron, No. 179, which in November moved to Gibraltar for patrols over the approaches to the Mediterranean, until 1944, when it returned to the UK to fly ASW patrols over the Bay of Biscay. By the end of the war Leigh Light aircraft had attacked 218 U-boats at night, and made 206 attacks on enemy shipping. Twenty-seven U-boats were sunk with this method and 31 were damaged. While the ratio of sinkings to attacks is not very impressive, only 12.38%; the effect of the *"verdammte Licht"* was not merely measured in terms of "kills" and damage but on the disruption to normal operations. Boats transiting through the Bay of Biscay were forced to remain submerged by night as well as day, which was not only uncomfortable for the crews and bad for morale, but meant that time in the operational area was reduced by five days or more. A significant reduction.

By 1942, most of the small early U-boats were being replaced by the ocean-going Type VII, with its 6,500-mile range, that were to become the most prolific in the North Atlantic. Over 300 were completed in 1942, of which some 10 per cent had been built in Dutch and French yards. The Axis powers had no fewer than 485 submarines in service, of which between sixty and seventy were Italian vessels. This enormous growth in the German submarine fleet encouraged Admiral Doenitz to boast, " We have the English by the throat." Nor, at the time was this boast idle, for even the defiant Sir Winston Churchill remarked that the British lifeline was in danger. Churchill later wrote :

"The only thing that ever really frightened me in the war was the U-boat peril ... our lifeline, even across the broad oceans, and especially in the entrances to the Island, was endangered. I was even more anxious about this battle than I had been about the glorious air fight called the Battle of Britain."

February 1942, recorded a loss of 679,632 tons, with U-boats responsible for the loss of 476,451. February, 1942 also marked the turning point in the Sea War, it was the start of many bad months with greatly increased U-boat activity, both the RN and and RAF were greatly over-stretched in particular Coastal Command. It was particularly unfortunate that with both services finding it hard to cope, that there was a significant rise in operational U-boat numbers. For the first time the number of operational U-boats exceeded 100 at 101 and continued to rise steadily throughout the year to 205 in November, dropping back to 203 in December mounting to a peak in May, 1943, at 239.

February 1942 to May 1943, saw the period of the great "wolfpacks" whose operations brought sinkings by U-boats alone to a total of 7,721,486 tons (1,412 ships). The 'packs' began operations in August, 1942, attacking convoys in the North Atlantic once the ships were outside air cover, and heavy losses were sustained in a whole series of convoy battles. Not unconnected was the Germans ascendancy at this juncture in the Intelligence war. In June, 1941, for the purposes of inter-communication between British, Canadian and the U.S. Navies, Naval Cypher No.3 was introduced. But without proper protection devices built-in by February, 1942, German Intelligence had reconstructed the codes and from then until 15 December was reading a large proportion of the signals sent, sometimes as much as 80%. From the 15 December due to a change in procedures the *B-Dienst* suffered a slight set-back but from February, 1943, it was again reading a large amount of the traffic, sometimes obtaining decrypts about convoy movements between 10 and 20 hours in advance. Most important between the period February, 1942 and 10 June 1943, it frequently de-cyphered the daily signal sent by the Admiralty estimating U-boat dispositions. Coincident on 1 February 1942, U-boat Command added a fourth wheel to its Enigma machine for the communications of its Atlantic and Mediterranean U-boats, and until December, 1942 proved very effective with Bletchley Park unable to provide information on U-boat locations, movements, or numbers.

It is for these reasons 1942, became known as the "dark night" of the U-boat war. In the first three months of the year, sinkings totalled 834,164 tons with 537,980 (over 64%) attributable to U-boat operations. The worse monthly total was in June, 834,196 tons, 623,545 in the North Atlantic, and no less than 700,235 to U-boats (nearly 84%). The largest U-boat contribution occurred in November : with 729,160 tons claimed out of 807,754 (over 90%). Churchill described this as "a terrible event in a very bad time".

It was against this background and events that AM Joubert kept up his protestations that Coastal Command could not operate effectively and efficiently without greater support from the Air Ministry. On 19 February, he told them, "the prospect of Coastal Command being able to work at reasonable efficiency appears to be coming more and more remote. The promise of centimetric ASV radar fitted to Liberators came to nothing, the one Liberator squadron with only five Mark 1s was being allowed to die out, along with the continual change in policy with regards to this long-range airplane". Further he added. "While fully aware of the importance of he sustained bomber offensive, it appears to me, if England is to survive this year, in which we are already losing shipping at a rate considerably in excess of American and British building output, some part of the bomber offensive will have to be sacrificed and a long-range type such as the Lancaster, diverted to the immediate threat on our Sea Communications.

The communique prompted Churchill to enquire of the Chief of Air Staff, what steps had been taken to compensate Coastal Command for the diversion of long-range airplanes to the Far East. AVM Portal replied, "I have avoided further allocation of Liberators to Coastal Command on the grounds that the Americans have already registered their discontent of Boeing B-17 Fortress (August 1942 - B-17As unsuitable for Bomber Command) aircraft deployed in Coastal Command on tasks other than high-level bombing raids, and he considered there would be serious trouble with General "Hap" Arnold, if Liberators were similarly diverted from the bombing role for which they were originally supplied to the RAF". He also added, he was strongly opposed to the transfer of either Liberators or Lancasters from the bomber offensive as the former were earmarked for the Middle East theatre, where they would be the only aircraft capable of bombing targets in Tripoli, Italy, and the Rumainian oil-fields, while the Lancaster was the only bomber available able to carry 8,000-lb of bombs to Berlin. He proposed, therefore to compensate Coastal Command by the transfer of A. W. Whitley aircraft until such time as Catalina strength reached a figure of 45 airplanes... So Joubert continued to suffer !

It was at this time, March, 1942, that he decided to make the difficulties facing the Command in its day to day operations more public; he introduced a bi-monthly (later monthly) *Coastal Command Review*. It was a serious professional review of the previous month's activities and was an important medium by which the squadrons were kept informed of what was going on throughout the Command and how the Air/Sea War was going. It detailed tactical lessons learnt during operations and discussed a whole range of professional activities of the Command in a way that they would be interesting as well as instructive to the crews. In it, Joubert put his public relations expertise to good use; the *Review* covered a wide spectrum of information, from the highly technical to matters of more general interest. The very first issue carried a detailed account of the antiquated, overworked A.W. Whitleys :

While engaged on an ASW sweep from Reykjavik, the Whitley aircraft F/612 sighted a U-boat on the surface at 11.25 am on 18 February at position 63°15' N. and 24° 30' W. The U-boat submerged when the aircraft approached to 300 yards, and the swirl of its dive could be clearly seen at the moment of attack. Six depth charges were dropped from 50 feet, each of 250-lb modified Mk III, with pistol modified Mark X, which had been preset to 50 ft. They fell 90 ft ahead of the swirl across the track of the U-boat; two were thought to have exploded 15 ft from the track of the U-boat, two others at 75 ft, two at 135 ft and two at 195 ft. After a couple of minutes a large oil patch was seen, about 250 ft in diameter, and lines of bubbles with thick streaks of oil. One minute later the U-boat showed on the surface and immediately submerged again. No wreckage or further signs of damage were visible, but there was a 35-knot wind at the time and the sea was rough. The aircraft circled round, getting a view over at least ten miles , and stayed an hour and a half. On the way home the port engine failed, and it was only just possible to reach land after reducing weight by jettisoning everything possible, including the camera with the photographs which had been taken. This is considered to have been an excellent attack which must, at least, have shaken the U-boat very seriously, and should have prevented it from doing further damage on its cruise.

From this report a number of important observations can be made; first it is a factual professional account; secondly, great care was taken not to make an unsubstantiated claim - owed in fact in all probability to the standards set by Peyton-Ward, in line with normal Coastal Command procedures. This, contrasting sharply with the "numbers game" played by the other Commands, taking into account the very different circumstances of an attack on a largely invisible enemy. Finally it should be noted that no U-boat was reported missing on the day of the F612's attack, which serves to show how very robust they were; the great strength built in to allow them to survive the pressures of the ocean depths enabled them also to survive what looks like certain death at the hands of their enemies. A problem that Coastal Command would be forced to overcome, if the attacks were to be more successful. It was obvious the Whitley was not the answer to AM Jouberts problems, and the addition of another squadron (No. 58, in May 1942) from Bomber Command, although fitted with ASV II, did little to ease the situation. In fact the position was becoming completely untenable, and as such he informed the Air Ministry of this on 30 March, 1942. He was in his own words, at one and the same time being, "metaphorically kicked by the Admiralty for not asking enough and blamed by the Air Ministry for demanding the impossible. The Air Council in an effort to placate Joubert, replied that on occasions AOC-in-C's views were at variance with the Air Staff, and this should not give rise to embarrassment by Coastal Command. At the same time he was allocated on loan from Bomber Command two more squadrons of Whitleys and two squadrons of Wellingtons, while two Bristol Beaufort squadrons which had gone overseas were replaced by H.P. Hampdens.

The addition of more Hudsons served only to emphasise the fact that still, the Command's equipment was far from adequate. In the last three months of 1941, anti-shipping strikes had succeeded in sinking 15 enemy vessels for the loss of 46 airplanes. The first four months of 1942, however, saw a an even greater decline in its success ratio with only 6 ships sunk, for the loss of 55 airplanes. Following a brief improvement in May, when the Command claimed 12 ships sunk for the loss of 43 airplanes, by the end of the year it was estimated one in four of all attacking aircraft were lost. A snapshot of No. 407 Squadron, RCAF equipped with Lockheed Hudsons served to demonstrate how desperate the situation had become.

Since this squadron became operational again on 1April, 1941, we have lost twelve crews, in all fifty persons either missing or killed. During the past month six crews have been designated missing or killed on operations with the loss of twenty-seven lives. This does not take into consideration the fact that after every major operation of this nature at least two or three aircraft are so very badly damaged that they are of no use to this or any other squadron.

In reality the fault was a tactical one with the daring strikes occurring at mast-head height. One pilot reported he had gone so low "that he struck a mast and hung one of the bomb-doors thereon", another pilot from No. 455 Squadron (RAAF), actually returned to base with several feet of mast attached to his aircraft. As more and more experienced crews left for the Middle East and German ships were equipped with anti-aircraft defences, it was clear low-level attacks were becoming too expensive both in terms of crews and aircraft. The only reason for them in the first place was of course the lack of a good low-level bomb-sight. Nevertheless eventually Joubert was forced to change tactics and resort to medium-level bombing; casualty levels reduced immediately, but, so did the sinkings ! By the end of the 1941, 45 ships were sunk for the loss of 251 airplanes, the only achievement being the Command was able to keep a degree of pressure on the enemies sea-going activities. Between April 1940 and March 1943, the Command made 3,700 direct attacks, sank 107 vessels (155,076 tons) for the loss of 648 airplanes — just over six airplanes for each vessel sunk. In contrast its most effective activity in conjunction with the Navy and Bomber Command was that of aerial mine-laying, with in the same period 369 vessels (361,821 tons) sunk for the loss of 329 aircraft — less than one airplane per ship.

Chapter 3 - The Coming of Age (1943)

Eventually in November, 1942, with the Sea War at crisis level in terms of Allied merchant shipping lost, with the RN and Coastal Command still desperately short of warships and aircraft to combat the threat. Joubert suggested some of the RAF's Bristol Beaufighters should be armed with torpedoes (the aircraft to be named 'Torbeaus'). As a result a 'Strike Wing' of Coastal Command was formed. Three Coastal Command Beaufighter squadrons were based at RAF North Coates in Lincolnshire, to operate off the Dutch coast. No.143 Squadron flew the cannon-equipped Beau-fighters, No.236 Squadron the Beau-bombers,while No.254 Squadron flew a mix of rocket-armed Beau-fighters,armed with eight 27 kg (60-lb) rocket projectiles and torpedo-armed Torbeaus. The plan was for the 'Strike Wing' to use up to thirty or more aircraft, each with its own particular role in the attack. The Torbeau's were to attack the merchant ships in the convoy while their escort fighters dealt with the enemy's escort vessels, with bombs, cannon-fire and rockets. The rocket-armed Beaufighters proved a formidable ASV anti-shipping weapon, as they did not have to hold to a steady course at low-level in order to launch their weapons.

In reality it was AM Slessor who reaped the benefit of Joubert's idea, as there was a considerable time lag between approval for the wing and its first action, in bad weather on 20 November, which was in essence a minor disaster. Joubert immediately withdrew the wing for further training and it was not until April 1943, after his departure that, the Beaufighter Wing began to show its true potential with two highly successful operations against German convoys at the cost of only one aircraft lost. Eventually under Slessors stewardship and despite demands for the airplanes to be deployed elsewhere, there were three very effective Beau-fighter strike wings, within Coastal Command.

In hindsight, the reality was, torpedo-bomber operations of WWII had a surprisingly small impact on the European war and the Battle of the Atlantic. In the first year or so of the war in Europe many of the torpedo-bomber successes came from operations of the Italian Air Force in the Mediterranean. It was the Italians who trained the first Luftwaffe torpedo-bomber pilots and who provided the German Air Force with their aerial torpedoes. Surprisingly the Germans did not make use of the torpedo at all when attacking the British Fleet off Norway in 1940, and even when attacking convoys in the Western Approaches, their attempts to use torpedo-bombers were spectacular unsuccessful. But by 1942, it was a different story when Junkers Ju 88 torpedo bomber squadrons, in co-operation with U-boats, inflicted heavy losses on Anglo-American convoys taking Lend-Lease materials and equipment across the Atlantic to Britain and Russia. (see details of Lend-Lease aircraft lost in transit at sea - in Appendix). Later unescorted torpedo-bomber units of the Luftwaffe in turn suffered heavy losses to ships' guns and to carrier-borne fighters protecting the convoys, losing many of their elite crews. It is difficult to realise in retrospect that numerically the Luftwaffe torpedo-bomber arm was stronger in the summer of 1944, than at any other stage of WW II. Based in France, following a year of intensive training in the Baltic, these Junkers Ju 88 and Heinkel 111 squadrons had more shipping targets offered them in the Mediterranean and the English Channel than at any other phase of the war; but the Luftwaffe lost air parity and the quality of the torpedo-bomber crews was inferior. In the end they were destroyed at their air bases in France in the summer of 1944, by B-17 Flying Fortresses of the 8th Air Force.

Neither land-based or carrier-based British torpedo bombers can lay claim to having played a decisive role in Europe and Mediterranean naval air warfare in WW II, though the attacks on Rommel's supply convoys in the Mediterranean certainly helped the Allied land Campaign in North Africa. One significant torpedo bomber success of British carrier-borne torpedo bombers occurred on 26 May, 1941, when Fairy Swordfish biplanes from HMS *Ark Royal* severely damaged the steering gear of the German battleship *Bismarck*. However, it would be true to say it was the Pacific War that provided the major success for the torpedo bombers in WW II, but that is another story...

Meanwhile, in mid-1942 in Britain, the AOC-in-C Coastal Command, AM Joubert was still grappling with his problems. It was a time of intense frustration for the Air Marshal and it seemed as though the only response possible to any request put to the Air Ministry, was "No". German fighter strength was increasing along the Dutch and Norwegian coasts, and normal reconnaissance was proving costly and it was not unreasonable to request some D.H. Mosquito fighters might be spared to assist with this essential work. The reply was that Mosquito production was entirely taken up in satisfying Fighter Command's prior need for night fighters. There were no Mosquitoes available for Coastal Command.

At the same time the U-boats were stepping up their attacks on the Atlantic convoys following the brief sojourn afforded, their concerted attacks on American coastal shipping, now over. The "packs" were back in increasing numbers with a total of 674,457 tons lost in April, amounting to 132 ships, of which 74 were sunk by U-boats and 705,050 tons in May, 151 ships, of which 125 were claimed by U-boats. What became glaringly apparent at this time was, if this intensity of raids was kept up, apart from anything else, there would be no bomber offensive. The primary target for the U-boats at all times was the oil tankers and British losses in the Atlantic in the first six months of 1942, amounted to 68, while the diversion of 49 more to the Indian Ocean to support the war in the Pacific, only served to worsen the problem. By the beginning of May, the Oil Control Board, were in a deep state of alarm, having calculated that their year end stock would be 2,000,000 tons below requirements, unless they got tanker reinforcements. They estimated they needed at least seventy, capable of sailing in convoys maintaining 10-knots and carrying 10,000 tons of cargo. A request to America for assistance was responded to most favourably with 45 tankers ceded for use, a surprisingly generous gesture to which Churchill promptly expressed his deep gratitude in the light that between January and June, 1942, the United States itself had lost no fewer than 73 tankers in the Atlantic. It now became patently obvious in the summer of 1942, that it was in the Atlantic that the war would lost or won.

The British Admiralty had no illusions of this fact, and indeed it was well aware of the need for greater support for Coastal Command in its efforts to contain the U-boat menace. On 23 June, the Naval Staff sent a despatch to ACM Portal, with a copy to Joubert : it was a detailed communique comprising several paragraphs - the first drawing attention to the fact, we had lost control over sea communications of the world with all that this meant in supply of raw materials and food for Great Britain, and the ability to take the offensive. The following paragraphs outlined the conception of maritime strategy which the Admiralty considered necessary to rectify the situation... It stated a major point that stood out clearly, was that ships were unable to maintain command at sea, and in line with the Air Ministry's own estimations that there was a current deficiency of aircraft for successful prosecution of the war at sea of about 800 machines of all types - of which the bulk were needed by Coastal Command. It concluded, the only outstanding problem was to find a means of fulfilling the agreed requirements as quickly as possible for "we cannot await the fruition of a long-term programme when our hopes of even fulfilling that programme are being daily decreased by our lack of command of the sea".

The stated airplane deficit amounted to almost the total inventory available to Bomber Command six months later, the Air Staff were staggered by the request. Even AM Joubert was somewhat taken aback; stating while he was in general agreement with the Admiralty's arguments and figures, "if there had been an unlimited number of aircraft available but, in light of the hard facts of shortage of aircraft in the RAF as a whole, he was against the demand for the immediate dissipation of RAF resources in order to strengthen Coastal Command alone. A view shared by the Chief of Air Staff and the Air Ministry. The Air Ministry were in a difficult position, desperate to meet demands from all branches of the service. In 1942, all branches of the service were suffering from an acute shortage of aircraft.

It is generally accepted that Coastal Commands ascendency in the Sea War occurred in May, 1943, at the time Air Marshal Sir John Slessor took over. Slessor himself quite reasonably stating "I hasten to disclaim any suggestion that this was cause and effect". In fact this in the main is true, and that the cause and effect occurred ten months earlier in July 1942, when AM Joubert was still in charge. Although like Slessor the turn around not directly attributed to Joubert but to AM Bowhill who had, had the foresight to let Squadron Leader Leigh pursue his ideas of fitting a powerful searchlight to long-range Coastal Command aircraft. Examination of U-boat losses from January 1942 to July 1942, reveals the impact of this important technical innovation. The facts are :

Between 1 January and 30 June 1942, 21 U-boats were lost, of the twenty-one lost only six were attributed to air action with a seventh shared. Of these, three were claimed by the United States air arms. For Britain all the Atlantic "kills" were made by RAAF or RCAF (No.10 Sqn and No. 461 Squadron) units operating from Britain, or RCAF bases in Newfoundland or Nova Scotia. Coastal Command claimed one, all British "kills" were in the Mediterranean; these being Italian submarines,not included in this survey.

This somewhat gloomy picture suddenly changed in July 1942, with 11 U-boats lost in the month, with 5 and one shared claimed by air action. The Americans claimed two and one shared, the RCAF one, and Coastal Command two, U-502 and U-751. The first, U-502 being the first Leigh Light equipped Wellington "kill" by No.172 Squadron on 5 July. From this point on, the number of U-boat kills in the Atlantic continued to rise, with 10 lost in August, 10 more in September and 16 in October — with ten and one shared claimed by air action. In total the second half of 1942, saw 65 U-boats sunk, 35 and one shared as a result of air action, equal to 53% of the total. RAF Coastal Commands share amounted to 18, fifty per cent, the Command had come of age. Only once in the following critical year of 1943, did the Command's total fall below 50% (47.3% in February). July 1942, can quite rightly be claimed as the 'new dawn' for Coastal Command, with the foundations laid by AM Bowhill and AM Joubert at last producing conclusive results.

The foregoing statistics are even more impressive when it is remembered in this achievement, each success is matched by hours, days and even weeks of unrewarding flying in some of the most inhospitable conditions in the world. It is sometimes said that "war is nine-tenths boredom", for Coastal Command there was no boredom each patrol usually meant long hours of arduous flying at low-level with the crew maintaining maximum vigilance. Probably the only comparable 'peacetime' missions being those flown by the weather reconnaissance crews of the USAF. Maximum attention and vigilance was demanded from the crew of each airplane not only to scan the skies for enemy aircraft but also not too miss the often indistinct silhouette miles away on the often monotonous surface of the sea. The action when it did come was often sudden, swift and precise, demanding an instant high state of readiness and action stations. In demonstration of the intensity of operations it is of interest to examine some operational reports of the period :

At 15.01 hours on 15 September, Whitley V 'B' of No. 58 Squadron flown by Sgt. B. F. Snell, sighted a U-boat (U-261) on the surface at a distance of seven miles, travelling at an estimated 10 knots. The aircraft turned and broke cloud at around 3,000 feet, and attacked from the U-boat's port quarter with five Torpex depth-charges released from 20 feet, with the U-boat fully surfaced. The depth-charges straddled the boat; three fell short to port, one made a direct hit on the bridge, and one fell beyond to starboard. As the depth-charge boils subsided the bows of the U-boat were sticking out of the water at an angle of 15°. Sgt. Snell turned the Whitley to make another attack. The bows of the boat slid under just before the remaining depth-charge was released, leaving on the surface an oil-patch some 90 yards long and 25 yards wide, in the centre of which were many bits of orange coloured wood (believed to be plywood), other debris and a black object which was assumed to be an oil-drum. The remaining Torpex depth-charge exploded in the centre of this oil and debris, 5 seconds after the bows disappeared from sight, and nothing further was seen of the boat. The Whitley dropped a submarine marker and flew away northward, returning to the scene about twenty minutes later, and following a square search nothing further was seen.

The practice of returning to the scene, known as "baiting" had first been used in 1918. After an inconclusive attack, when the U-boat had vanished into the depths, the attacking aircraft would fly away from the scene and stay away for sometimes an hour or more, then return, preferably through cloud cover or down sun. It was not unusual to catch the U-boat surfaced again, and so the attack was renewed. In the case of *U-261* the "baiting" was probably somewhat superfluous in the light of the amount of oil and debris appearing on the surface following the U-boats disappearance.

The dramatic turnabout in U-boat losses at this time soon prompted Admiral Doenitz contrary to his earlier statement about the 'crow and the mole' , to say, "U-boat traffic round Scotland and in the Bay of Biscay is gravely endangered by daily, even hourly, hunts by aircraft. In the Atlantic the enemy's daily reconnaissance covers out as far as 20° W, which forces U-boat dispositions far out into the centre of the Atlantic with consequent higher fuel consumption, shorter operational periods, and greater difficulty in finding the enemy convoys in the open Atlantic. If developments continue at the present rate, these problems will lead to irreparable losses, to a decline in ship sinkings, and consequently to reduced chances of success in the U-boat warfare as a whole".

He also drew attention to the effect already produced by even a small number of very long-range airplanes in protecting convoys, quoting U-boat captains saying that successful attacks were possible "only as long as Allied aircraft were not in evidence". Which of course was no more than the truth. A patrolling long-range B-24 Liberator, had the dual effect of defence for the convoy by guiding it to the right areas, and the positive offensive function of forcing U-boats to dive and stay submerged, often preventing them from making an attack at all. In order to counter them in the Atlantic, Doenitz requested reinforcement with Heinkel He 177 "Greif" twin-engined heavy bombers which he considered "the only aircraft which have a range and fighting power capable of acting as a reconnaissance and combating English aircraft in the Biscay area". Luftwaffe needs on the Eastern Front of course negated this, until October 1943, when along with a few Blohm und Voss BV 222 six-engined "Wiking" flying-boats, an allocation of a few He 177 proved less than satisfactory. However, earlier in September, 1942, Doenitz did receive a *Staffel* (equivalent to RAF squadron of nine aircraft) of the heavily armed Junkers Ju-88C-6. With a maximum speed of 300 mph and a powerful armament fit of three 20mm cannon and three 7.9mm machine guns fixed for forward firing, two fixed up-firing 20mm cannon and one flexible aft-firing 13mm machine gun.

The Ju-88s (with a second *Staffel* added in October and two more in November, to form V/KG 40), proved a formidable adversary for many of Coastal Command's older and slower types of aircraft. There were 44 combats over the Bay of Biscay alone in September, 1942. Even the Wellington's were not exempt and on 11 September,a Wellington was lucky to escape following an attack by four Ju 88s when their first attack pierced the hydraulics of the rear turret, which thereafter could only be turned by hand. And a second attack by three Ju-88s together, when two passed overhead and either side with the third opening fire at 300 yards as it approached from dead ahead, climbing steeply to avoid collision. But, as its nose pointed upwards the Wellington's front gunner fired a long burst into the belly; the fighter-bomber peeling of to port with smoke bellowing from both engines, after a few seconds crashed into the sea. The remaining three Ju-88s then reformed and repeated the attack, except this time the third aircraft attacked from astern. These tactics were repeated three more times, while the Wellington took evasive action by climbing from sea-level to 300 ft dropping to sea-level and climbing again and turning from port to starboard. Eventually one of the attackers made off towards the French coast, leaving a thin stream of black smoke trailing from its port engine. The two remaining Ju-88s making two more attacks from the quarters but did not approach within 600 yards. Finally having took up positions above and to starboard they shadowed for three minutes or so, until the Wellington disappeared into a patch of sea fog. The Wellington survived although it had sustained many hits, luckily none of the crew were hit. In October, 1942, with Doenitz's reinforcements, operational Junkers Ju-88C-6 airplanes destroyed sixteen Coastal Command aircraft, but help was at hand with the introduction of the Bristol Beaufighters of Nos 235 and 248 Squadrons :

Already on the 17 September, 1942, at 17.55 hours eight Beaufighters of No. 235 Squadron on interceptor patrol were flying at 200 feet in loose formation in the Bay of Biscay, when a Focke Wulf Fw 200 Condor was sighted. It was flying one mile to starboard on a reciprocal course over an armed 300-ton fishing trawler. The three leading Beaufighters 'E', 'P' and 'N' attacked the Condor on the port side, while Beaufighter 'O' dived from 2,000 feet to make a head-on attack, and the remainder attacked from the starboard quarter. The attack tactics which had been discussed at an earlier briefing worked perfectly. However, the trawler opened fire bringing down Beaufighter 'C' into the sea. Beaufighter 'J' then attacked the Condor for a second time from the port quarter and 'E' followed with a third attack from starboard, then broke away and attacked again from the port beam. The Fw 200 now burst into flames and dived into the sea with a series of explosions. A dingy was released and seen in the sea with one man trying to climb in and three floating in the water. The seven remaining Beaufighters reformed and resumed their patrol at 18.10 hours.

Ten minutes later flying at various positions with six miles between the first and last aircraft, three Ju 88s were seen ahead, circling at 1,000 feet above a fishing vessel flying a French flag. The Beaufighters climbed to 1,000 feet and attacked simultaneously from various directions. One Ju 88 was hit in the port engine and tail, and dived nose down into the sea. Beaufighters 'N', 'O' and 'E' attacked a second Ju 88; flames appeared from in the cockpit and a large piece of cowling fell off. This airplane also plummeted into the sea, enveloped in flames. Meanwhile Beaufighter 'A' followed the third Ju 88 and attacked, but it took evasive action and disappeared in a cloud. Beaufighter 'A' flew through cloud and re-sighted the Ju 88 attacking and losing it again. When the attacking Beaufighters turned for home two Ju 88 tailplanes could be seen bobbing in the sea.

There were many encounters of this nature at this time with the victories ebbing and flowing first one way then the other. V/KG 40 continued to threaten operations, but not without cost to itself. Introduction of the more powerful Torpex filled depth-charges, linked to a reliable 25-foot pistol-setting, at last gave Coastal Command weapons of true lethality. However, true to life it was in September 1942, that the honeymoon period enjoyed by the ASV Leigh Light equipped Wellingtons came to an end with the introduction of the German *Metox* receiver. Produced under orders by the Nazis by French firms, *Metox* was a simple receiver, designed to detect ASV transmissions from patrolling Allied aircraft. In the U-boats radio room, the receiver operator heard the aircrafts radar transmissions as a continuous buzz in his earphones. Thus warned of an approaching radar-equipped attacker, the submarine crews could dive to safety before the attack developed. The German submariners commented favourably on the new receiver : it picked up transmissions coming from aircraft more than 30 miles away — more than twice the distance at which an airborne radar operator could detect a submarine... By September, 1942, several German submarines had been fitted with the *Metox* receiver, and often these would act as escorts for their less fortunate colleagues making the dangerous crossing of the Bay of Biscay. By the wars end most of the German U-boats were fitted with the receiver. So by the end of 1942, another round in the technical war on the U-boat had been opened.

At the same time the problem of the "Gap"; several hundred miles of open sea in the north-east Atlantic, roughly south of the point of Greenland, left Allied shipping extremely vulnerable to the U-boat packs. It was in this "Gap" that a great many of the U-boats kills were occurring. At this time Coastal Command had only five VLR Liberator Is of No. 120 Squadron based at Reykjavik, Iceland, to counter the threat. It is perhaps important to note that with a combat radius of 2,400 miles it was only the Mark I Liberator that was a true VLR airplane. The Mark II which was also on No. 120 Squadrons inventory was a bomber variant with a range of 1,800 miles and was rated as a long-range airplane and not a Very Long Range (VLR), airplane. Similarly the Mark III also designed as a bomber with 1,680 miles range, was also on No.120 Squadron's inventory but required extensive de-modification for the VLR, low-altitude, ASW operation : the self-sealing liners to the fuel tanks and most of the defensive protective pieces of armour plating were removed, as were the turbo-superchargers for the engines, and the lower power-operated gun turret. This weight reducing programme made it possible for the airplane to take-off carrying more than 2,000 gallons of high octane fuel, in addition to its offensive load of eight 250-lb depth-charges.

Nevertheless No. 120 Squadron bears testimony to the maxim it is the man and not the machine that counts. The man in this instance was Ulsterman Squadron Leader Terence Bulloch, who by the end of July, 1942 had logged 2,300 hours flying time and was assessed as an "exceptional" pilot and above average navigator. In addition he was a dedicated adversary of the U-boat. He was deeply interested in his airplane and every part of its equipment; imparting his knowledge to his crew, thereby forming a close-knit highly professional hunter-killer ASW team. His dedication and leadership did not go unrewarded for long : on 16 August he encountered *U-89;* only lack of a proper 25-foot setting for his depth-charges saved her from certain destruction. Two days later he attacked *U-653*, damaging her so severely she was forced to return to base. His first "kill" came on 12 October, at 12.18 hours when piloting Liberator 'H' in the Atlantic south-west of Iceland, a radar contact was made eight miles away to starboard; at 12.23 the boats wake was seen some eight miles away. Approaching from the sun Bulloch approached the U-boat, which was travelling at about 10 knots, just 15 miles from an Allied convoy :

Diving to attack from the U-boats port quarter at 15° to the track, six Torpex depth-charges were released from 75 feet while the U-boat was still on the surface; two more of the aircrafts depth-charges hung up. *U-597* was completely covered by the stick of depth-charges, both in line and range, from bows to stern. During the explosion of the first depth-charge on the stern, three large and several small pieces of metal were thrown up into the air, and one large oval piece of metal flew past the Liberator's rear turret. As the third and fourth depth-charges were exploding amidships close up to the starboard side, the U-boat shuddered and lifted out of the water, leaving the deck clearly visible with water pouring off it. As the spray cleared the conning tower and the periscope were visible for around seven seconds until sinking vertically without trace. Almost immediately a small white cylindrical object was observed bobbing up and down in the water and subsequently oil and other wreckage including a further greenish-grey cylinder studded with bolts, measuring about a foot in diameter and projecting about five feet out of the water, were seen floating in the oil patch, and was still there half an hour later when the Liberator left the scene. It was assumed the object was an airtight part of the submarines exhaust system. Photographs confirmed the accuracy of the attack evidenced by the amount of wreckage, oil and other debris on the surface in the area of attack. *U-597* and her entire crew had sunk to the bottom of the Atlantic Ocean.

For Squadron Leader Bulloch this was only the start of a long and successful campaign in his assault on the German submarine menace. In the course of the next three weeks he and his crew sighted four U-boats and attacked two. Bulloch was in operation again on the 5 November, 1942, the day following the tragic lost of fifteen ships of Convoy SC 107. He had been accredited with sinking *U-132* on this day, but subsequently it has been established she was sunk as a result of the attack on her final victim, the ammunition ship *Hatimura,*being in the radius of the resultant massive explosion. However, the vessel he did attack on this day, was forced to submerge in order to escape the scene. The following month on the 8 December, he was escorting Convoy HX 217, which came under attack by two packs totalling twenty-two U-boats. These had just sunk a merchant ship in the half-light of the dawn when the 120 Squadron Liberator arrived on station. Throughout the next five and half hours of the patrol Bulloch made eight U-boat sightings attacking seven times. The Liberator that replaced him flown by Squadron Leader Desmond Isted, also sighted at least five U-boats and attacked four, sinking *U-611* finally making the attack on Convoy HX 217 a complete U-boat failure.

The unqualified failure of the wolfpack attack on HX 217 was attributed by the U-boat captains to "the arrival of air patrols in unusually large numbers". Although the reality was the repeated attacks by No. 120 Squadron Liberator's gave an understandable delusion that the skies over the Atlantic were full of airplanes; in fact the reality was very small numbers were producing very big results. One German Petty Officer told his captors :

"British air reconnaissance was particularly dreaded by U-boats. He said, if on the surface you see a plane, the plane has probably seen you and it is already too late : you are done... Survivors told of the British air reconnaissance flights which forced them to spend much time submerged... Others stated that while in the Atlantic they were constantly forced to dive to avoid attracting the attention of aircraft patrols.

Further proof of the effectiveness of air attacks at this time came in the closing months of 1942, when the air menace had grown to such an extent that Admiral Doenitz instructed his crews should "fight it out", on the surface. To enable them to do so, special gun platforms known as "bandstands" were constructed on the U-boats to carry a single or (later) multiple 20-mm cannon, with a maximum rate of fire of 150 rounds per minute, and multiple machine-gun mountings. Later in 1943, the *Kriegsmarine* introduced the "submarine aircraft-trap", *U-441* was converted to carry two armoured "bandstands", one forward and one aft of the conning tower; her armament consisted of two quadruple-barrelled 20-mm guns and a semi-automatic 37-mm gun, with an increased crew of 67, from the normal compliment of 50. *U-441* made two cruises; in both she was so badly damaged that the "aircraft-trap" experiment was abandoned. Although heavily armed U-boats continued to operate. The addition of bulky armament, which included heavy armoured shields for the gun-crews, inevitably affected the submarines underwater performance. While the boats were successful in shooting down or seriously damaging a number of airplanes, the tactic left the U-boat vulnerable on the surface longer than normal, a fact referred to in *Coastal Command Review,* which suggested :

"namely that if a U-boat engages with gun or cannon fire she is obviously not going to dive. If the U-boat is not going to dive there is no longer any need to attack in the shortest space of possible time. The aircraft can break off the attack before getting dangerously close, then fly round the U-boat at about 800 yards range and bring all guns to bear. These tactics usually produce a high mortality rate among gun-crews on the upper deck, resulting in a sudden decision on the part of U-boat captain to *zum Teufel gehen,* i.e. "get the hell out of it", leaving the aircraft with a "sitter".

So, as fortunes swung first one way then the other in 1942, by the end of the year one thing was certain, now, air power was a force to be reckoned with. Shipping losses continued to the end of the year to the unprecedented level of 1,794,489 tons lost in the last quarter. But, on the other hand, at last air power was playing a significant part in the increasing serious losses to U-boats. But, still in November 1942, 134 ships were sunk, 83 of them in the Atlantic. At the same time Germany failed in its quest to interfere with Operation *Torch,* with the U-boat fleet humiliated, by 19 November, having lost seven U-boats in 12 days. Doenitz was forced to withdraw his U-boats towards the west, this in itself an admission that they no longer ruled supreme, and there was worst to come...

As 1942, drew to a close, development of the much improved ASV III centimetric radar was providing a detection range of some 40 miles for convoys and 12 miles for surfaced submarines, with greatly improved resolution. The main problems at this time were in production and priority, and with only limited supplies available, the question was, who should have first call on the equipment. Bomber or Coastal Command. Nevertheless following months of wrangling by headquarters staff, by January 1943, the first Coastal Command Liberator was carrying ASV III on daylight patrols, and at night when complemented with the Leigh Light. The operational successes of 1943, obviously owned much to the introduction of ASV and the Germans inability to introduce an effective countermeasure, *Naxos-U* which came into operation too late in October, 1943. Even more so, was the success at Bletchley Park at the turn of the year, when it finally cracked the Germans "fourth wheel" enigma machine. Almost the whole of 1942, was spent in this pursuit, in fact Rear-Admiral Clayton, the head of its Operational Intelligence Centre, remarked in November that the U-boat war was :

the one campaign which Bletchley Park are not at present influencing to any marked extent - and it is the only one in which the war can be lost unless B.P. *do* help. I do not think that this is any exaggeration.

Once Bletchley Park had "cracked it". The Admiralty, at the time, were greatly relieved as the importance associated with the de-cyphers of operational instructions sent to the patrolling U-boats was enormous. The communications included information about the departure and return of U-boats, the numbers and types of U-boats at sea, the movements and disposition of their patrol groups and their operational orders. As except when a U-boat sailed on a special mission or to a distant venue, its destination and operational orders were relayed to it by W/T after it had put to sea. That the communications were so comprehensive was related to U-Boat Command's desire, to keep close control of the North Atlantic offensive. Not only did returning U-boats always signal their expected time of arrival; every outward-bound U-boat reported clearing Biscay or, if leaving from Norway or the Baltic, after crossing 60°N... No U-boat could deviate from its orders without requesting and receiving permission, and without requesting and receiving permission none could begin its return passage. The control exercised by U-boat Command over the U-boats while they were searching for and attacking convoys was also rigid. It constantly ordered the formation and re-formation of the patrol lines between specified geographical positions at regular intervals, addressing by name each U-boat commander who was to take place in the line and giving him his exact position in it. This was the great weakness of the "Doenitz system", of Command and Control. Too much and too specific and too often. Which, in itself did pose a problem for Bletchley Park even when it had cracked the "fourth wheel" code. There was a vast mass of signal traffic, and it took a considerable time until this could be read sufficiently fast enough for the decrypts to be of full operational use, and it was not until August, 1942, that this was achieved,when, "from this time till the end of the war all the W/T traffic for each day was read as a matter of course with little or no delay".

AM Joubert handed control of Coastal Command to AM Sir John Slessor, on 5 February, 1943. Following two terms of office and having presided over the worst of the dark night of the U-boat war, but by the time of his departure, he had the satisfaction of having brought about the turn in the Command's operational effectiveness. It now had effective lethal weapons, and it knew how to use them; there were more to come - ASV III was entering service and the use of rockets was in the offing, along with large calibre guns and other devices. The Commands inventory had also increased in numbers; it now had 43.5 operational squadrons, in addition to Photographic, Meteorological and Air Sea Rescue units and six squadrons forming, re-equipping or training - a total of 59.5 squadrons with an inventory of 839 airplanes and a daily availability of 469.

Coastal Command Operational Inventory circa February, 1943.
The main weakness in the above still the distinct lack of VLR aircraft - with only two Liberator squadrons with

Operational Squadrons : Aircraft type	Authorised Establishment	Actual Establishment	Average Daily Availability
12.5 flying-boat units (inc 1 US Navy)	126	118	49
18 anti-U-boat GR squadrons (inc 2 Bomber Command and 2 USAAF)	304	293	161
13 anti-shipping GR and long-range fighter units	238	260	145
6 Photo-recce units	91	85	54
1 Meteorological Sqdn plus 4 Flights	68	49	34
2 Air-Sea-Rescue Sqdns	40	34	26
Total	867	839	469

a total of 14 aircraft. The struggle to obtain more, would prove a major uphill task for AM Slessor. Meanwhile he benefited from another of Jouberts contributions by way of the - "Planned Flying and Maintenance" , as described in *Coastal Command Review* No. 6, October, 1942. The plan introduced in August, 1942, strove to anticipate operational requirements so that maintenance could be carried out in the most economic and profitable manner (the *Review* pointed out that it was standard peace-time practice in American civil airlines); the effect was to compensate some part of the weakness in numbers by increased use of resources that did exist.

AM Slessor, highly regarded as a rising star in the RAF, took over in an "exceptionally violent" winter, "the ice coming down almost as far as Newfoundland and hurricanes and severe gales prevailing throughout the North Atlantic". This atrocious weather in effect afforded the Command some respite : the U-boats finding it exceedingly difficult in locating the convoys, with single ships even more difficult to locate in the fog and sleet. The total sinkings in January 1943, were reduced to 261,359 tons (50 ships), of which U-boats claimed 203,128 (37 ships). However, as might be expected air operations were also severely hampered, with aircraft if not grounded virtually blinded by the prevailing conditions; only six U-boats were sunk in the whole month of which only two in the North Atlantic, one by unknown causes, one (*U-337*) credited to No. 206 Squadron on 16 January. As weather conditions eased in February, losses increased : 403,062 tons lost, with U-boats responsible for 359,328 (63 ships out of a total of 73); the U-boats suffering nineteen losses, nine to air action, of which Coastal Command claimed seven.

At the Casablanca Conference held in early 1943, to assess the problem of invading Europe — the final report declared : The defeat of the U-boat must remain a first charge on the resources of the Allies. With Germany producing U-boats at a rate of twenty a month, while only seven a month were being sunk, rather belatedly and as it proved, ineffectually, Bomber Command had now turned its attention to bombing the U-boat bases, and other targets such as Bremen, Hamburg, Kiel, Rostock, Lubeck, Augsburg and Flensburg - all places closely associated with U-boat production. Dropping huge numbers of ordnance on the 16-foot thick reinforced-concrete roofs of the pens, where "they made no more than a slight indentation in the surface". In total between January and March 1943, a total of 3,056 bomber sorties dropped 4,178 tons of high explosive on the main U-boat bases, losing 67 aircraft in the process; 1,825 sorties (2,848 tons dropped) against the U-boat yards cost 74 aircraft. Not a single U-boat was even damaged by any of these raids.

Throughout 1942, AM Joubert had become aware that the Allies needed a unified Atlantic Command to match that of Admiral Doenitz, he was also aware his main adversary in this matter was the US Navy's Commander-in-Chief of the Fleet and the Chief of Naval Operations, Admiral Ernest King. King firmly believed that, for the United States, the Pacific was the theatre that mattered. Nevertheless an Allied Atlantic Convoys Conference in March, went some way to resolving the problem of unifying the Anglo-American effort, when the system of convoy cover was re-organised, and most important of all, it was agreed VLR squadrons of the RCAF and USAAF would operate out of Newfoundland. The US Navy agreed to allocate escort carriers to the convoys, this closer co-operation going some way to closing the "Atlantic Gap", with the additional protection affording air cover all the way. Albeit the thorny problem of establishing a unified command remained unresolved.

Coastal Command continued to keep up the pressure on the U-boat's activities but in the first few months of 1943, twenty eastbound ships from convoys HX 229 and SC 122 were sunk in four days most in areas unprotected by aerial patrols. At the beginning of March, Doenitz (now Grand Admiral and Commander-in-Chief of the German Navy) had fifty U-boats operating in the North Atlantic. They were formed into three packs, which with the aid of U-boat Command in Paris, he was able to place them with absolute precision. He assembled forty in two packs for the main assault on convoys HX 229 and SC 122 which began on 16 March. Even so, the atrocious weather almost turned the whole operation into a complete fiasco; it was only by chance that *U-653* on its way home with engine trouble, found itself in the midst of HX 229 that the packs made contact. At the same time the other U-boats looking for HX 229, found SC 122. By the morning of 17 March, twelve ships had been sunk and the whole U-boat concentration was preparing for a final assault on the remaining ships. Fortunately, just-in-time three Liberators of No.120 Squadron reached the area of SC 122, they sighted 11 U-boats and attacked six, and largely as a consequence, only one ship was lost that day. But, not having Leigh Lights, as darkness fell the Liberators were forced to withdraw and two further ships were lost. The next day No. 120 Squadron returned to the scene with five Liberators, they sighted seven U-boats and attacked five; the convoy suffered no loss that day. But the less well protected HX 229 lost two more ships. During the night what remained of the two convoys (originally SC 122 contained 60 ships and HX 229 contained 40) joined up making a very large collection in a very small space with eighteen escort vessels.

By now the Liberators of No. 120 Squadron were joined by seven Fortresses of No. 206 Squadron and three Sunderland flying boats in addition to six other Liberators. Even so, two ships were sunk, and with Deonitz realising the odds were mounting against them the U-boats withdrew, with two badly damaged. For the Germans it was to be their most successful of all convoy battles. Twenty-one ships from the two convoys had been sunk; it was "the biggest convoy disaster of the war". The Admiralty was to state, 'The Germans never came so near to disrupting communications between the New World and the Old as in the first 20 days of March, 1943. The month of March , saw the U-boats at their most successful, in the most atrocious weather conditions, with constant storms with heavy seas following, a number of U-boats themselves finding it difficult to remain afloat. During the month, 693,389 tons of Allied or neutral shipping was lost; 120 ships. Over 90% of the losses was attributed to the U-boats, 627,377 tons, 108 ships. U-boat losses dropped from 19 in February to 15, of which only 10 were sunk in the North Atlantic or the Bay of Biscay. Of the 15 sunk, nine were claimed by air attack, two in the Mediterranean, the rest to Coastal Command. The most worrying aspect was that in the first twenty days of the month, out of 85 ships sunk by U-boats in all areas, 67 were lost while in protected convoys. In the whole month, in the North Atlantic, 32 were lost while in actual convoy, and 10 were stragglers.

Fortunately with operational U-boat numbers still on the increase (231 March, 237 April, and 239 in May) within days the situation changed dramatically again, and from then on the U-boats appeared to be fighting a losing battle. With Bomber Command having abandoned their offensive against the Biscay bases and construction yards in April, it was pleasing 41 U-boats were sunk in May (six in one night),seventeen in June and 37 in July, with German figures showing 35% of these losses were from air attack, while surfaced in W/T communication with Submarine Command, a further 20% while in the vicinity of the convoys they intended to attack and another 19% were sunk by combined naval and aircraft operations. These figures included RAF Coastal Command operations, and the losses inflicted by the Royal Navy's Fleet Air Arm, USAAF and US Navy planes

With better tactics, better aircraft with longer patrol ranges (there were 70 VLR aircraft available in May), with centimetric radar, more effective depth-charges, more bases and escort carriers all helping to tip the balance in favour of Allied air power at last. There was also better intelligence with the Bletchley Park team now managing to unscramble the operational code Triton that the Germans had introduced to replace their original Hydra code. Ship-based high frequency radio direction finding (HF/DF), also profited from the enormous amount of communications traffic generated by the "Doenitz system"; during one convoy action in early 1943, there were over one hundred transmissions from U-boats noted by the Allies in a period of seventy-two hours. The "fixes" from these transmissions enabled ships or aircraft to pin-point the presence and whereabouts of the U-boats, to possibly sink it or make it dive. In addition during March, 1943, Sir Max Horton, the new C-in-C of Western Approaches formed the first five convoy Support Groups, with the Americans, later, supplying a sixth and a carrier *Bogue,* to work in close co-operation with the convoys and in close conjunction with Coastal Command. At the same time after extensive studies by Commander Peyton-Ward and the Operational Research Section, a new directive was issued in regard to the stick spacing of depth-charges. Following analysis of some 300 attacks from every aspect, it was clearly shown that a universal stick spacing of 100 feet (in place of the existing 36 feet for large aircraft and 60 feet for Lockheed Hudsons) was optimum both for outright "kills" and infliction of damage. The spacing was therefore standardised at 100 feet from the 14 March, 1943.

At first the order was not popular with pilots and bomb-aimers, because it seemed to be a reflection on their skill and efficiency, and an article in the March, 1943, issue No. 11, of *Coastal Command Review* carefully explained the reason for the change.

Referring to an analysis of 43 36-foot spacing attacks for which there was photographic evidence taken at the time, it concluded — there is, therefore, absolutely no doubt that 100-ft spacing is better than 36 foot. The *Review* article entitled "Depth-Charge Stick Spacing", reported of the 43 attacks analysed, photographs showed that "owing to errors in range, 18 sticks overshot completely and four sticks undershot completely". Based on this analysis, the odds against straddling a U-boat (when near enough to the surface to be vulnerable to the 25-ft depth setting) with a stick of six depth-charges spaced at 36 feet proved to be roughly four to one against in beam attacks, three to one against in attacks close to track".

The proof of these findings and implementation of the new directive was in the successes: with 83 attacks in May, 1943, using the 100-foot spacing, resulting in 14 U-boats sunk and 13 damaged. A further major technical innovation at this time was the introduction of the what for security reasons was known as the "Mark 24 Mine". This was, in fact, an air-launched torpedo, with an acoustic homing head, developed in the United States. Coastal Command began to receive deliveries in May and the Liberators of Nos. 120 and 86 Squadrons were carrying the weapon, with No. 86 Squadron making its first "kill" on 12 May. Deployment of the Mark 24 Acoustic torpedo evened the score as the Germans introduced their FAT (*Flächenabsuchender* torpedo), the "zig-zag runner", with the ability to home on a target from all angles and their new magnetic torpedo pistol. In addition for the Allies there was Ultra, in June, at last, in the fourth summer of the war there was enough evidence from this source to convince the Admiralty that its Atlantic cipher was compromised and should be replaced by one that was secure. Although at this time Ultra could not supply operational intelligence as quickly as was necessary, it was, supplying more general information of the U-boat effort.

Significantly as early as February, 1943, it had been noted that the growing band of inexperienced U-boat commanders were on occasion reporting torpedo failures, made unsubstantiated claims and betrayed signs of timidity, particularly in the face of air attack, and there had also been a noticeable increase in the occasions on which U-boats developed debilitating defects during their outward passage of the Bay of Biscay. These, the first signs of cracks in the *Kreigsmarine's* morale.

On the 4 April the *Löwenherz* pack of 14 U-boats sighted convoy HX 231, and mounted an attack which resulted in the loss of six ships. Following, two of the U-boats were sunk south-west of Iceland, one *U-635* on 5 April, by a Liberator of No. 120 Squadron, and the other *U-632* the very next day, in the same area, by a Liberator of No. 86 Squadron. Ultra recorded U-boat Command's dissatisfaction with this situation, at the same time as a reprimand was issued to all U-boat captains for the excessive use of wireless. Five days later, the *Lerche* pack sighted convoy HX 232 and sank three ships, all on the first night, although after there were no further losses, and Ultra heard U-boat Command voicing there suspicions that the U-boats were not mounting their assaults vigorously enough. It reminded them they should display "the healthy warrior and hunter instincts". It also found disturbing, frequent references to their fear of attack from the air and to the efficiency of escort craft in following up aircraft sightings and by the 19 April, U-boat Command were heard conceding they could no longer use "wolfpack" tactics against convoys which had air support.

On the 19 April, British Admiralty's Operational Intelligence Centre, issued the following statement, there appears t o be an "incipient decline in U-boat morale". The action against three further convoys, HX 234, ONS 3 and ON 178 between 20 - 24 April, actually reinforced this when only four ships were sunk at the cost of three U-boats, with No. 120 Squadron again in the thick of things. The month's final tally reflecting the abrupt change in U-boat fortunes. The total tonnage lost was less than half the previous month's figure (344,680 tons; 64 ships), and if U-boats claimed 95 percent of this, their own score was halved at 327,943 tons ; 56 ships. Their own losses on the other hand amounted to 15 boats, the same as the month of March. Eight of these were as a result of air attack, six by Coastal Command.

The major turning point in U-boat fortunes occurred in May. Even with some 60 boats operational in the North Atlantic. The weather was again atrocious, with gales, snow squalls and enormous seas, not only hampering the U-boats, but causing even greater difficulties for the convoys and their escorts. It was impossible to refuel the navy destroyers at sea; as they ran low on fuel, all but two of those protecting ONS 5 were forced to return to port. This, setting the stage for the last major attack on a convoy by a U-boat pack : 13 ships were sunk between 1 - 5 May. But not without loss, six U-boats were sunk and four badly damaged. The atrocious weather dictated the battle was dominated by the Royal Navy, with only a flying-boat of the RCAF claiming a sixth.

However; from this time on things were very different, with aircraft, land and carrier-based, accounting for more than two thirds of the U-boats lost. In the battle of HX 237 and SC 129 between the 9 - 14 May, with Bletchley Park and German Intelligence both vying for ascendency, a total of 36 U-boats sank only five ships losing five of their own in the process. It was in this battle that the Acoustic Homing Torpedo was used for the first time, when three Liberators from No. 86 Squadron in action on the 12 May, were equipped with two of the new weapons in addition to their normal payload of depth-charges. At this time of course the squadron had no experience of the operational use of the weapon, the question being when and how to use them. Due to its possible susceptibility to enemy countermeasures there was already rigid rules on its use in action : since any countermeasures might cause it to run ashore and be captured, its use close to enemy-held shores was forbidden, in addition it should not be used in any situation where observation from the target or other enemy craft was possible.

With this in mind, Liberator 'B' of No. 86 Squadron flown by Flight Lieutenant J. Wright sighted a surfaced submarine in poor visibility, near to convoy HX 237. The U-boat (*U-456)* dived on seeing the aircraft but having released his torpedo Wright circled the area to see what happened. For at least two minutes the answer was, nothing; then a small upheaval was seen (similar to a weak depth-charge) about 900 yards from the boats diving point. Soon afterwards the boat reappeared on the surface, but by this time, the Liberator was coming to the limit of its endurance and Wright broke away informing the convoy's SOE that the vessel lay wallowing on the surface. Immediately a destroyer was despatched to investigate, but by the time it reached the spot the boat had gone, having sunk or been scuttled by the crew. Two days later a No. 86 Squadron Liberator attacked *U-403* with another homing torpedo, which escaped undamaged, but a Catalina of US Navy Squadron VP-82 was more successful the previous day, the 14 May, when it sank *U-657* with an acoustic homing torpedo, in the same area south-west of Iceland.

By now the increased U-boat losses were of great concern to the German Naval High Command, it was reported to have complained : "We can see no explanation of this failure". Of even greater concern was the apparent inability to sink more merchant ships and the perceived further decline in morale among the U-boat crews. But, the next two battles were the most decisive of the Sea War; both resulting in serious defeats for the U-boats, the first not merely a defeat but a complete disaster. This was the attack by 33 boats on SC 130, between the 17 - 19 May, when six U-boats were sunk and not one ship from the convoy was lost. This unmitigated fiasco was attributed by U-boat Command to "inexperienced captains", which to a degree was true and indeed on the 21 May prompted the following signal :

If there is anyone who thinks that combating convoys is no longer possible, he is a weakling and no true U-boat captain. The Battle of the Atlantic is getting harder but it is the determining element in the waging of the war...

At this time this was quite an amazing message, which was read with deep relief and immense satisfaction at Bletchley Park and the Submarine Tracking Room. The attacks of the following days, against convoys ON 184 and HX 239 served only to confirm the situation. On the 22 May, *U-569* became the first U-boat to be sunk by a US Navy hunter-killer team flying TBM Avengers operating from escort carriers. On the 23rd *U-752* that had been shadowing HX 239 was sunk by a Fairey Swordfish of the FAA. Swordfish 'G' of NAS 819, flying from escort carrier *Archer* had already sighted *U-752's* periscope, and was turning to attack when it came to the surface directly in front of the Swordfish. By the time the look-outs reached the conning tower they had sighted their attacker and relayed the fact to the captain who immediately gave the order to dive. By then the Swordfish had released a bomb that penetrated the boats No 4 tank and blew a hole in the pressure hull. A stream of water entered the wardroom and *Kapitänleutnant* Karl-Ernst Schroeter ordered the boat to surface, intending to fight it out. But by now a Grumman Martlet 'B' of NAS 892 had joined in the attack, and strafed the bridge with cannon fire. Schroeter and his midshipman was killed, the remaining incumbent gave the order to abandon ship and to open the main vents to sink her. *U-752* was the first U-boat to be sunk by rockets, the weapons only being issued to No. 819 NAS three weeks before the engagement, in which no ship from either convoy was lost. On 24 May, noting 31 U-boats had already been lost to date, Admiral Doenitz wrôte in his War Diary wrote:

Losses, even heavy losses, must be accepted if they are accompanied by proportional success in tonnage sunk. But in May one U-boat was lost for every 10,000 GRT (gross registered tons) sunk, where not so long ago one U-boat was lost for 100,000 GRT sunk. Thus our losses so far in May have reached an intolerable level. The enemy air force played a decisive role in inflicting these high losses.

So, on that day the 24 May, Admiral Doenitz called off the Atlantic convoy battle and ordered the U-boats to deploy to an area south-west of the Azores. The deadly peril was over. The Germans conceded the Battle of the Atlantic had gone to the enemy. In the month of May, the convoy battles alone, had claimed 20 U-boats lost, nine sunk by aircraft alone, of which eight were due to Coastal Command. The full total of the U-boat losses in that month was 41; of these, aircraft claimed 16 (69.5%). Shipping losses during the month dropped to 299,428 tons (58 ships) of which U-boats still claimed the lion's share : 264,852 tons (50 ships). But this total was never repeated and only once was it even nearly matched.

In July, 1943, when U-boats accounted for 252,145 tons (46 ships) out of a total of 365,398 tons (61 ships). But of the U-boat total only 123,327 tons (18 ships) were sunk in the North Atlantic. 97,214 tons (17 ships) were sunk in the Indian Ocean. At the same time, more ships were being built than were being sunk, a very significant factor... That the U-boat fleet collapse had come so swiftly was of great surprise, except perhaps, by those associated with the Ultra decrypts, those who had lived with the situation hour to hour and day to day. In fact Commander (later Captain) Roger Winn RNVR the brilliant head of the Submarine Tracking Room, had predicted that a collapse would occur, and it would be sudden. The combined effects of good Ultra, skilled escorts with sophisticated equipment, aircraft carriers and VLR airplanes all working together, with the harmony of experience was quite simply — to much for a U-boat fleet most of whose best men were dead.

This did not, of course, mean the U-boat war was over; there could be no relaxation against the enemies determination, no stand-down of the naval section at Bletchley Park, the Submarine Tracking Room, the naval escorts or Coastal Command. But it was a very significant point in the war, it meant Britain would not starve, would not run short of supplies and equipment. British industry would not be starved of vital raw materials; Bomber Command's offensive would not be stopped due to lack of fuel, and the armoured forces could continue their build-up for future operations such as "Bolero" and Operation *Overlord*. For some who were only too aware of the facts that had brought the turn around about, there was a sense of elation and for those at Western Approaches Command and Northwood, relief and pride for all associated with the sea and air operations. AM Slessor was quick to pass on ACM Portal's message made on 1 June, in *Coastal Command Review*, which said.

I wish to express to you and all under your command my admiration and warmest thanks for your achievements in the anti-U-Boat war during the month just ended. The brilliant success achieved in this vital field is the well deserved result of tireless perseverance and devotion to duty and is, I am sure, a welcome reward for the aircrews and others who have spared no effort during long months of arduous operations and training. Now that you have obtained this remarkable advantage over the U-Boats I know you will press it home with ever-increasing vigour and determination until, in conjunction with the Royal Navy, you have finally broken the enemy's morale.

AM Slessor himself informed Coastal Command crews : "It is difficult to over-estimate the importance in Allied strategy of these results... He pointed out that Dr Goebbels had been promising the German people a victory at sea, and he asked : "what will happen when the Nazis at last hoist in the fact that their last hope of avoiding a decisive defeat has disappeared largely through the efforts of Coastal Command". Although additional comments, in the statement indicated Slessor himself was not entirely aware of the importance of the victory Coastal Command had won. In continuing the extract from his statement he said :

"Many of us in Coastal no doubt sometimes envy our friends in Bomber and Mediterranean Air Commands their share in the shattering offensive which has been such a heartening feature of last month's news. But if we can keep up this rate of killing against the U-boats, or anything near it, we are doing as much as anyone to hasten the collapse of the Axis. If we could really kill the U-boat menace once and for all". Unlike Joubert, AM Slessor's allegiance appeared to lie with bombing, and in his own words AM Harris's mounting offensive was "true air warfare". It was plain he underrated his own Command's victory, or the victory that AM Bowhill and Joubert had prepared for him... Even at the end of the year, he told the Command that "1943 will have many claims on history", he continued :

For us this has been primarily a defensive victory. The main objective of the operations against the U-boat was to prevent us losing the war"... This somewhat blinkered view actually revealed a strategy which had found both Bowhill and Joubert continually at odds with the air staff for allocation of resources. This view reiterated in An Official History of the RAF 1939-45, published in 1954, which stated :

Coastal Command was essentially a defensive organisation and should therefore draw as little as possible on limited resources which should be devoted to the offensive.

The irony being of course, the most important Allied land battle of WW II, without doubt Operation *Overlord* could not have taken place without the Atlantic victory to which Coastal Command made such a magnificent contribution. By the end of 1943, Coastal Command had had an outstanding year, of the total of 219 U-boats destroyed, no fewer than 84 were accredited to Coastal Command. The crow was now definitely fighting the mole... Throughout the year aircraft of the FAA including Fairey Albacore and Swordfish and Grumman Avenger units operating from the escort carriers had operated under Coastal Command and participated in the attacks against the "E" and "R" boats with torpedos and mines. There is no doubt Coastal Command was as essential to the Allied offensive at this time, as it was during the great offensive in Europe that was to come.

It should be said that Doenitz's decision to withdraw from the North Atlantic in May, 1943, did not bring any respite for Coastal Command and after a very quiet month of June, as the U-boats were redeployed, July saw a sharp increase in shipping losses in the South Atlantic, the Mediterranean and the Indian Ocean. However, in order to reach these operating areas five out of six submarines had to pass through the Bay of Biscay, making them vunerable to Coastal Command patrols operating from Gibraltar and the UK, who aware of the move south, now concentrated their attentions in this area. The U-boat commanders chose to cross the Bay in groups, submerged at night but prepared to fight it out with aircraft on the surface during daylight hours. To do this their defensive armament was increased and some were fitted out a flak boats. This inevitably led to some heavy engagements not only between the U-boats and ASW aircraft, but also between D.H. Mosquito fighters of Fighter Command and Luftwaffe Junkers Ju 88s and Focke Wulf 190s endeavouring to afford some sort of cover to the U-boats in the Bay of Biscay, an area covering some 300 miles by 120. As result, at one time in the summer of 1943, Coastal Command was losing an average of one aircraft each day in this area.

In an attempt to arrest the situation a Royal Navy surface hunting group was dispatched to the Bay and a period of very successful joint anti-U-boat operations ensued, reaching a climax in July when of the total submarines attempting to transit the area, fifty-five were sighted. Six were forced to return to port and seventeen were sunk — all but one by air attack. Fourteen Allied airplanes were lost, but again the Germans decided the losses were unsustainable and another change of tactics was necessary. The idea of fighting back on the surface was abandoned, when it became clear that the advantage lay in attacking the aircraft, especially if as was common with the advent of the Strike Wings, they attacked in large numbers.

At the same time the U-boats began to make the crossing by hugging the coast of Spain and remaining submerged. This of course meant Allied air operations were forced closer to the Luftwaffe bases in France, which soon resulted in the loss of one of the RN surface hunters and severe damage to another forcing the remainder further out to the west. Although to some degree this was fortuitous as again the Germans appeared to be concentrating their efforts in the North Atlantic. By this time the Germans had suffered a number of losses to their submarine refuellers (Type XIV "Milch Cows"), this in itself severely restricting long distance U-boat operations. In total in the three months from June to August 1943, losses amounted to a total of 79 U-boats, while in the same period only 82 ships had been lost to submarines in all areas. Nevertheless there were still enough operational U-boats available to make another attack on the main Atlantic convoys again, and starting in September, 1943, a force of twenty-one submarines launched what was to be one of the last successful operations in this respect.

Two convoys comprising 79 merchant ships and 14 escort vessels were afforded heavy air cover from shore-based and escort carrier airplanes; but bad weather reduced the effectiveness of the air patrols and the resulting convoy losses were particularly heavy at a time when the Allies appeared to be gaining the upper hand. Six ships were sunk and and three escort vessels were lost and a further two seriously damaged. One reason for this was that not for the first time in the technological race the Germans went ahead with the introduction of a new acoustic torpedo. But, it was not long before the Allies had developed an effective countermeasure to the new torpedo in the form of a towed "noise generator", which was soon put to good use. Although not to be outdone the Germans decided to cease production of all existing types of U-boats to concentrate on the new Type XXI and XXIIIs. The first able to travel at a maximum speed of 16 knots submerged, though only for 25 miles. The second smaller boat could travel at 10 knots submerged up to 40 miles.

Until these boats were available a number of older types were fitted with *Schnorchel* (Snorkel) a pre-war Dutch invention, enabling submarines to remain submerged and run on their diesel engines instead of their batteries, with the small size of the exhaust pipe that remained above the surface still making it extremely difficult to sight visually or by radar.

Chap 4 The Sea War Continues (1944-45)

With the advent of the Allies invasion of Europe, and the war on the convoys abandoned, Admiral Doenitz drew up his plans for using his U-boat force to sink the invasion convoys, that he knew would soon be in the Channel, but the *Landwirt Group* of 40 submarines that were to be in action on D-Day or D+1 were known about and the Allies put in place 10 Naval Attack Groups to deal with them. Every square mile of the Channel was covered by patrolling anti-submarine ships and aircraft and checked every 30 minutes. Doenitz's U-boats were unable to have any impact on the course of events in June, 1944, and he lost nearly half their number.

In the three weeks before D-Day the Germans endeavoured to move up reserves of submarines from bases in Norway but their every move was anticipated. In addition in the continuous daylight of the northern summer, where the battles were fought off the coast of Norway and areas further north, many submarines were lost or damaged. The main U-boat battles of 1944, were fought in the English Channel and Western Approaches. This campaign began on D-Day when the German Biscay submarine fleet made its way to the western approaches of the Channel on the surface. This fleet, which Ultra had revealed, would comprise 40 U-boats, was constantly engaged by Coastal Command which, during the first four critical days from D-Day, made 38 sightings that resulted in many successful attacks, although not without the U-boats fighting back. Most of the U-boat attacks at this time were decisive, with the Command flying on average, 30,000 flying hours a month on ASW patrols.

With 51 squadrons and three flights of Coastal Command deployed along with the Royal Navy, to guard the western and northern flanks of the massive D-Day sea armada, it was the South-Western Approaches that posed the greatest danger from the U-boat bases in the Bay of Biscay, and no fewer than 30 squadrons comprising, Liberators, Sunderlands, Catalinas and Wellingtons, supported by Strike Wing Beaufighters and Mosquitos and FAA Swordfish,were assembled under No. 19 Group. With Ultra and Bletchley Park serving the Group well, as usual, the aircraft knew exactly when to make their attacks as the U-boats completely relaxed and off guard transited to the area on the surface. With Ultra supplying the time and roughly the location, ASV III supplying the exact location, the Leigh Light illuminating the target by night, and depth-charges or cannon (this included the 57-mm equipped "Tsetse" Mosquitoes), were available to make the "kill".

On 6 June, the Germans had 35 U-boats available to attack the Allied armada (of 6,939 vessels), nine of them fitted with *Schnorkel*; 16 were ordered to the Channel, but No. 19 Group monitored them all the way. One was sunk on the night of the 7 June, three more on the 8th, and one each on 9th and 10th. The first of these *U-955* had already been unsuccessfully attacked on 5 June, and a search had been made to find her... Following, on the 7 June a Short Sunderland flying-boat of No. 201 Squadron flown by Flt Lt. Baveystock DFC, DFM, obtained a radar contact which he illuminated with flares. However, the boat dived and Baveystock lost contact so he decided to use "baiting" tactic, in the hope it would surface again. Which sure enough when a second contact was made at 03.00 hrs it proved to be the same U-boat. Six depth-charges were dropped, one of which seemed to explode directly under the boat. The "blip" on the ASV radar screen then disappeared, the submarine sank with no survivors.

The following day the Command achieved a hat trick, with Flt Lt Moore (RCAF) flying a No. 224 Squadron Liberator, claiming two of them. At 02.11 hrs he sighted a U-boat (*U-629*) which had first been located by ASV radar. The crew did not use the Leigh Light as there was sufficient moonlight, and an attack was made in which six depth-charges were dropped in a straddle, three landing on either side of the conning tower. The explosion lifted the boat out of the water and when Flt Lt. Moore flew over the site, oil and wreckage could be seen in the water... Less than half an hour later the Liberator made another radar contact and a visual contact was made at 2.5 miles range, confirming a U-boat (*U-373*). Descending to a height of just 50 feet Moore dropped another six depth-charges of which four fell to starboard and two to port. After the attack the boat was seen listing to starboard and sinking by the stern. After the boat had sunk, three dinghies and a number of survivors were seen in the oily water, later being picked up by a VP boat. For this quite amazing sortie with two U-boat "kills" in less than thirty minutes Flt Lt Moore was awarded the DSO and US Silver Star. The third "kill" on the 8th was *U-970* achieved by a Sunderland flying-boat of No. 228 Squadron flown by Flt Lt. C. G. Lancaster DFC. The initial contact had again been by ASV radar, and the U-boat was then illuminated by flares. Following the attack she disappeared and Lancaster was unsure if his attack had been successful. The "kill" confirmed the next day when the German air-sea-rescue service was observed picking up survivors.

On the 9th it was the turn of *U-740*, located in the English Channel to the south-west of the Isles of Scilly by a Liberator of No. 120 Squadron, flown by Flt Lt. A. K. Sherwood. When located it was some five to six miles away and diving. Flt Lt Sherwood dropped six depth-charges ahead of the diving swirl and after the explosion oil was seen rising to the surface. A sonobouy was dropped, and breaking-up type noises were heard; these ceasing after about fifteen minutes. The next day *U-821* was attacked by four D.H. Mosquitos 'T', 'S', 'V' and 'W' of No. 248 Squadron of the Banff Strike Wing, led by Flt Lt. S. G. Nunn (details are related later in this chapter). Following on the 10 June, Admiral Doenitz U-Boat War Diary recorded : "on account of the large number of air attacks and the extensive damage suffered, above all on U-boats without *Schnorkel*, all further sailing of these boats has stopped for the present"...

Introduction of the rocket-firing D.H. Mosquitos and Bristol Beaufighters, together with the Mosquito XVIII, all of which entered squadron service in 1943, but not announced officially until early 1944, made the anti-shipping strikes even more devastating. The first attack on an enemy submarine by a Mosquito XVIII was made early in November, 1943, against a surfaced U-boat returning to Brest from a patrol. From then on, even the waters close to the French coast were no longer safe for unescorted surfaced submarines and shortly after the first attack the Germans were forced to provide escorts for surface ships and fighter aircraft cover for submarines entering or leaving port.

During the twelve months from 31 March, 1943 to March 1944, Coastal Command made 4,500 sorties on anti-shipping operations and from April, 1944, onwards these attacks increased. The effects of the attacks by Bomber Command and the Second Tactical Air Force on enemy communications forced the enemy to make increasing use of coastal shipping resources thereby presenting Coastal Command with more numerous targets. These targets were attacked with torpedoes, bombs, rockets and cannon so effectively that the enemy was forced to supply his convoys with protection and it was estimated that some 40% of the German naval strength was deployed on escorting inshore shipping. As many as twenty escorts were provided for one merchant ship. The Norwegian coast proved a particularly good hunting ground for Allied ASV patrols, and Axis shipping along the coasts of Denmark, Holland, Belgium and France, was attacked day and night.

Strike Wings of torpedo-carrying or rocket-firing Beaufighters and Mosquitos were usually accompanied by a large escort either of cannon-firing Mosquitos or by aircraft of Fighter Command. Frequently the torpedo-carrying Beaufighter "Strike Wings" would be escorted by long-range heavy calibre cannon-equipped Beaufighters. The escorting aircraft would go in first to shoot up the enemy escorts and "flak" ships with cannon and rocket projectiles, reducing the opposition and enabling more accurate attacks to be made by the "Torbeaus". During June, 1944, a total of 8,000 sorties was flown by Coastal Command, more than 3,000 on reconnaissance and anti-shipping sorties during which some 600 vessels were attacked. In July, 2,000 sorties were flown against enemy shipping with 550 individual attacks made against some 225 vessels.

As mentioned one of the early Strike Wing successes occurred on 10 June, 1944, when four D.H. Mosquito's of No. 228 Squadron, led by Flt Lt. S. G. Nunn, when flying at low level over the approaches to Brest, they spotted a U-boat break the surface approximately 2.5 miles ahead. It was apparent the U-boat had not seen the aircraft as they were flying at only 30 feet above sea level. Each Mosquito attacked in turn and after a series of strafing runs the crew were seen abandoning the boat which appeared to be sinking by the stern. An attack by a No. 206 Squadron Liberator which dropped two depth-charges made a certain Coastal Command "kill". However, this was not the end of the incident as later that afternoon six No. 248 Squadron Mosquitos that had returned to the scene were fired on when they overflew the survivors in a VP launch, and one aircraft was damaged causing it to crash. In the meantime the other five airplanes, two of which were armed with six pounder Tsetse guns attacked the launch and blew it out of the water... Another prominent member of the Strike Wing at this time was No. 455 Squadron RAAF, with rocket-firing Beaufighter X's which operated off the Dutch coast between March and October, 1944, when it returned to Scotland to join the Dallachy Wing to continue attacks off Norway, until the end of the war.

The command also played an important part in the battle for the French ports at this time, especially the U-boat bases in the Brest Peninsula. Immediately the fall of the ports appeared imminent Coastal Command aircraft and surface vessels of the Royal Navy threw a ring around them, thus preventing them receiving reinforcements. In addition destruction of a large proportion of the Germans mine-sweeper fleet operating in this area, meant air and surface craft prevented the movement of U-boats and other enemy shipping. In three weeks, Mosquito, Beaufighter and Halifax aircraft made nearly 300 attacks on 150 separate targets from Ostend to Bordeaux, during which more than 30 enemy vessels were sunk, damaged or set on fire.

The largest force of Beaufighters ever engaged on a shipping strike was assembled on 25 September, 1944 to attack a concentration of some twenty enemy vessels in the heavily defended anchorage of Den Helder, the most likely "escape port" for German forces trapped in Holland by the British Army. More than 70 Beaufighters, escorted by North American Mustang and Hawker Tempest fighters of Fighter Command, made sea-level attacks on the ships and on shore batteries and radio installations with cannon, rockets and torpedoes.

The liberation of Belgium provided a new base for Coastal Command aircraft, including Swordfish III of No. 119 Squadron, and towards the end of the year the main battle area was concentrated round the Dutch and Norwegian coasts. The hours of darkness brought the enemy no respite, with the ASV III-equipped Swordfish and other strike planes co-operating with flame-dropping aircraft to continue the attacks at night on U-boats and small ships which were particularly targeted in a campaign of individual night attacks. A new technique was adopted for these night attacks known as the "Drem" system. This consisted of a striking force of Beaufighter aircraft armed with torpedos or rockets and Halifax or Wellington flare-dropping aircraft which went out singly under cover of darkness to patrol areas round the Norwegian coast. When targets were located powerful flares were dropped by the Halifax and Wellingtons to indicate the position of the enemy ships and guided by these lights, the striking force of Beaufighters, closed in for the attack.

The statistics for 1944, show well how the momentum of the war at sea was kept up on the enemy : a grand total of 1,045,629 tons of shipping was sunk - just 13.4% of the massive total of 1942. Significantly sinkings by U-boats fell to 773,327 tons (132 ships out of 205), and even more significant, in the whole year sinkings by U-boats in the North Atlantic amounted to no more than 175,913 tons (31 ships). The greatest losses as might be expected were associated with Operation *Overlord*, (266,442 tons ; 65 ships), which served to show what might have been had not the Royal Navy, Coastal Command and other Allied air arms concentrated their efforts in the English Channel and Western Approaches at this time. It was also during this period without doubt, that Ultra proved itself; from August 1943 onwards, the ability to read the U-boat signal traffic greatly expedited interception of returning boats by aircraft and naval offensive groups, just at the time they believed they were in range of the safety of their home ports. Ultra also permitted the destruction of the U-tankers (the "Milch Cows"). In fact in hindsight it is quite remarkable that the *B-Dienst* did not suspect their U-boat W/T traffic was regularly intercepted and de-ciphered. In all probability the arrogant belief that Enigma was perfectly secure and could not be broken did not trigger the thought, that it may have become insecure. As one academic was prompted to comment "it is always difficult for experts to prove themselves wrong" !

To some degree, the failure of the *B-Dienst* to grasp the reality of the situation, must go to the Allies and the deception techniques applied. Not least of these the standard procedure of covering every Ultra-guided attack by the concentrated use of air patrols, so that a good reason for the subsequent U-boat attacks would be apparent. It is all credit to Coastal Command that these decoy patrols, merely to register a presence, often requiring many hours of tiring unrewarding flying over inhospitable waters, went undetected.

Technological ascendency throughout the period see-sawed backwards and forwards almost to the end;new weapons and new tactics making constant appearances. On the Allied side the advent of ASV III centimetric radar and sonobouys; linked to the introduction of improved depth-charge stick-spacing and the acoustic homing torpedo proved fatal for the U-boat fleet.

By the end of 1944, the situation in the Battle of the Atlantic might have appeared a stalemate, for with the U-boats now having to transit from northern ports and with Allied convoys routed south of Eire, successes by either side were few and far between. Nevertheless anti-shipping activities continued into 1945, when Coastal Command introduced a new phase. Under Air Chief Marshal Sir Sholto Douglas, who had succeeded AM Slessor as AOC-in-C Coastal Command in January 1945,twenty-nine squadrons from No.19 Group alone, with 350 Beaufighters, Halifaxes, Mosquitos, Sunderlands and Wellingtons, covered the whole area to such effect that any surfaced U-boat was certain to be detected on radar within thirty minutes. On 4 February, 1945, Leigh Light Liberators attacked enemy submarines and destroyers in the Baltic port of Danzig. This attack, the first of its kind to be made by the Command, involved a flight of more than 1,600 miles. However, this situation did not continue for long, soon the coastal waters around the British Isles were selected by Admiral Doenitz as the area in which his forces could most profitably be deployed and more than 40 U-boats entered the area in February, 1945.

Anti-U-boat patrols steadily increased again as the enemy made a last ditch attempt to interfere with Allied shipping operations in Northern Europe. In February, sorties from home bases involved over 16,500 hours and in March the total increased to 28,000 flying hours, although in April this dropped back to 27,000 hours. In the end the U-boats had only limited success and lost 12 boats in February, and a further 15 in March. Technical innovation continued on both sides with the Germans introducing two new types of *Schnorkel* equipped U-boats (the Type XXI and the Type XXIII) with three times the battery power and increased submerged range; while the Americans introduced the 'sono bouy' which when dropped in an area of sea where a U-boat was suspected to be travelling, would transmit the boat's propeller noises back to the aircraft. The Mk 24 Acoustic Torpedo could then be dropped to home on to the source of the noise.

It should be said, in the light of Germany's perilous situation at this time, April 1945, it was amazing that the rate at which new U-boats were being commissioned surpassed losses, and it was in general the older boats that were being sunk rather than the new high-tech types. U-Boat Command had placed orders for 290 Type XXI U-boats for delivery by February, 1945. In fact 90 had been launched, of which 60 were in service by December, 1944. In addition 31 of the smaller Type XXIII boats had been launched, and 23 were in service. At the beginning of May, it was estimated some 91 of the Type XXIs were at sea undergoing trials or crew training, the first operational Type XXI having put to sea on 30 April, and had succeeded in evading a RN submarine hunting group with ease. Luckily before it could launch a torpedo in anger the signal came from Grand Admiral Doenitz announcing the German surrender, and ordering all U-boats to give themselves up in designated ports.

Fitted with Snorkels of advanced design, these new boats were recognised to be a serious threat and Coastal Command introduced two new measures to counter it. The first was the obvious one of improving the skills of the airborne radar operators in recognising the very small "target" returns from the Snorkel tube, and then to improving the effectiveness of the attacks. The other measure involved improved technology, involving the introduction of sonobouy which although technically still in the experimental stage ten Liberator squadrons were equipped with them. Indeed in March, 1945, two U-boats were sunk as a result of location by sonobouy, although the war was over before the sonobouy's full potential could be realised. The weapon subsequently becoming part of the post-war anti-submarine warfare armoury. In spite of this the new U-boat types that were at sea by this time did have some success, with seven Type XXIII sinking seven ships without loss early in the year, without even being detected or attacked. By the end of April, one of the smaller Type XXI had become operational with by this time another 111 either being fitted out or working up to enter operational service. There is no doubt if the boats had entered service before the cessation of hostilities the threat posed would have been as great if not greater at any time throughout the duration of the war.

Meanwhile, the old Type VIIs were still operating in or near British waters, although it should be said with the same lack of success they had experienced the previous year. In February, 1945, there were 51 Type VIIs operational but they managed only to sink 11 ships for the loss of 22 U-boats. In March, 10 ships were sunk for the loss of 15, with the total for the month far in excess of this, with thirty-two written off in total, thirteen having been severely damaged from heavy bombing raids on German bases. In total in the first five months of 1945, Type VIIs had sunk 46 ships for the loss of 56 U-boats.

The main occupation of Coastal Command in the month of April, 1945, was shipping strikes in the waters between Scandinavia and Germany where more than 1,650 anti-shipping sorties were flown and 234 targets were attacked. The grand finale of shipping destruction by the Allies took place on the 3 and 4 May 1945, when the enemy was attempting a frantic evacuation from his remaining Baltic ports to Denmark. Every type of vessel from ocean-going liners to midget submarines was involved and Coastal Command joined in the massive wrought of these vessels. During the final weeks of the war, U-boat losses were unrelenting. Fifty U-boats were sunk in the Baltic or its approaches with another 33 sunk in other areas. As already stated bombing raids on German bases accounted for many others, while Beaufighter and Mosquito attacks sank many others as they attempted to escape from the Baltic to Norway. The last U-boat "kill" of the war was rather appropriately made by a Consolidated Catalina 'X' of No. 210 Squadron flown by Flt Lt. K. M. Murray, who attacked *U-320* in the Norwegian Sea, west of Bergen on 7 May at around 04.45 hrs. Four depth-charges were dropped, after which oil was seen on the surface. Flt Lt. Murray then dropped a pattern of sonobouys and hammering noises were heard as if the crew was trying to effect repairs. The hammering noises were still audible many hours later but with the Catalina at the end of its PLE (Patrol Limit Endurance), it was forced to leave the area. On 9 May, *Oberleutnant zur See* Heinz brought the stricken submarine to the surface ordering the crew to abandon ship before she was scuttled.

Coastal Command's WW II achievements stands for all time : starting with their two "kills" in 1941, by the end of the war the Command had claimed the destruction of 192 U-boats plus a further 19 jointly with the Royal Navy. In addition another 40 "kills" were attributed either to US operated aircraft or shared with other Allied naval forces (American and Canadian). The Command had also been responsible for the sinking of 4 Italian submarines (two in the Atlantic), with one shared, and 343 enemy merchant ships of the total of 437 vessels sunk; RAF Bomber Command and Fighter Command accounting for 25 and 69 "kills" respectively.

It had been a long wearisome and costly battle for Coastal Command, which by the end of the war comprised seven Groups, including No. 17 Training Group, No. 106 Photographic Reconnaissance Group and No. 247 Group in the Azores, in addition to the two independent Headquarters, one in Gibraltar, and the other in Iceland. U-boats had sunk more than 2,200 ships, 14 million tons - most of it in the Atlantic. It had cost the German Navy 784 U-boats (plus a further 154 destroyed in harbour or during construction) with more than 28,000 casualties, almost the same as the British Merchant Navy. In the final issue of the *Coastal Command Review* in June, 1945, it was stated that, in the course of the whole war, 1,511 aircraft of Coastal Command had been lost to enemy action or were missing. If fatal crashes of aircraft returning from operations is included, the total rises to 1,777, an average of one aircraft for every day of the war, in 240,000 sorties flown by Coastal Command aircraft. 741 of the Command's wartime aircraft losses were as a result of anti-submarine (ASW) sorties. The Command lost 6,022 personnel killed in action and a further 2,852 killed in accidents - some 5,866 of these were pilots and crew (1,630 from the Dominions). Such were the hazards of the tasks undertaken by Coastal Command...

While it can be said the Allies won the Battle of the Atlantic, the U-boats were never quite defeated. At the end of the war the U-boats were still preparing to launch a new offensive with twenty-five in British coastal waters still the direct concern of 400 Allied ships and some 800 aircraft. RAF Coastal Commands wartime activities came to an end on 4 June, 1945, when the 2,853rd and last convoy protection patrol was completed.

Chapter 5   Very Important Bases - "Pee Dee" and Dunkeswell   (FAW 7)

The county of Pembrokeshire's location in south-west Wales, made it an ideal location from which the militaries front-line units could launch their war on the U-boat, in both World Wars. In WW I the county was in the forefront of activities to combat the U-boat. In 1915, Milton Aerodrome was constructed as a part of the RNAS attempt to combat the U-boat threat in the western approaches to the British Isles. Five S.S. Z Type airships were based at the aerodrome, which were used for long-range patrols. On 29 April, 1917, a RNAS unit was formed at Milton (RNAS Pembroke), initially with Sopwith 1½ Strutters and then six Airco D.H.6 bombers used for coastal patrol duties. Although the unit reported a number of U-boat sightings in 1918, no U-boat sinkings were recorded. Another of the county's bases during WW I was the RNAS Seaplane station at Fishguard. Two Coastal Patrol Flights, Nos. 426 and 427 equipped with three Fairey Hamble Babies and three Short 184 Seaplanes carried out anti-submarine patrols over the southern half of the Irish Sea.

In WW II the county again became an ideal location to base the RAF's front-line units to fight the new Sea War.
Its prominent position, meant aircraft could protect not only the South Wales ports or shipping lanes around the Welsh coast but could patrol and escort shipping in the Atlantic and Bay of Biscay. The main operational bases utilised were Brawdy, Dale, Talbenny, St Davids and Pembroke Dock. With a number of other support and training airfields operated in support of Coastal Command operations. In 1939, there was only one airfield and two seaplane bases in the county. The airfield, Carew Cheriton — near to the original RNAS base at Milton was equipped with Avro Anson Is of No. 217 Squadron. However, by the end of the year three different squadrons of Ansons were based at Carew (Nos. 48, 217 and 321 Squadrons and No.3 OTU at Haverfordwest). Followed in 1940, by detachments of Bristol Blenheim IVFs of Nos. 236 and 248 Squadrons, with the purpose of protecting convoys in the Irish Sea from enemy aircraft. Later No. 248 Squadron deployed its Beaufighters to combat the long-range Fw 200C Condors and Junkers Ju 88s patrolling the area.

Later Carew Cheriton's role in front-line WW II operations changed to training crews for Coastal Command and in November 1940, the Coastal Command Development Unit was transferred to Carew from Ballykelly in Northern Ireland. The Development Unit was responsible for service trials of new airborne signalling equipment using a variety of airplanes like Hudsons, Beauforts, and Whitley bombers, as well as Sunderlands based at nearby Pembroke Dock. Also the testing of ASV radar, bomb and depth charge attack techniques on both surface vessels and submarines in day or night were carried out by the unit. The night attacks were carried out with the aid of parachute flares and Leigh Lights that were gradually being introduced into service. Another valuable trial by the unit was the introduction of the Beam Approach Beacon System, conducted at Pembroke Dock in the Haven to assist flying-boats to land and take-off at night. All the trials eventually helping develop operational systems to combat the U-boat menace in the Atlantic.

Other airfields like Brawdy, Dale, Talbenny and St Davids did not become operational until 1942-1943, and were mostly involved with anti-submarine and anti-shipping strikes in the Bay of Biscay. Two Vickers Wellington Squadrons transferred from Bomber Command to No. 19 Group, Coastal Command in June 1942; No. 304 Polish moved to Dale on the 15th, and No. 311 (Czech) to Talbenny on the 12th. Both squadrons soon saw action against U-boats in the Bay of Biscay, as well as shipping attacks in the Gironde Estuary. Because of the bombers vulnerability to fighter interception, two squadrons of Bristol Beaufighters TF.X : Nos 235 and 248 were based at Talbenny in 1943, tasked with escorting the Wellingtons on their anti-shipping strikes.

In March, 1943, the two Wellington units returned to Bomber Command, leaving Dale to be taken over by the Fleet Air Arm and Talbenny by RAF Transport Command to be used by No. 302 Ferry Training Unit. Two other new Pembrokeshire airfields which became operational at this time in September, 1943, were St Davids and Brawdy, its satellite airfield, in February, 1944. During the construction of St Davids, it was originally planned that a squadron of US Navy PBY4 Consolidated Liberators were to be based there for long-range North Atlantic patrols. However, the squadron went to Dunkeswell, and St Davids became a base for a detachment of B-17 Fortresses from Nos. 206 and 220 Squadrons, the bomber from Boeing, better suited in RAF service to maritime patrol work than strategic bombing. However, the Fortresses stay was short and finally in March 1943, the airfield was vacated and became the base for H. P. Halifax Mks II, III, V and eventually the maritime G.R. II variants of No. 517 (Met) Squadron on (26 Nov 43), No. 58 Squadron (6 Dec 43), and finally No. 502 (Aux) Squadron on 10 December, 1943. In addition to weather flights No. 517 Squadron flew anti-submarine patrols over the Western Approaches, using Tiree as an advanced base for the northern sectors.

During their stay at St Davids and Brawdy the squadrons were credited with a number of U-boats either destroyed or severely damaged. Most attacks were in the Bay of Biscay or off the French coast, before they had ventured into the Atlantic. The squadrons undertook a number of notable operations at this time, as the Sea War intensified. On 26 April, 1944, a Halifax made a radar contact with a U-boat which dived as the aircraft dropped its bombs, with one finding its target cutting the U-boat in half. Later in the year on 20 August, No. 58 Squadron lost its C. O., Wing Commander Grant, during a heroic attack on surfaced U-boats off the French coast. Another mission involved Halifax "F" for Freddie of No. 502 Squadron which having sighted *U-413*, dropped its four 600-lb anti-submarine bombs, damaging its conning tower, thereby depriving it of its ability to submerge. The airplane then made four more attacks with .303 machine guns but on the fifth run it received a direct hit on its port outer engine. The Halifax managed to limp home to St Davids on three engines while the U-boat made off to the safety of its base. The Halifax was in action again within twenty-four hours but the U-boat requiring extensive repairs to its conning tower, did not sail again for three months. In August, 1944, the Halifax squadrons were transferred to other bases, and St Davids and Brawdy became home to two squadrons equipped with Consolidated Liberator G.R.VI and G.R.VIII variants, with a No. 220 Squadron Liberator piloted by Flt Lt Wallace scoring a definite U-boat "kill" on 26 September, 1944.

Pembrokeshire's most famous base was the seaplane base at Pembroke Dock which was officially opened on 1 January, 1930. Throughout the 1930s the base was gradually built up with concrete slipways, two spacious C Type hangars and permanent accommodation for the base personnel. The first units to be permanently based there were Nos. 210 Squadron with Supermarine Southampton II flying-boats in May 1931, and No. 230 Squadron which reformed at the base on 1 December, 1934, being the first unit to receive Short Singapore IIIs in April, 1935. When No. 228 Squadron reformed on 15 December, 1936, with Saro London Is and a number of other types, it also took up residency at Pembroke Dock. From 1936 to 1946, there were at least nine flying-boat units at one time or the other based at 'Pee Dee'. Including :

No. 10 Squadron (RAAF)   12 Aug 1939 to Apr 1940 and 28 May 1941 to Dec 1941
No. 119 Squadron (RAF)   4 Aug 1941 to Nov 1941 and 6 Sep 1942 to 17 Apr 1943
No. 201 Squadron (RAF)   8 Apr 1944 to Nov 1944
No. 209 Squadron (RAF)   16 Jul 1940   to Dec 1940 and 10 Oct 1941 to Mar 1942
No. 210 Squadron (RAF)   7 Aug 1936 to Sep 1937 and 18 Dec 1937 to Sep 1938 and
                           8 Oct 1938 to Oct 1939
No. 228 Squadron (RAF)   15 Dec 1936 to Sep 1938 and   9 Oct 1938 to Sep 1939 and
                           28 Aug 1941 to Oct 1941 and   4 May 1943 to 4 Jun 1945
No. 422 Squadron (RCAF)   4 Nov 1944 to Jul 1945
No. 461 Squadron (RAAF)   21 Apr 1943 to 20 Jun 1945
No. 4 (Coastal) Operational Training Unit.   1941 to 31 July 1947

In the period known as the 'Phoney War', No. 228 Squadron based at Pembroke, was quite busy, flying an average of 35 sorties a month. On 9 September, 1939, Short Sunderland serial L2167 of No. 228 Squadron attacked a U-boat which had sunk the merchant ship SS *Vancouver City*. On 17 September, Sunderland serial L5798, claimed another U-boat damaged. On 16 August, 1940, F/O E. R. Baker won a DFC for flying a 13 hour patrol in Sunderland serial PD9024 during which time he contacted and attacked *U-51* with bombs and machine guns, resulting in severely damaging the submarine forcing it to limp back to its base where it was out of action for some time.

No. 461 Squadron (RAAF) also based at Pembroke on various occasions during the war, carried out patrols over the Bay of Biscay, and was involved in a number of notable operations and incidents. On 29 March, 1943, a squadron Sunderland T9114 flown by F/O Gordon Singleton rescued the crew of serial JM675 which had crashed. However, having taken the surviving crews members on board Singleton's airplane was unable to take-off due to the extra weight, but luckily a French sloop *La Combattante* was able to take the extra crew. Unfortunately this was not the end of the drama as having endeavoured to get into the air in the prevailing heavy seas, T9114 sustained damage to its hull and was unable to land in the Haven, at Pembroke Dock. Instead it made history by landing on grass at nearby Angle airfield with surprisingly little extra damage sustained.

During a patrol on 2 June, 1943, a No. 461 Squadron Sunderland flown by Flt Lt. Colin Walker, was attacked by eight Junkers Ju 88s. After continuous pounding by cannon and machine gun fire the aircraft was so badly damaged, that all the instruments were unserviceable, the port inner engine was out of action, the hydraulic system to the turrets was damaged and could only be worked manually. The rear gunner was wounded and one of the waist gunners was dead, but the aircraft managed to shoot down three of the attacking aircraft. However, the condition of the flying-boat and its crew caused Flt Lt. Walker to break off the engagement, and return to base. But the chances of reaching 'Pee Dee' some 300 miles away were not good, so he headed for the nearest UK *terra firma* and set the aircraft down at Pra Sands in Cornwall. The squadron was in action again on 30 June, when a Sunderland flown by Flt Lt. Dudley Morrows joined with other RAAF aircraft in an attack on a surfaced U-boat. Flt Lt. Morrows aircraft attacked *U-461*, diving through a barrage of flak dropping his depth-charges on the submarine cutting it in half but instead of climbing away to safety, the aircraft returned to drop a life raft to the survivors. On the homeward flight the Sunderland's crew attacked another U-boat without success, but was severely damaged by heavy flak put up by the submarine. The flying-boat was too severely damaged to reach Pembroke Dock and an emergency landing was made at St Mary's in the Scilly Isles. Two weeks later Flt Lt. Morrows was in action again. This time his Sunderland was attacked by six Junkers Ju 88s. Following a concerted attack the Ju 88s broke away and the Sunderland was left to limp home, but it was so badly damaged Morrow's was forced to ditch in the sea. Luckily all the crew were picked up safely by a Royal Navy destroyer.

No. 201 Squadron was another busy flying boat unit operating out of Pembroke Dock. Most notable of the squadrons pilots was Flt Lt. Baveystock with three U-boat "kills" two while with No. 201 Squadron. One in June, 1944, and the other on 18 August. Aircraft also flew up to 1,800 miles into the Atlantic from 'Pee Dee' to meet and escort the convoys carrying vital wartime supplies.

Already in July 1942, the Battle of the Atlantic was in the balance with the British in desperate need of a long-range maritime patrol aircraft. The situation was eased somewhat in March 1943, when President Roosevelt ordered 135 U.S. Navy and Army Air Force Liberators to help close the Atlantic (air) Gap. Among these were four squadrons of Colonel Howard Moore's 479th Anti-Submarine Group, USAAF. In the interim, since November 1942, the 1st and 2nd (Provisional) Squadrons of the 480th AS Group had helped out, with a number of successes including *U-752* attacked on 10 February 1943, and *U-211* seriously damaged on 20 February. However, in March 1943, both these units left for the Mediterranean, to be replaced in July 1943, by the 4th and 19th AS Squadrons, which from 6 August operated out of RAF Dunkeswell, near Honiton, in Devon, in the south of England. Dunkeswell somewhat unique in WW II being the only operational US Navy base in Britain. Later in the month the 4th and 19th AS Squadrons were joined by the 6th and 22nd AS Squadrons. Although their stay was short-lived they shared the honours with the RAF and RCAF units, accredited with the destruction of *U-404*, *U-558* and *U-706*. Unfortunately for the lost of five Liberators and most of their crews.

Whilst the presence of the USAAF AS Squadrons were invaluable, behind the scenes long-standing differences as to which US air arm was best suited to undertake ASW duties was finally resolved in 1943, when a deal was struck and on 1 September 1943, the USAAF exchanged its ASW-equipped Liberators for an equal number of un-modified Naval B-24D bombers. Almost immediately fifteen PBY-5A Consolidated Catalinas of Patrol Squadron 63 (VP-63) flew into Pembroke Dock to carry out ASW patrols. But VP-63's UK mission lasted only a few weeks as in December 1943, it was redeployed to Morocco, to assist with operations in the Mediterranean. VP-63 losing one PBY-5 in its short stay at Dunkeswell when Lt Tanner's airplane (P-10) was attacked by eight Junkers Ju-88 on 1 August 1943, with seven of the ten crew losing their lives.

Meanwhile, among the first US Navy Liberator types to operate from the UK in WW II in October 1943, was the PB4Y-1 Liberators of Fleet Air Wing 7 (FAW-7) which comprised naval squadrons VPB-103, VPB-105, VPB-110 and VPB-111. Patrol Bombing Squadron 103 (VPB-103) arrived at St Eval, Cornwall, on 17 August 1943, for familiarisation training with RAF Coastal Command. Accompanied by personnel H.Q. Squadron to set up FAW 7 H.Q. at Plymouth under Commodore William T. Hamilton US Navy. Already an experienced maritime unit VPB-103 had commissioned at San Diego in March 1943, and since had completed 268 missions amassing some 2,400 hours on convoy escort duties in the South Atlantic operating out of Argentina. Next to arrive was VPB-105, which in May 1943, had redesignated from VP-31, having seen operations in the Panama Canal Zone and the Caribbean. Both units became operational at Dunkeswell in mid-September, 1943, to assume all the duties of the earlier AS Squadrons USAAF except the 4th who had agreed to stay until a third US Navy squadron arrived. This was to be VPB-110, commissioned at Norfolk, Virginia, in July 1943, equipped with Martin Mariners. The unit arriving at St Eval in late September to begin patrols on 30 October. With FAW 7 up to strength, the USAAF Liberators flew their final mission on 1 November 1943, and finally moved out to join the 8th Army Air Force in Europe.

On 2 September 1943, two days after operations commenced from St Eval, VPB-103 lost its first Liberator in combat. Flown by Lt. Keith Wickstrom the airplane disappeared without trace, after an attack by a mass formation of Junkers Ju-88s. Unfortunately this was to be only the beginning with VPB-103 losing a further nineteen airplanes by VE-Day, many disappearing without trace. As well as enemy actions there were a number of problems with the airframe. With four turbo-charged 1,200 hp Pratt & Whitney Twin Wasp engines, and its 3,000 U.S gallon fuel load giving 12 to 13 hours endurance with a 4,000-lb bomb-load, although making it idea for long-range maritime patrol it was not the easiest airplane to fly, exhibiting a tendency to stall in a sharp turn or fast climb. Often operating at excessively high weights the wing-tips had a tendency to twist, reducing cruising speed by 15%. The high aspect wing was particularly intolerant to icing and after around 500 flying hours the entire airframe was often found out of true. Fuel leaks, a weak undercarriage and the close proximity of hydraulic lines to electrical wiring compounded the problems.

Most of FAW 7s PB4Y-1 Liberators were fitted with Erco front nose turrets, though some retained the original B-24D glasshouse nose. Other special equipment for ASW duties included APS-15 radar, LORAN, sonobouys and provision for carrying Mk 24 acoustic homing torpedos (nicknamed FIDO or ZOMBIE).

Until March, 1944, chronic spares shortages for the US Navy Liberators made it difficult for FAW 7 to prepare twelve aircraft for operations each day. In addition inexperienced ground crew led to a number of maintenance related incidents, as for example when a visiting RAF Whitley was written-off on the airfield when struck by an accidental burst of gunfire from a parked Liberator. On another occasion a recently serviced airplane lost its radar antenna and radome when after a pre-dawn take-off the airplane's captain ordered the radome to be lowered and the crew were amazed to see it disappear completely out of the airplane to the sea below. The fitters the previous day having forgotten to put the mechanical stops in. This incident triggers this author to recount a similar incident that occurred at RAF Khormaksar, Aden, in 1964, when a Hawker Hunter FGA 9 on returning from a Radfan Valley rocket firing sortie landed, only to have its radome drop forward to dangle off the nose-mounted Ranging Radar transmitter/receiver unit as it taxied in, the radome not having been properly secured after servicing the previous day. In returning to the Liberator incident further trouble prevailed when having survived a near-miss from another Liberator nearby testing its guns, it was decided to dump depth - charges for a quick return to base, whereby it was found the bomb-bay doors failed to open although eventually depth charges and doors joined the radome in the sea. On returning to base after just thirty minutes the airplane was given a triumphant welcome, as with its gaping holes, trailing cables and other debris ground personnel thought the airplane had survived an enemy attack. From that time on its crew were chided with remarks such as "radome gone, bomb-bay doors away" !

At this time missions were flown every fourth day, always providing sufficient personnel were available. These were particularly arduous with the crews exhausted by 12-13 hour long sorties,which were often made even worse by bad weather, as well as fighter attack and flak from the target areas. On return to base there was no respite as frequently the crews were faced with an airfield approach with no nav-aids and low cloud base or worse a diversion to a remote unfamiliar airfield. Unfortunately several airplanes met their end in this manner. On 28 December 1943, Lt Bill Parrish and his crew lost their lives when serial 63926 hit high ground near Okehampton in zero visibility. Almost three months later Lt Meihaus in serial 32210 crash landed at Chivenor, Devon, with three engines out, although luckily this time all survived. At other times some airplanes hardly got off the ground into the air - as on 10 September 1943, when Lt G. Brown of VB-105 went into the sea off Cornwall during a fighter affiliation exercise and a little over a month later Lt John Hillman's aircraft suffered a sudden loss of power on take-off with the airplane consequently exploding in a fireball half a mile from the Dunkeswell base.

A number of other airplanes were forced to ditch in the sea, - six days after operations commenced Lt James Alexander and his VB-103 Squadron crew were attacked by six Junkers Ju-88s. The Liberator although downing one Ju-88 and badly damaging two others, eventually ditched about 40 miles off the Spanish coast, before being picked up by a local fishing boat next day. Lt K. L. Wright and his crew were less fortunate on 14 February, 1944, when having been shot up by Junkers Ju-188s and severely damaged, with only one engine functioning it came down in the sea about 65 miles E.N. east of Lands End. Two radio operators died and the ordnance man died of his injuries until the remainder of the crew were picked up by RAF rescue launch at 13.15 hours the following day.

Meanwhile on 23 July, 1944, Special Air Unit One arrived from the United States to carry out attacks on the German V-1 launch sites in occupied France, under the code name "Project Anvil". The operation was launched at short notice using two PB4Y-1s of VPB-110 Squadron which were flown by VPB-110 volunteer pilots. The aircraft were taken off with a pilot at the controls and flown to 20,000 feet then switched to automatic pilot and the pilot baled out (similar operations had been undertaken earlier using Boeing B-17s). This particular operation took place on 12 August, 1944, with two pilots in the PB4Y-1 - Lt Jospeh P. Kennedy (brother of J. F. Kennedy), and Lt Wilford J. Willy. Escort airplanes were to be a US Navy PV-1 Ventura and a USAAF B-17, for radio control of the drones to the target. Unfortunately twenty minutes after take-off, the PB4Y-1 (serial 32271/T exploded at 15,000 feet off the Suffolk coast killing the pilots, as a result of a malfunction in the fuse system. Undaunted a second PB4Y-1 (serial 63954/S) of VB-105 piloted by Lt Ralph Spalding was launched against Heligoland's submarine pens on 3 September, 1944, and was again unsuccessful, falling short of the target. Even though Lt Spalding had left the airplane successfully. Unfortunately he was killed later in a crash in Morocco while ferrying one of VB-105's airplanes back to the United States.

Subsequently, US Navy PB4Y-2 Liberators flew a number of missions against enemy submarines in the Atlantic. With the first submarine *(U-249)* to surrender after the cessation of hostilities, to raise its black surrender flag to a PB4Y-2 Liberator operating near the Isles of Sicily, on 9 May, 1945.

The previous year two weeks before Christmas 1944, in atrocious weather, low on fuel and with radio failure, Lt Charno and crew baled out safely from 5,000 feet over Boston, Lincolnshire. Their airplane flying on to fall to earth near Manchester ! At the beginning of the year of 9 February, 1944, Lt Schaffer, managed to land at St Davids on three engines as did Pearl Harbour veteran, Lt Charles "Whiskey" Willis on 20 January. With his No.2 engine and the hydraulic system out of action, after having been hit from "friendly fire" from a British naval vessel, Lt Willis managing to land the airplane on one main wheel with little further damage or injury to the crew. In addition to these incidents in the air, two of the units enlisted men were lost on 30 January 1944, when a Wellington bomber crashed on the armoury where they were working at RAF Talbenny, in South Wales.

There were also successes, as on 10 November, 1943, all three of the Wings squadrons were in action against *U-966*. Following an attack by an RAF Wellington, Lt Wright's Liberator serial 32035/E *Muck's Mauler* attacked the submarine with depth charges and further action by Lt Parrish in Liberator 63926/E and a Czech-crewed Liberator from No. 311 (Czech) Squadron RAF resulted in the U-boat being scuttled near La Coruna, Spain. Two days later, Lt R. B. Brownell USNR, flying 32032/C sent a U-boat contact radio message, but nothing more was heard from the aircraft which was posthumously accredited with *U-508*. In the first major encounter with surface ships on 28 December, PB4Y-1 (63935/V), and (63938/X) of VB-105 encountered a group of ten German destroyers en-route to meet the blockade runner *Alsterufer*. The two Liberators shadowed the group and directed two British cruisers which sank three destroyers in the ensuing action aided by a force of five VB-105 airplanes, one of which claimed a probable Luftwaffe Focke Wulf Fw 200 "Condor" recce plane. One month later, Lt C. A. Enloe's Liberator serial 32211/E straddled a surfaced U-boat with six depth charges, taking return fire. Initially accredited with a "probable sunk" which was later confirmed by a German intercepted naval signal reporting the loss of *U-271*. Next day Lt Norman Rudd's Liberator serial 63952/E damaged *U-592* which was finished off by the Royal Navy as she approached St Nazaire.

US Navy PB4Y-1 as operated by FAW 7 - Dunkeswell

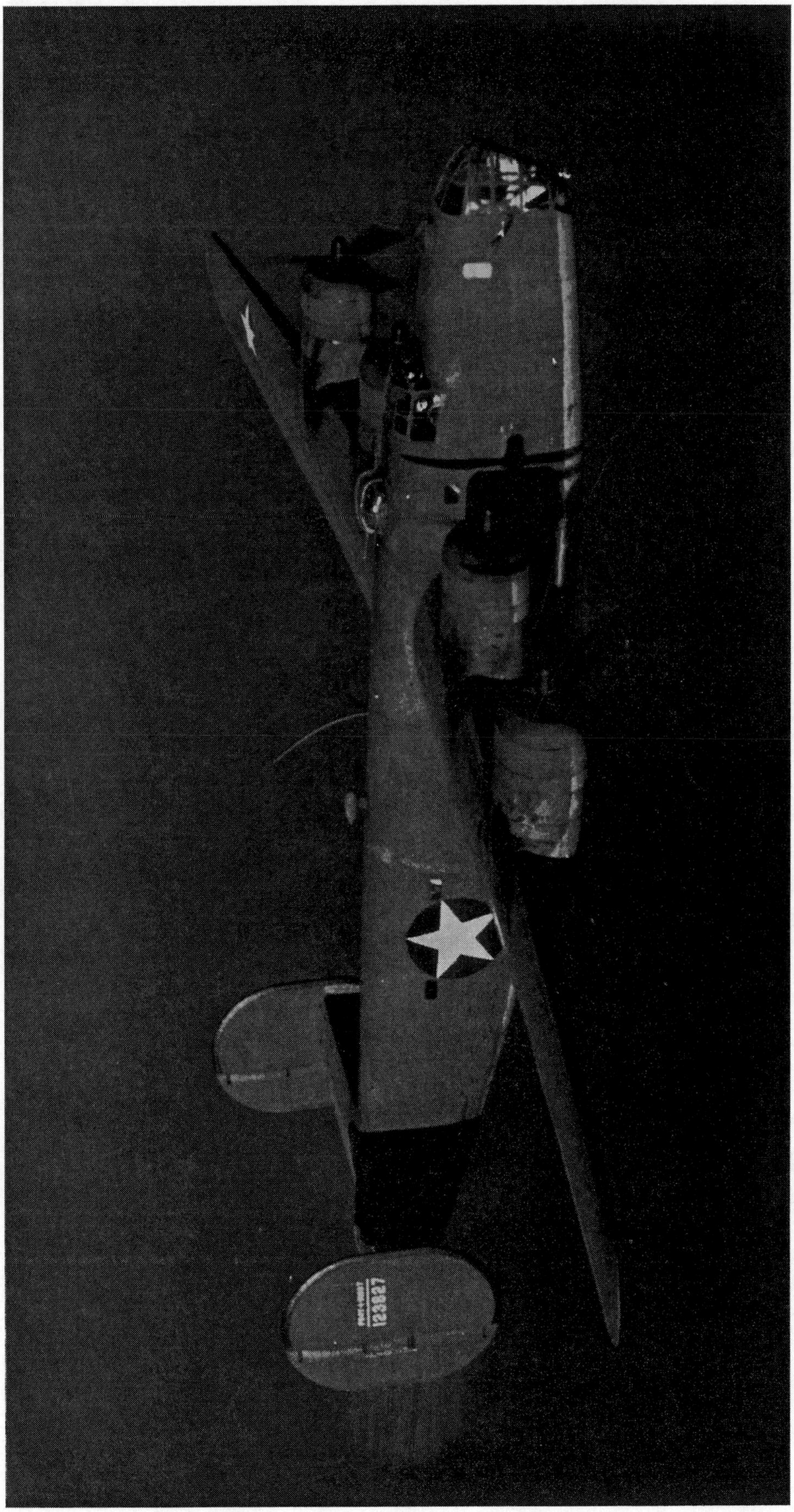

In the period leading up to D-Day as opportunities for anti-submarine action lessened, attacks on enemy surface shipping increased although often this was interrupted by attacks from Luftwaffe Junkers Ju-88s. However as the Allies moved through France denying U-boats access to their bases, they occupied the English Channel more, to harass the shipping lines, remaining submerged for long periods using their snorkel to monitor surface activities. The first "snorkel" sighting was achieved by Lt-Cdr J Munson of VB-110 on 18 June 1944, and although his attack was not successful due to faulty depth-charges, photographic evidence was obtained for Allied intelligence. Lt Cooledge in a VB-105 Liberator 63933/T helped finish off *U-243* on 8 June, following an attack by two No.10 (RAAF) Squadron Sunderland flying-boats. After two run ins when the bomb-bay doors failed to open on a third attempt with the co-pilot opening the doors by hand, a successful depth-charge attack was pressed home. Finally the Wing's most significant operations were undertaken by VB-103 crews - on the 11 March, 1945, when Lt Russell N. Field caught *U-681* on the surface west of Bishop's Rock undertaking a successful "kill" for which he received both the American and British DFCs. In a similar manner Lt Dwight Nott's Liberator, sank *U-326* with a homing torpedo on 25 April, 1945. Until the wars end in the short period of operations FAW 7 Liberators had sunk five U-boats and played a part in the destruction of three others as well as taking the first post-war U-boat surrender on 9 May, 1945, as detailed previously.

To counter the increased U-boat activity in British coastal waters in January 1945, two more PB4Y-1 Liberator squadrons arrived in the UK to operate from nearby RAF Upottery. VB-107 from Ascension Island and VB-112 from Morocco, formed the Wings Patrol Group 2. Until early 1944, RAF Upottery had operated USAAF 439th Transport Groups C-47 Dakota's in support of the invasion. In November/December 1944, the base also supported the squadrons from Dunkeswell temporarily while its runways were repaired. But by the time the new units were settled in, U-boat contacts were rare and the only action of note occurred on 27 February, 1945, when VB-112's Lt O. B. Denison flying Liberator serial 38886/H, sighted a submerged snorkel and directed surface ships to the area which after tracking the submarine through the night, eventually caught and sank *U-1208*. In addition a detachment of three Consolidated Catalina from VP-63 in Morocco were successful in co-operating with British destroyers to sink three U-boats and on 30 April 1945, Lt. F. G. Lake piloting a "Cat" sank *U-1107* south-west of Ushant.

Missions continued until the spring of 1945, by which time with much of Europe back under Allied control FAW 7s job was nearly done. On 11 July, the Wing's H.Q. was temporarily transferred to Dunkeswell before returning to the United States at the end of the month. At the height of operations Dunkeswell was home to 5,000 Americans and during their time at Dunkeswell, FAW 7 squadrons completed 6,454 missions totalling 62,247 patrol hours, and flew in excess of 10.5 million miles, in an attempt to ensure "almost every pint of water in the Bay of Biscay was covered every half hour".

FAW 7s WW II losses amounted to twenty-three airplanes, seven from VB-103, six from VB-105 and ten from VB-110. At the wars end of the sixty-nine US Navy Liberators remaining at Dunkeswell awaiting repatriation to the United States, thirty-four were broken up after an offer for sale to the British Government for a few thousand dollars was countered by an offer of $50 each. Being unacceptable to the U.S. Government the airplanes were broken up by a team of Seebees using bulldozers and steel cables looped around the mid-section fuselages.

British and American Base Locations in the UK in WW II (Note: Coastal Command bases underlined)

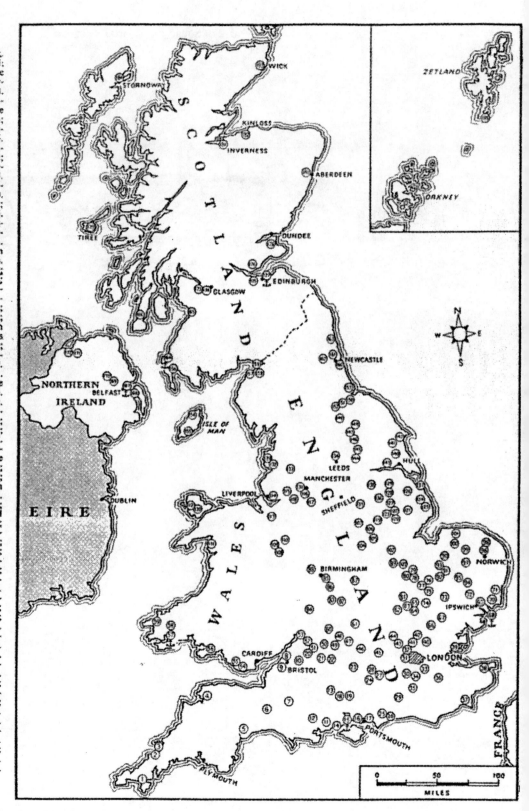

GR VI Liberator Liberator - Line Drawing

No. 220 Squadron Coastal Command

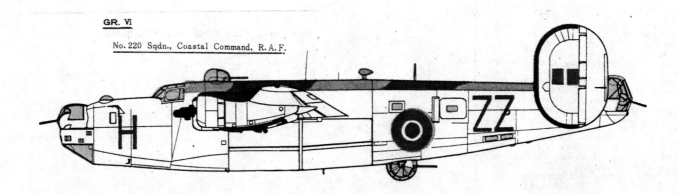

GR. VI

No. 220 Sqdn., Coastal Command, R.A.F.

Chapter 6 - Air Sea Rescue and Other Missions

Rescuing the crews of military aircraft forced down in the sea during WW I was often carried out on an *ad hoc* basis, with the airmen often left to their own devices. Occasionally marine craft, floatplanes and flying boats that could be spared from their primary duties were brought to bear. The same arrangements continued in the RAF between the wars and it was not until WW II that the military authorities gave any serious thought to creating an air-sea-rescue organisation. Following the outbreak of WW II, 12 Westland Lysander airplanes, able to drop survival packs to aircrew in the sea, and more than 20 high-speed launches were deployed on ASR duties. Then in February 1941, the RAF Air Sea Rescue Service was formed under the operational control of Coastal Command.

Before this, in September 1939, only eight days after the outbreak of war, Coastal Command had carried out its first air-sea-rescue. Flt Lt. Barrett and his crew from No. 204 Squadron were on U-boat patrol when they heard from other Sunderland aircraft of No. 228 Squadron in the area that the cargo ship SS *Kensington Court* had sent out an SOS it had been torpedoed and was sinking. One of the No. 228 Squadron aircraft - N9025 piloted by Flt Lt. Thurston N. W. Smith, landed alongside the lifeboats, as did the No. 204 Squadron aircraft and between them they picked up all the crew and flew them home. In WW II both the Sunderland and the Catalina flying-boats gave proof of their value in the air-sea-rescue role. In fact the Sunderland extended its heroic activities into the Korean War, when just a handful completed over 1,500 sorties.

Also in September, 1939, the SS *Blairlogie*, under fire from a U-boat, sent out an SOS. A Sunderland flying-boat went to the rescue. Four and half hours after leaving base and some 300 miles from the nearest land, the Sunderland located the crew in boats, with the ship sunk. The aircraft directed an American vessel to the scene and stood by until the rescue had been made, returning to base late in the evening after a round trip of over 1,300 miles. The following year on 2 March, the SS *Domala* was bombed and set on fire 14 miles off Selsey Bill in the Channel. A passing destroyer was led by an Avro Anson general reconnaissance plane to a raft, the only one of four with anyone on it.

In the Sea War against the U-boats as well as air attacks and other missions Coastal Command was also called on to go to the rescue of airmen adrift after a forced landing in the sea or seamen adrift after their boats had sunk. On other occasions aircraft on long-range patrol duties, being about their business over large expanse of ocean could, by timely warning, often help ships avoid running into dangers ahead. On several occasions ships unwittingly steaming into minefields had been given such warnings. As for instance in March, 1940, a number of mines had been seen by a patrolling aircraft directly in the path of a Dutch vessel, the *Stadtschiedam*. The visual signals made were ignored, but the ship was eventually persuaded to change course by the airplane firing a burst of machine gun fire across its bows.

On 2 July, 1940, a Sunderland was sent to find the survivors of the *Arandora Star*, torpedoed in the Atlantic when carrying a large number of prisoners to Canada for internment. Thirteen lifeboats packed with survivors were located soon after 11.00 hours. Near by them, scattered over a wide area, were rafts, pieces of wood and other wreckage to which other many other survivors were clinging. The Sunderland dropped *Mae West* life-jackets, first aid kits and food packages. Two hours later the flying-boat found a destroyer of the Royal Canadian Navy, the *St Laurent* and guided it to the lifeboats. The aircraft then flew round and round overhead for more than three hours guiding the destroyers boats by means of flares to where the survivors were floating.

On 16 July, a Sunderland saw the mast and upper superstructure of a destroyer and a merchant vessel protruding through the thick fog which lay over the sea off the coast in north-east Scotland. The ships, which were making for a port of anchorage, were about to run into a small island, but the airplane flashing the International sign U-U-U, meaning "you are running into danger", followed by the signal "turn to port" ensured they entered harbour safely. Later that same day the same Sunderland reunited a RN destroyer with its flotilla when it had lost touch with its six companions. Similar shepherding missions were not uncommon in the severe weather often encountered in the areas of operation.

On 25 September, a Sunderland returning to base from convoy escort duty, sighted a lifeboat in the sea. Flying lower the Captain saw that some of the persons on board were children. One of them a small boy, began to wave a white rag, spelling out the letters the *City of Benares*, — a passenger liner, the Captain knew had been torpedoed eight days before which had been carrying children from the UK to Canada. The Sunderland turned back towards the convoy it had left, signalled details to its relief, another Sunderland, and then low on fuel, returned to base. The other Sunderland then located a warship and led it to the lifeboat, to pick up forty-six survivors. A month later, a Stranraer flying-boat found a lifeboat with 25 survivors of the SS *Pacific Ranger* on board. Nineteen of them were rescued by destroyer. On 26 October, a Sunderland helped naval units to pick up survivors from the *Empress of Britain*. During this operation three Bristol Blenheim fighters provided protection from enemy air attack. A similar operation was undertaken a few days later by a Sunderland when all the survivors from the *Laurentie* were picked up.

Other ASR missions, involved providing assistance to submarines and surface vessels of the RN which had suffered damage by mines or in action with the enemy. On 27 November, 1939, the British submarine *Triad* reported that she was in difficulties off the Norwegian coast. Three Hudsons sent out to locate her, soon lost her again in the atrocious weather conditions, although she was located again by other Hudson airplanes that had been sent out to provide protection for two destroyers and another submarine, the *Triumph,* which had gone to her assistance. A month later, the *Triumph* herself was in difficulties and needed assistance when she was struck by a floating mine in the North Sea. On both occasions the Hudsons kept enemy aircraft seeking to attack the stricken submarines at bay, while they made for the safety of their home port.

On the night of 10/11 May, 1940, the destroyer HMS *Kelly* was torpedoed in the North Sea during an encounter with enemy E-boats. The *Kelly* was part of a force making to take part in operations off the Dutch coast and was taken in tow by HMS *Bulldog,* which had rammed and sunk one of the E-boats. The ships requested air protection and Hudsons were despatched to escort the vessels, but by 06.00 hours the *Kelly* was listing so badly that her starboard decks were awash. Even so, she was not abandoned by her crew and throughout the day the Hudsons patrolled the skies in relays above, leaving only as darkness fell. The next day a Short Sunderland flying-boat arrived at dawn to carry out an ASW patrol in the area. While Admiralty tugs took over the task of towing the *Kelly,* and Hudsons once more took over protection duties. In fact, they were unable to prevent two Heinkel bombing attacks, but their presence ensured that no bombs fell near their target. The Hudsons kept up their protection flights throughout the day and half the next until the *Kelly* was towed into port with little more than her upper superstructure showing. In total forty-nine aircraft had taken part in this operation, which was completed at 13.00 hours on 13 May, 1940.

In July, 1940, an aircraft of Coastal Command discovered HMS *Whirlwind* which had been badly damaged by a U-boat. It directed another destroyer to the scene and the crew were rescued. On 1 September, the same year further Coastal Command assistance was given to Royal Naval ships HMS *Ivanhoe* and HMS *Express.* The following year on 22 August, 1941, the Free French submarine *Rubis* found herself in grave difficulties off the Norwegian coast. Bristol Blenheims of Coastal Command found her in the morning and constant patrols were maintained over her. The next day she was seen to be stopped and reported to a Bristol Beaufort aircraft by signal that her batteries were destroyed but she was water-tight. A Short Sunderland and two Catalina aircraft were despatched to pick up the crew, as it was impossible for surface vessels to reach the stricken submarine owing to the presence of an enemy mine-field. In the event it was not necessary to implement this rescue as she succeeded in starting her surface engines and began to make slowly for her base. Surface escort was provided by the RN and air cover was provided by Coastal Command Blenheims and Beaufighters.

By 1941, the method of rescuing a ship's crew by flying-boat was well established, and followed similar methods to those employed to take off the crew of the stricken SS *Kensington Court* mentioned earlier. Three Sunderland flying-boats converged on the vessel at once. It was arranged for one to remain on guard overhead while the others landed to pick up survivors. There were 34 in two of the ships' boats, but the heavy swell prevented them from approaching the Sunderlands too closely and a shuttle service of small rubber dinghies had to be established until all the survivors were on board, 21 on one aircraft and 13 on the other. In the case of the *Kensington Court* the survivors had only just taken to their lifeboats, but when an attempt was made on the 16 October, 1941, to rescue 21 men from the *Stagrant* they had been in their lifeboat for three and half days. They had been spotted by a Sunderland, which had dropped a container with food and cigarettes, on 14 October, as sea conditions prevented the flying boat from landing. Two days later the same airplane set out again and it was still dark when one of the gunners reported a red light on the sea some miles away... The pilot discussed the possibility of landing in the dark with his co-pilots, and having decided it could be done the flying-boat was set down on the calmest sea possible and took the men aboard safely, from their lifeboat.

In March, 1941, a Coastal Command Whitley found survivors of the SS *Beaverbrae*, the victim of an enemy aircraft. On 10 June, two Coastal Command Vickers Wellingtons each sighted a lifeboat with survivors off the coast of Northern Ireland. Later over 40 men were rescued by destroyers. Later in September, 1941, a British submarine had stopped the Norwegian vessel *Tropic Sea*. On board was a German Prize crew who were endeavouring to take the vessel into a French port. But on appearance of the British submarine the vessel was scuttled with the Norwegian crew escaping in one boat and the Germans in another. Later a Sunderland with an armed crew was sent to pick up the survivors, but only the Norwegians were found, and rescued.

On 10 February, 1942, a Lockheed Hudson sighted a raft with two survivors upon it. A trawler was directed to the spot and reached the raft on the next day, having been helped in its location of the raft by a Catalina flying-boat. The two rescued men, a Swede and a Dane had been torpedoed a month before ! They appeared fit and well when picked up due in the main to the construction of the life-raft, which had been made by the ships carpenter. It could float either way up and was well stocked with water, provisions and blankets. The men had even been able to cook hot meals on it !

Such airborne rescues continued throughout the Sea War, and the foregoing are just but a few examples of what was involved. The work continued right until the wars end, with about 3,000 persons adrift in the sea sighted and helped to survival by Coastal Command aircraft in 1939/1940 alone. The Commands ASR operations peaked in 1944, with some 169 airplanes dedicated to the task. A wide variety of airplanes were used for ASR, including Supermarine Walrus amphibians, Westland Lysanders, Boulton Paul Defiants and Supermarine Spitfires. The Walrus of course could alight on the sea to pick up survivors, the other airplanes could only drop rescue packs and summon help of the ASR launches or other vessels. However, Lockheed Hudson and Vickers Warwick types were specially modified to carry an airborne lifeboat, which could be parachuted to survivors in the sea. Other rescue aids included the Thornaby Bag, and Bircham Barrel, buoyant containers filled with survival gear which could be dropped by virtually any aircraft. The Lindholme equipment, comprising a dingy pack with attached buoyant supply containers was even more efficient, and remains in use today.

With weather conditions in the North Sea usually bad, with gale force winds on at least ten days every month throughout the year, and fog and mist on more than half of the days of summer and only slightly less in winter, when the days are much shorter. Flying an ASR sortie at sometimes 50 feet, for up to four-and-half to five hours looking for small life rafts and dinghies was to say the least both tiring and arduous, especially with the Warwick A.S.R. I with an Airborne Lifeboat underslung was quite heavy and sluggish on the controls.

During WW II the RAF Air/Sea Rescue Service is reported to have saved 13,626 lives and a number of specialised ASR squadrons were maintained for a period post-war.

It is of interest as well as the rescue missions the Command was called on to undertake a number of special missions. On 22 June 1941, Hitler launched his attack on Russia. On the 24th two Coastal Command Catalina flying-boats arrived at a base in North-East Scotland and took on board an official Mission to the Government of the USSR. It included high ranking officers of the Army and the Royal Air Force, the British Ambassador to the Soviet Government and other important persons. The next day the flying boats flew to Archangel, a 18 hour flight. This was just one of a number of many long-distance flights by Coastal Command airplanes to transport Government officials of all kinds to places all over the world. A number of special ferry service flights were made after the collapse of France. On 18 June, 1940, for example, a Sunderland flying-boat took the First Lord of the Admiralty and the First Sea Lord to Bordeaux and brought the first Sea Lord back on the following day. Some days later General Sikorski was brought to the UK in a Lockheed Hudson airplane.

On 25 June, another Sunderland carried the Minister of Information and General Lord Gort VC on a mission to Rabat. They were commissioned by HM Government to go to French Morocco, where several French statesmen, personal friends of Mr Duff Cooper, were reported to have arrived, in order to discuss the new situation with them and with the local British representatives as to what were the prospects of continued resistance in French North Africa. The Sunderland took-off about 09.00 hours and arrived at Rabat at 19.00 hours. The landing was made in difficult circumstances, as the river on which it had to set down was no more than 150 feet wide. Immediately on touching down the pilot had to use his rudder in order to round a bend of the river. A number of French Air Force officers took the pilot and his passenger to the Customs Wharf and then on to the British Consulate. Later the Sunderland took-off just before dawn to fly to Gibraltar to off-load its passengers before returning to the UK. There were many long-range special missions undertaken by Coastal command throughout the duration of the war, details of which remain scant.

A little known role undertaken by the Command's Sunderland flying-boats was the dropping and picking up of agents at night. The Sunderland would fly into a previously arranged location off the coast at night where a boat would come and pick up, or return, the agent from the flying-boat. Both the Norwegian coast and the many coves and bays in the Mediterranean were ideal for these clandestine missions, and both Nos. 228 and 230 Squadrons became quite adept in these missions. No. 228 spent a short while operating out of Malta, but the German offensive in the area made the island a less than desirable base for flying-boat operations.

ARMSTRONG WHITWORTH
WHITLEY

The Armstrong Whitworth Whitley was a large, all-metal, twin-engined monoplane. The wings had a sharp angle of incidence and with a long fuselage and a tailplane with twin rudders mounted inboard it was a sturdy but not very attractive airplane. It was built to Air Ministry Specification B.3/34, and the prototype flew in March, 1936. The first Whitley I was delivered to the RAF in March, 1937. It gained immortality in RAF service being the first RAF bomber to fly over Berlin, the first to fly the leaflet raids in September 1939, and the first to drop bombs on Germany in May, 1940. It was also the first Allied airplane to bomb Italy on 11 June 1940, when it bombed Genoa and Turin and was involved in the first Allied paratroop operations over southern Italy in February, 1941.

In Coastal Command the first Whitleys to enter service were the normal bomber variant when No. 58 Squadron was transferred from Bomber to Coastal Command for temporary duty on 30 September, 1939, beginning convoy escort patrols on 10 October. Later having returned to Bomber Command to receive Whitley Vs in April, 1942 the squadron transferred to Coastal command again to fly ASW patrols from St Eval, Cornwall. the unit later receiving H.P. Halifaxes remaining with Coastal Command until the wars end flying its last patrol of the war on 23 May, 1945.

In the autumn of 1940, Whitley Vs replaced No. 502 Squadrons Avro Ansons at Aldergrove, Northern Ireland. In November 1940, Whitleys of No. 612 Squadron were added to Coastal Commands battle order, the first Whitley patrol flown in February 1941, although it was not until November that year that the Ansons were finally withdrawn. Later during the course of Whitley V production for Bomber Command a special Coastal Command variant the Whitley G. R. VII was produced for Coastal Command, fitted with long-range ASV II radar. It was to be Whitley VII 'B' of No. 502 Squadron flown by F/O R. G. W. Holdsworth who dropped three depth-charges to score Coastal Commands first 'ASV' "kill" when he sank U-206 on 30 November, 1941 in the Bay of Biscay, West of St Nazaire.

Unfortunately the Coastal Command Whitley VII was still powered by two 1,145 hp R-R Merlin X engines, but the weight of the radar installation, increase in crew from five to six men, and the additional drag caused by the four above fuselage ASV 'goal post' antenna greatly reduced the airplanes top speed. It was not long until most Whitleys had been re-assigned to No 10 Coastal Command OTU at St Eval, Cornwall, where some were still in use as late as July 1943.

Whitley VII (LA 794) with A.S.V. aerials. (*Imp. War Museum Photo.*)

BLACKBURN
BOTHA

Named after General Botha, the Boer General and first Prime Minister of the Union of South Africa, the Blackburn Botha general reconnaissance and torpedo bomber was one of a trio of new types that had been chosen to re-equip Coastal Command in the late 1930s, just before war broke out. The other aircraft included in this scheme were the Bristol Beaufort and Saro Lerwick flying-boat both discussed later. The Botha was intended to operate on general reconnaissance or torpedo bombing duties. An order for 442 aircraft was placed 'straight off the drawing board', in December, 1936, with further contracts for an additional 814 issued to Blackburn in 1940, which later, after only 138 were built, was cancelled.

The urgent need for aircraft dictated the first two series airplanes doubled as prototypes and L6104 and L6105, made their first flights on 28 December 1938 and 7 June 1939 respectively. The first flight was made by company chief test pilot Flt Lt. H. Bailey, who later died in the fatal accident to the Dumbarton-built Blackburn B-20 retractable-hull seaplane on 7 April, near the Isle of Bute. Viewed 'head-on' from the front the Botha or "why bother", was distinctive and somewhat unusual in that the prone bomb-aimers position in the nose was offset with asymmetric glazing to port. The rather derogatory nickname is believed to have arisen on account that the design suffered a number of accidents in its early life that were not fully understood or explained. The reason for this was that the AIB (Aircraft Investigation Branch) was not called in to investigate these accidents either during company flying or service use until mid-1940.

The first accident had occurred during company test flying when L6129, with company test pilot B. R. Rolfe, together with his flight test observer J. B. E. Johnson aboard had plunged to earth at Flixborough, Scarborough, Lincs., during a production test flight from the factory at Brough on 5 March, 1940, and did not survive. Soon afterwards there were another three fatal accidents: L6377 crashed on 26 May and L6390 on 12 June, both during production test flights from Abbotsinch, and L6205 on 8 July, on test from Brough. The cause of one of the four accidents (not identified) was reported to have been caused by possible aileron instability. Nevertheless the first service deliveries had been made in June 1940, when almost immediately service pilots found it to be seriously underpowered, the company having been forced to use the 850 hp Bristol Perseus X engine due to the unavailability of other more powerful types, and that the airplane also had a number of other shortcomings.

It had poor single-engine performance even though it had been given clearance by A&AEE Boscombe Down. It also had a number of unique and at the time novel features, such as a retractable undercarriage and hydraulically operated flaps and brakes, electric trim gear, interconnected throttle and mixture controls, electric engine starting, an automatic pilot and a fuel jettison system. It could be said it was slightly ahead of its time as through no fault of Blackburn's chief designer G. E. Petty, RAF crews were trained and used to relatively unsophisticated airplanes in the late 1930s. What they did like about the new general reconnaissance torpedo-bomber was that it had a spacious cockpit for the crew of 4 and colour-coded engine control levers. One disturbing aspect for the pilot and navigator must have been the close proximity of the rotating propeller tips to the sides of the fuselage. Just how close was recounted by Albert Guy, an LAC aero-engine fitter who recalled when Pilot Officer Barrett returned to the flight line with a loose engine cowling on putting his arm out of the cockpit window to indicate this, had his hand severed just above the wrist.

The only front-line unit to receive the Botha was No. 608 (Aux) Squadron, Coastal Command based at Thornaby-on-Tees. In June 1940, the Botha joined with the units remaining Avro Anson Is, to fly anti-submarine patrols over the North Sea until 6 November, when after having flown only 308 operational sorties they were withdrawn. The type was never issued to other operational squadrons as planned, but was subsequently instead, employed on operational training duties..! When despite being declared obsolete in August 1943, it remained in use until September 1944.

Much underpowered and with many other shortcomings, the Perseus-engined Blackburn Botha GR and torpedo-bomber was ordered 'off-the-drawingboard': 138 were built and flew with No 608 Sqdn and some training units between 1940 and 1944.

BRISTOL
BEAUFORT

The Bristol Beaufort was the standard torpedo airplane of Coastal Command for three years, from 1940 to 1943. The Beaufort went into full Coastal Command service with No. 22 Squadron based at Thorney Island, near Emsworth, Sussex, in November, 1939. Already with a reputation as a difficult airplane to fly, with unreliable engines and no development potential. Eventually things marginally improved when its two Bristol Taurus VI radial engines were replaced by the more reliable — Pratt & Whitney Twin Wasp radials — except the additional performance gained was gradually stripped away as essential operational modifications, such as more guns, better armour protection, etc, increased the weight of the airplane. It is true to say had it not been for dogged determination of both air and ground crews the Beaufort would have suffered the same ignominious fate as its close relative the Blackburn Botha, banished to operational training duties.

Problems with the airplane were apparent from the start — Cyril Unwins Bristol Aeroplane Company's chief test pilot, made the first flight of the prototype on 15 October, 1938. This was a short flight as was the two succeeding flights the whole three amounting to no more than thirty minutes of flying time, until the airplane serial L4441 was returned to the workshops for modification.

The chosen Bristol Taurus radial engines had been fitted with close-fitting low-drag cowlings, with the cooling air drawn through cylinder banks to exit via controllable slots in the nacelle sides under the wings, the intent being this would afford some thrust augmentation. But the initial flights soon showed this was not working and the engines were rapidly overheating. There were a number of other problems to be addressed - the interaction of the airflow around the deep forebody of the aircraft and over the engine nacelles caused buffeting on the tail unit, and the big 'flat-plate' fairings on the main gear legs could induce severe drag problems, exaggerated by the lack of co-ordinated response during retraction and extension. L4441 remained in the workshops for five months undergoing modification and finally emerged with more orthodox engine cowlings with controllable trailing-edge cooling gills, enlarged oil cooler air intakes and numerous other improvements.

Finally in this form it was delivered to the A&AEE at Martlesham Heath, near Ipswich, on 17 April 1939, for preliminary handling and performance trials. With minimum payload the airplane achieved a top speed of 304 mph at 15,000 feet, and 246 mph at sea level. But on return to Filton the airplane was returned to the experimental workshops for further work on engine cooling and areas associated with low-speed instability brought to the fore during the A&AEE trials. Attention to these problems took another three months.

Meanwhile, the second prototype serial L4442, flew on 3 July 1939. This airplane was fitted with revised design engine cowlings and oil cooling system and the first issue of some operational equipment — in due course it went to the A&AEE, by now relocated to Boscombe Down - on 17 October, 1939. The third airplane to be produced L4443, was retained by the manufacturer to further investigate the engine cooling and performance problems and was later sent to India, for tropical trials. But, the declaration of war in September, 1939, saw the A&AEE give the Beaufort a limited clearance certificate for entry into operational service with RAF Coastal Command who were desperately short of aircraft at this time. Even though the reality was the type was still suffering horrendous engine problems. With two of the prototype's written off after engine failure (L4442 at Filton on 21 May 1940), and other aircraft having to undergo major rectification work after having been forced down due to engine failure, the type soon became one of the most unpopular to fly for the company test pilots at Filton.

Much time and effort was expended by the Bristol Engine Company to rectify the problems with the small Taurus engine but even when its reliability was improved, as late as 1942, Pilot's Notes carried a warning "In the event of complete failure of one engine during, or shortly after, take-off, no attempt should be made to remain in the air unless a height of at least 500 to 1,000 feet has been reached and the flaps have been raised. Otherwise, close the throttles immediately, ensure that the undercarriage is not coming, if there is time, lower the flaps, switch off the ignition and land straight ahead.

Originally the airplanes all-up weight was limited to 17,500-lb, but by the time of its entry into operational service in early 1940, this had risen to 18,500-lb; with the modification of the Tauras engines to give slightly greater output to compensate, this continued to rise to 20,000-lb then to 21,000-lb for the Mk I Tauras-powered variant and 21,500-lb for the Mk II American P&W Twin Wasp engined airplane. The torpedo launcher bomber was an all-metal mid-wing monoplane which could also be used for general reconnaissance duties, replacing the Anson. It carried a crew of four — pilot, navigator/bomb-aimer, wireless operator/air gunner and air gunner. The control surfaces were fabric covered. The main bomb and torpedo load were carried in the bomb-bay under the forward body, and bombs could were also be carried under the outer wings.

Armament varied but mainly comprised a fixed machine gun in the port outer wing, augmented by a second gun in a similar position in the starboard wing in later aircraft; while twin machine guns fired by the navigator could be installed on gimbal mountings in the nose. In earlier variants a single under-defence machine gun firing aft, was fitted under the starboard nose (later an ASV radar antenna was fitted here); two independent beam machine guns, one each side of the rear fuselage, were carried and the dorsal power turret had, in early versions, one gun, and - later - two Brownings. All the guns were of .303-in calibre.

The Beaufort I was powered by two Bristol Tauras II, VI, XII or XVI sleeve-valve engines, and the Mk II by two American Pratt & Whitney Twin Wasp R-1830-S3C4-G or SC3-G overhead-valve engines. The P&W engines were, initially civil-rated reconditioned engines and some were later replaced by Lend-Lease R-1830-90 and -92 units with military ratings. A comparison of performance characteristics is shown :

	Bristol Tauras	**P & W Twin Wasp**
Take-off	1,085 bhp at 3,100 rpm	1,200 bhp at 2,700 rpm
Max at specified height	1,030 bhp at 3,100 rpm at 3,500 ft	1.200 bhp at 2,700 rpm at 4,900 ft
Max speed	250 mph	250 mph
Aircrew used	de Havilland varible-pitch constant-speed	Curtiss Electric constant-speed fully feathering
Max range	1,500 miles	1,500 miles

The first Beaufort arrived at Thorney Island, on 15 November, 1939, but due to ongoing engine problems and the crews difficulties in converting to an airplane with less than desirable handling characteristics due to lack of fin area, it was not until the 15 April the following year that it took off on its first operational sortie, mine-laying off the mouth of the Elbe, during which one of the new airplanes were lost. In the next few weeks No. 22 Squadron operated from diverse bases all over the UK; from Wick, Lossiemouth and Sumbrugh in Scotland, St Eval, Cornwall, Kaldadarnes in Iceland and Skitten, Scotland. The squadrons first anti-shipping strike occurred on 7 May 1940, when three airplanes bombed an enemy destroyer off Norderney, but again one airplane was lost and another was badly damaged. However, within a month or so the squadron had lost no less than 13 airplanes (only four to enemy action), and as a result all Beaufort's were grounded.

For the next two months, while the Bristol Aeroplane Co., endeavoured to sort the problems (mainly engine) No.22 Squadron remained inactive operationally, and then in mid-August the unit was informed it would be receiving the new fast American Martin Maryland bomber. The first of these were received on 22 August and "C" Flight began to train on them. But within a few days the Beaufort's were cleared for operations to begin by the end of the month, and "C" Flight was detached to Thorney Island to become No. 431 General Reconnaissance) Flight, later moving to Malta.

No. 22 Squadron resumed operations on 31 August 1940, with a bombing attack on the Seaplane Station at Amsterdam, following this with its first torpedo strike at shipping off Ostend on 11 September. Four days later, the unit carried out its first night torpedo attack on Ijmuiden. The squadron continued on operational duties until the end of the year and into 1941, for the loss of thirty-three aircraft... Then on the 6 April 1941, operating from St Eval, Cornwall, it launched an attack on the German battle-cruisers *Scharnhorst* and *Gneisenau* at Brest. Six airplanes - three with bombs and three with torpedos set out on the raid, but bad weather meant only two airplanes reached the target area. One, serial N1016 coded OA-X piloted by Flying Officer Kenneth Campbell — although hit again and again by heavy flak put up by the two ships, managed to launch its torpedo which struck the *Gneisenau* causing severe damage putting it out of action for many months. Unfortunately The Beaufort was shot down by the air defences in the vicinity of the heavily defended Brest Harbour, and the crew were killed — Flying Officer Campbell being awarded a posthumous Victoria Cross.

On the 25 June, 1941, the squadron moved back to Thorney Island, but detachments continued — on e was based at RAF Luechars, Scotland, to attack shipping off the Norwegian coast. But on 2 January, 1942, the squadron stood down from operations in the UK to prepare to leave for the Far East. Although in the event it was soon in operation again in the Middle East carrying out its last torpedo raid in conjunction with No. 39 Squadron which resulted in the loss of five of its Beauforts shot down and three badly damaged airplanes forced to land at Malta.

Meanwhile in the UK, further developments at Filton had led to the first flight of the prototype Beaufort Mk II with Twin Wasp engines, on the 9 November 1940; the first series production airplane serial AW244 taking to the air on 17 August, 1941. The first Mk II had been received by No. 22 Squadron on 5 November 1941, before it left for overseas. Others were delivered to No. 42 Squadron another torpedo-bomber unit.

No. 42 Squadron had received its first Beaufort I on 2 April 1940, at Bircham Newton, moving south to Thorney Island on 16 April, maintaining detachments in Scotland, at Sumburgh and Wick. Operations from Thorney began on 5 June, but on 21 June the squadron had a hard time when its detachment at Sumburgh attacked the German battle-cruiser *Scharnhorst* off the Norwegian coast. As with No.22 Squadron all its airplanes were grounded during July and August, until resuming mine-laying operations along the coast of northern Europe. No. 42 Squadron had moved to Wick in Scotland on 19 June, 1940, and moved again a year later to Leuchars, on the 1 March, 1941. Attacks were made mainly in the Norwegian coastal area. A significant success was scored by Flt Sgt. R. H. Lovett flying serial L9939 code AW-Z when his torpedo struck the German heavy cruiser *Lutzow* off Norway, on 13 June. On 3 August 1942, No. 42 Squadron moved south again to Thorney Island, to be told it was to proceed overseas to the Far East — and its aircraft started to leave for the Middle East en-route on 13 August, where it lost its identity with its airplanes dispersed to other units.

The third UK unit to receive Beauforts was No. 217 Squadron which received its first Beaufort Is in May, 1940. But the troubles that had plagued the other units came to the fore and the type was not used operationally until 25 September operating alongside the units Avro Ansons until December, 1940. On moving to Thorney Island from St Eval on 28 October, 1941 — the squadron had a hard time attacking the Atlantic coastal ports of Brest and Lorient until resuming convoy patrols, but losses continued. It transferred to the north of Scotland at Skitten, on 16 February, 1942, and then to Leuchars two weeks later on 1 March. In May along with the other Beaufort units, it was notified of its move to the Far East, and the Beauforts began to leave for overseas on 7 May. But the desperate need for anti-shipping strikes on Rommel's re-supply convoys in the Mediterranean saw No. 217 take up station at RAF Luqa, Malta. But the unit sustained heavy losses and by September, 1942, its remaining airplanes were distributed among other units, with the groundcrew moving on to Minneriya, Ceylon, to form the basis of a Lockheed Hudson unit, in October 1942.

The next unit to receive Beauforts in the UK was No. 86 Squadron who had been flying Bristol Blenheim IVs on convoy escort duties off the East Anglian coast since 28 March, 1941. The first Beaufort was received on the 9 May 1941, and the squadron began mine-laying operations on 15 July — torpedo training followed and anti-shipping strikes began on 11 November, the first torpedo attack flown on 12 December — all being flown from RAF North Coates, to which the unit had moved on 12 May, 1941. As with the other Beaufort squadrons No. 86 took its turn on the various UK detachments until what remained of the unit was reduced to a cadre in August 1942, soon after which in October, it re-equipped with Liberators. Of note is the fact, No. 86 Squadron's Beauforts played an important part in trying to prevent the 'Channel Dash' by the German battleships *Gneisenau, Scharnhorst* and *Prinz Eugen,*early in 1942.

Two Dominion units equipped briefly with the Beaufort, did not use the type operationally. No. 489 Squadron (RNZAF) formed at Luechars on 12 August 1941, and a few days later received some Beaufort Is and Blenheims to begin torpedo training, but the shortage of airplanes, led to the squadron losing its Beauforts at the end of January 1942, to re-equip with torpedo-carrying H.P. Hampdens in March. The other was No. 415 Squadron (RCAF) which suffered a similar fate, re-equipping with Hampdens in January, 1942.

Of the 1,013 Beaufort Is delivered more than 50% had been lost by the end of 1942, not all to enemy action. The improved Mk II faired somewhat better with 415 built by 1944. Bristol's proposed a Mk III variant to be powered by two 1,280 hp R-R Merlin XX engines, but it never got beyond the design stage.

BRISTOL
BLENHEIM

Early in 1941, daylight raids against enemy shipping was entrusted to Bristol Blenheim airplanes. The twin-engined all-metal mid-wing monoplane powered by two 840 hp Bristol Mercury radial engines carried a defensive armament of a fixed Browning machine gun, installed on the wing and a Vickers K machine gun, installed in a semi-retractable turret in the fuselage. The bomber could also carry up to a maximum of 454 kg (1,000 lb) of bombs.

The assaults which began early in the year, by Blenheim squadrons seconded to Coastal Command (Nos. 82 and 101 Squadrons Bomber Command), were continued throughout the summer and early autumn of 1941, by No. 235 Squadron Coastal Command. They sought enemy convoys, and on occasion single ships moving up and down the coasts of Holland, Belgium and France, which were divided for the purposes of attack into a number of 'beats'. It was the practice of the Blenheims to fly these 'beats' until an enemy convoy was sighted then to attack immediately. This was not always as easy as might be expected as often the patrols were made in poor weather, with moderate or poor visibility desirable as no fighter escort was provided. The aircraft flew low over the water and on sighting the convoy each picked a target and delivered its attack from mast height, the bombs swinging almost horizontally into the ship's quarter. They then made a 'skidding' turn as opposed to a sharp turn which would have exposed the aircraft's vulnerable underbelly to the fire of the ships gunners — and made for home.

A three-ship Blenheim formation led by the units C.O. that set out in early September 1941, to seek a large enemy merchant ship off the coast of France, relates; "We did not see the big ship, but after turning to port and flying the prescribed length time along our beat we saw a convoy just on the horizon. At that moment, too, we saw a big ship, probably the one we were after, but as we were in the wrong position to attack her we went on for the convoy. I chose a ship of, I judged, between 3,000 and 4,000 tons. I had a flak ship to starboard. Both it and the flak ship opened up. The air in front became full of black puffs with red sparks crossing them. That was tracer and it all looked as though it was going straight towards us, only to turn away at the last moment and hit the water. It was my first attack on a ship and I pulled up a bit late and only just missed the mast. We then found we were rushing over a destroyer and that a Messerschmitt Me 109 was 400 ft above us. He fired a few bursts and then went off. The Wing Commander must have got his ship, because we saw a big one with its decks awash just after our attack".

A month later the same crew, in the company of two other Blenheims, found a convoy ten miles off the Frisian coast. The attack was made from the direction of the shore, and the Blenheims, flying very low, got well into the convoy so that the ships if they opened fire, ran the risk of hitting each other. They did not do so until the attackers were clear of them. Two of the Blenheims made of after dropping their bombs and the third dodged in and out, 'weaving among the ships' till its pilot found a gap and slipped through.

Occasionally in 1941, even the Stirling bombers were deployed against enemy shipping. In the afternoon of 24 November two Stirling's sighted seven German ships off the island of Borkum. While attacking them, they were themselves attacked by eight Me 109s. They accounted for three of the enemy aircraft in an engagement that lasted for 25 minutes. One of the Stirlings was badly damaged by flak before the action, and fought it, with bomb doors hanging open and a starboard engine dead. Soon after the port outer engine stopped, but the Striling got back to base on the two remaining. Such attacks by Bomber Command against German shipping from the Bay of Biscay to Norway, were not uncommon. and in six months during 1941, they sank more than seventy ships.

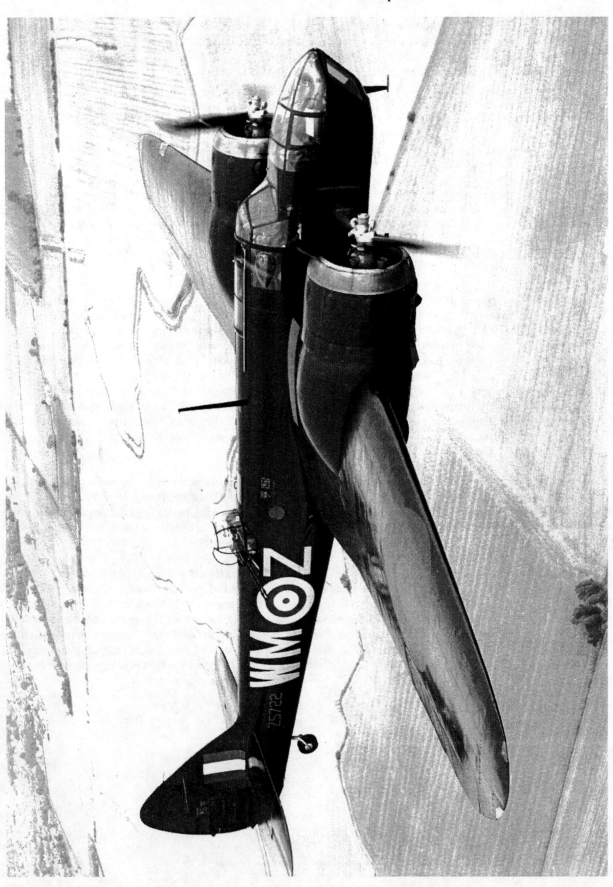

BRISTOL
BEAUFIGHTER

Design of the Beaufighter began at Filton, Bristol, at the end of 1938, the plan being to quickly produce a high-performance long-range fighter utilising the wings, rear fuselage, tail unit and other components of the Beaufort torpedo-bomber offered up to a redesigned front fuselage and higher-powered 1,425 hp Bristol Hercules radial engines. Initial flight trials proved very successful, few modifications were needed and series airplanes began to leave the production lines in July 1940, reaching RAF Squadrons in September and in March 1941, the Mk IC long-range fighter variant for Coastal Command entered service with No. 252 Squadron at RAF Chivenor, north Devon. The Mk IC featured extra radio and navigation equipment for long-range daylight missions over water. In April 1941, No. 252 Squadron moved to Northern Ireland for convoy patrols and on 1 May, fifteen of its airplanes were sent to Gibraltar en-route for operations on the hard pressed island of Malta.

Meanwhile, training and patrols continued from RAF Aldergrove, until all remaining airplanes were used to reform No. 143 Squadron on 15 June, 1941 as a long-range fighter unit in Coastal Command. In July the squadron moved to north-east England and then to Scotland for convoy patrols along the east coast. The next Beaufighter variant to enter service with Coastal Command was the Mk VIC with uprated 1,670 hp Bristol Hercules VI or XVI engines, and a backwards firing Vickers K gun installed in the navigators cockpit. The long-range fighter had already proved its worth with Coastal Command and squadrons operating from St Eval, Cornwall, had enjoyed many successes against Junkers Ju 88 over the Bay of Biscay. The Mk VI saw the airplanes versatility as a Coastal Command aircraft further enhanced. Rockets and torpedos now became part of the airplanes armament. In early March, 1942, a Beaufighter (X8065) had been successfully tested as a torpedo-carrier at the Torpedo Development Unit at Gosport,Hants, and in September 1942 a Mk. VIC (EL329) became the first Beaufighter to be armed with rocket projectiles fitted with 25-lb explosive warheads. In November 1942, the first Beaufighter "Strike Wing" was formed at RAF North Coates, consisting of No. 143 Squadron with long-range fighters, No. 236 Squadron with bombers and No. 254 Squadron with torpedo-bombers (Torbeaus). Their first successful operation against enemy shipping was on 18 April 1943. The rocket-firing variant entered service in May 1943, and the first operations occurred on 22 June 1943. In the Mediterranean the first rocket-firing Beaufighters were used by No. 603 Squadron in November, 1943 and No. 252 Squadron followed soon afterwards. Although at this time, No. 47 Squadron still carried torpedos, the number of large enemy vessels which justified the use of this heavy weapon were on the decline. No. 227 Squadron was deployed in the light bombing and fighter escort role with No. 16 Squadron SAAF equipping with the new Beaufighter X in December, 1943.

The Torpedo-Fighter X or TF X powered by two 1,770 hp Bristol Hercules XVII air-cooled radial engines was the best anti-shipping fighter of the war, able to deliver a formidable quantity of rockets, bombs, torpedoes and cannon fire over very long ranges and at high speed. The main external distinguishing features over earlier marks were the thimble nose housing the centimetric radar, and the dorsal fillet, extending the fin up the fuselage to improve stability.

A major operation of note involved sixteen Beaufighters from the five eastern Mediterranean squadrons, was one of the last operations that justified the use of torpedoes. On 22 February, 1944, aircraft from Nos. 47, 227 and 603 Squadrons, together with four NA B-25 Mitchell bombers of the U.S. 340th Bomb Group attacked the German merchant vessel *Lisa* of 5,343 tons carrying vital supplies to the garrison on Crete. She was escorted by two torpedo boats and protected by Junkers Ju 88, Messerschmitt Bf 109s and Arado Ar 196s. Eight Beaufighters of No. 47 Squadron lead by Wing Commander William D. L. Filson-Young flew over the island from North Africa together with eight Beaufighters of Nos 227 and 603 Squadrons and the four Mitchells of the USAAF. In the ensuing engagement one Mitchell bomber and three Beaufighters were shot down, but *Lisa* was torpedoed and sank after a large explosion on her starboard bow. Following the raid on the 15 March, No. 47 Squadron was sent to India to form part of a strike wing to operate against Japanese shipping.

Meanwhile the other units continued operations in the Eastern Mediterranean, even though bad weather hampered operations in early March. An operation of note was flown on 6 March, by Flt Lt. Alexander P. Pringle of No. 603 Squadron when during a night intruder mission he spotted two warships off the island of Dia, near Herakilon. He fired eight rockets fitted with 60-lb warheads (normally Beaufighter VICs used rockets with 25-lb solid-shot warheads) at the leading vessel. Immediately fires broke out followed by a huge explosion, it was soon discovered that Flt Lt. Pringle had sunk the German TA15, a former Italian destroyer of 970 tons. A number of minor anti-shipping operations continued throughout April and May with a number of small vessels sunk and a number of aircraft lost. In the meantime decrypts of enemy signals revealed the Germans intended to send three vessels to transport military supplies to Crete, the vessels to set sail from Piraeus on 31 May. In response the largest anti-shipping force ever assembled by the RAF in the Mediterranean was readied, consisting two groups; 12 Martin B-26 Marauders of No. 24 (SAAF) Squadron with 18 Martin Baltimores of Nos. 15 (SAAF) Squadron and 454 Squadron (RAAF), escorted by 13 long-range Spitfires and four NA Mustang IIIs, to be followed five minutes later by 24 Beaufighters of Nos. 252, 227, 603 and 16 Squadron (SAAF).

The result was absolutely devastating. The first wave hit one of the merchant vessels, the *Sabine* of 2.252 tons, but one Baltimore was shot down. The Beaufighters also hit the same vessel, as well as the *Gertrud* (1,960 tons) and *Tanais* (1,545 tons). They also sank the submarine hunter UJ2105 and badly damaged torpedo boat TA16. Four Beaufighters were shot down. Unfortunately all three vessels reached Heraklion, but *Sabine* burnt out and a fire in *Gertrud* could not be extinguished. Following which, the port was attacked in the night by Vickers Wellingtons and Liberator bombers, setting oil tanks ablaze. It was raided again the following night by Baltimores, which hit the blazing *Gertrud* causing her to explode at the same time the blast sinking TA16. The only survivor of the three merchant ships was the *Tanais*, which was subsequently sunk by a British submarine on 9 June.

Following the successful operation, Beaufighter Xs of No. 252 Squadron continued to hunt for what remained of the German merchant ships, in the Aegean and on 19 June eight of the squadrons airplanes found torpedo boat TA19 south-west of the island of Kalymnos and damaged her so badly she was forced into dock near Athens for repairs. The next month shortly before midnight on 2 July two more 252 Squadron Beaufighters found two merchant vessels *Agatha* (1,259 tons) and *Anita* (1,165 tons) near Rhodes. They sank the former, but the latter escaped. To be sunk later by a submarine on 14 July. By this time there were very few German vessels left in the area for the Beaufighters to attack and on 15 July, No. 227 Squadron was taken off ASV duties and became No. 19 Squadron (SAAF) to operate from Italy, alongside No.16 Squadron in August, the units becoming part of the Balkan Air Force.

The two remaining Beaufighter squadrons Nos. 252 and 603, in this theatre, concentrated their attacks on the ships evacuating the German troops from Greece. On 6 September, eight Beaufighters of No.252 Squadron attacked the merchant vessel *Carola* (1,348 tons), which had left Leros for Piraeus escorted by two flak vessels. All three were badly damaged but did not sink, and reached port, where *Carola* was eventually sunk by the Germans as a block ship. A week later 16 Beaufighters of the two squadrons sank the mine-sweeper *Nordstern* (240 tons) at Paros and eight of No. 252 Squadron airplanes sank the tanker *Elli* (272 tons) at Andros, on 19 September. On the 22 September, the troop transport *Drache* (1,870 tons) was destroyed at Leros by 12 airplanes of both Beaufighter squadrons. Twelve aircraft put the transport *Orion* out of action at Denusa the following day, and eight No. 252 Squadron aircraft sank the transport *Helly* (314 tons) at Andros on 27 September. Later as the Germans scuttled what remained of the ships and the islands were liberated, a number of garrisons surrendered following attacks by rocket-firing Beaufighters. At the end of November, 1944, No. 603 Squadron came off operations and returned to the UK, while No. 252 Squadron remained in North Africa until moving to Hassani, Greece, on 18 February, 1945, where it remained until disbandment on 1 December, 1946.

By the end of 1943, two other Beaufighter units, Nos. 39 and 272 Squadrons were active with their improved torpedo-carrying T.F.Xs which they had received in June that year. But on 20 November 1943, as part of the North-west African Coastal Air Force, No 39 Squadron began a new phase in its anti-shipping operations. In December, it handed over its torpedoes to the Royal Navy to begin training with powerful new rocket projectiles as part of the Mediterranean Allied Coastal Air Force constituted on 19 December. While some RAF "top brass" at this time still advocated the use of torpedoes, No. 39 Squadrons C.O. Wg. Cdr. Nelson. B. Harvey, was a strong supporter of the new weapons which improved the types effectiveness, negating the need to fly the airplane at slow speed in order to aim the torpedo, instead, the pilots could dive on enemy vessels at high speed to deliver their rockets with less risk to themselves to being hit by flak. Having completed its rocket-firing training by the end of the year, on moving to Marrakesh, Morocco, for the first eleven days of 1944, the squadron was tasked with the protection of Prime Minister Winston Churchill's delegation attending the Casablanca Conference. The delegation had flown to Tunisia on 12 December, 1943 as guest of U.S. President Franklin Roosevelt. During this period the squadron was deployed on the air defence of Marrakesh in co-operation with the ground defences, until they were replaced by Supermarine Spitfires of No. 32 (F) Squadron.

On return to Reghaia, east of Algiers, the squadron flew convoy escort patrols protecting Allied convoys from attack by Junkers Ju 88s. At this time their was very heavy Allied shipping passing through the Straits of Gibraltar en-route to Italy, being extremely vulnerable to both enemy U-boat and air attacks. The possibility of air attack often given away by the presence of enemy reconnaissance airplanes in the area. The attacks usually took place at dusk, the planes flying from their bases in southern France, when the Germans would head for the Spanish Balearic Islands which they used as a landmark before positioning themselves for attacks on passing convoys to the south of the islands. However, fully aware of the Luftwaffe tactics, by positioning themselves close the islands, No 39 Squadrons Beaufighters were rewarded with a number of successes. Of note was an interception which took place in the late afternoon of 1 February, 1944, when Flying Officer Neill D. Cox led six Beaufighters on a patrol, which came upon a swarm of forty enemy planes near the island of Ibiza. This included Junkers Ju 88s of Zerstörer 1, escorting Heinkel He 177s and He 111s of Kampfgeschwader 100 and 26 both armed with guided bombs and torpedoes preparing to attack convoy UGS 30. In the ensuing air battle, Flt Sgts. W. Pryce and F. A. Cooper each shot down a Ju 88, while the other four squadron Beaufighters damaged three more German planes. Unfortunately Flt Sgt. "Freddie" Cooper was shot down and another squadron airplane forced to return to Reghaia, crash landed. Cooper and his navigator, Sgt. A. V. Bridle, were picked up by air-sea-rescue launch the following day along with a downed Ju 88 pilot. In total the Luftwaffe lost two Heinkel He 111s and four Junkers Ju 88s, most to the heavy flak put up by the convoy's ships. Two days later No. 39 Squadron was ordered to move to Alghero in north-west Sardinia, to join No. 272 Beaufighter Squadron commanded by Wg Cdr. Donald H. Lowe who had only arrived themselves at the beginning of the month. Following a period of familiarisation of the area and fighter sweeps, mostly flying in very unfavourable weather conditions, two squadron airplanes were lost in heavy rain storms when returning to base with both crews losing their lives. The arrival of No. 39 Squadron saw No. 272 re-assigned to its maritime role to provide protection against enemy flak for rocket-firing Beaufighters.

The two units began training together on 24 February, and practise flying continued for about a fortnight until the squadrons formed an anti-shipping Strike Wing carrying out their first operational mission on 10 March. No. 39 Squadron led by Canadian Sqn Ldr. N. R. J. Butler provided four Beaufighters while No. 272 Squadron put up six led by a Belgian Flt. Lt. René G. Demoulin. Thirty miles west of Marseille the strike planes intercepted a merchant vessel of about 3,000 tons escorted by two motor-torpedo boats. Attacking with cannon and rocket salvos the merchantman, through the smoke, appeared to be damaged and listing, but the before the final outcome could be seen, the Beaufighters at the end of their endurance were forced to return to base unscathed.

The Strike Wings next attack on the 12 March, result when four rocket-firing airplanes of No. 39 Squadron accompanied by four No. 272 Squadron airplanes led by another Belgian Squadron Leader Charles L. Roman sighted three vessels near the mouth of the River Ebro in Spain. Two of the ships were identified as Spanish and the other was a former French ship *Killissi* of 3,723 tons known to being used by the Germans to carry - from Spain to Marseille - an ore containing tungsten, known as "Portuguese wolfram" used in the hardening of steel in the manufacture of weapons, such as tank shells. The *Killissi* was heavily armed with 75mm guns and four machine-guns, but some of these were soon silenced by the cannon-firing Beaufighters while the rockets firing airplanes soon set the vessel alight along its entire length. The ship was forced to head for the beach where it was lost along with two Frenchmen and four Germans of the 66 man crew. The ship according to Spanish shipping records carrying oranges from Valencia.

At the same time a few minutes after the attack on the *Killissi* was made, a second Strike Wing echelon of eight Beaufighters led by Flt. Lt. D. Charles sighted one of the Spanish vessels, and misunderstanding Flt Lt. Charles's instructions over the R/T, attacked the *Cabo San Sebastian* instead of the French vessel, with only Charle's himself so doing. The Spanish vessel was badly damaged by three rocket hits on the port side below the water-line, two of which went through the starboard side. The bridge and part of the upper superstructure was also extensively damaged. The Spanish authorities claimed if the vessel had been further out from shore she would have sunk, but in the event it was towed into port at Barcelona for where temporary repairs were effected. Five of the crew were wounded. The German propaganda machine had a field day, as the attacks had been made in neutral Spains territorial waters. Although no mention was made that the *Killissi* which was under German control. Or that the Spanish had allowed the Germans to set up radio-navigation and meteorological stations around their coast. Or that some German merchant vessels were sailing under neutral countries flags of convenience. At this time also, British Intelligence was well aware Spanish waters were regularly being used by German U-boats and merchantmen to shelter from attack from the strike planes.

Four days later, Flt Lt. Charles led five No. 39 Squadron Beaufighters accompanied by four No. 272 airplanes to a position off the Rhône Delta, the airplanes force accompanied by an Vickers Warwick ASR airplane of No. 284 Squadron that had arrived in the area two days before to lend support and rescue facilities if needed. On this occasion the Beaufighters found two German merchantmen, the *Kabyle* of 1,881 tons and *Maure* (the former French *Polemis*) of 1,475 tons. Both vessels were equipped with 75mm and 30mm guns, and also fired "parachute and cable" (PAC) rockets. These devices consisting of a cable 100m (300 ft) long, fitted with explosive charges which unfolded in the air then dropped slowly to explode amid low-flying attackers. Although in this instance the defences were ineffective and both vessels were hit by cannon fire and rockets. The smaller sank, while the larger was damaged beyond repair. The attacking Beaufighters were fired on by shore-based flak batteries and Axis fighter planes were seen taking off from a nearby airfield. Three Messerschmitt Bf 109 fighters pursued the Beaufighters and attacked one of No. 272 Squadron's airplanes, setting its starboard engine on fire, before it was seen diving into the sea. Sgt. Peter F. Bishop and Sgt Philip W. Leach losing their lives. No. 39 Squadron suffered it first casualties in these operations on 27 March, when a Beaufighter returning to base after a sweep when no targets had been found was shot down. Ironically the crew Flying Officer John C. Yorke and Flying Officer Walter B. Mathias, who both lost their lives had survived a similar incident on 15 September 1943, to return to their unit to fly again...

On 6 April, four airplanes from both squadrons set off on another sweep off the Spanish coast. They spotted a vessel near the the border with France, but it was identified as Spanish and was not attacked. While it was investigated further a No. 272 Squadron airplane flown by Squadron leader Demoulin broke away and attacked a small vessel which appeared to be a fishing boat. As he raked the vessel with cannon fire suddenly his starboard wing crumpled and flames came from the engine although no fire was seen from the small boat. The stricken Beaufighter hit the water about 50 yards behind it, and both Demoulin and his navigator Flt Sgt. John S. Barker, were killed.

As German shipping losses continued to escalate, they took the precaution of sailing their ships only at night. In response the Beaufighter strike wing timed their attacks for first light or dusk, in the hope of catching the vessels at the start or end of their sailings. In the early morning of the 19 April, 1944, Wg Cdr. Lowe of No. 272 Squadron led a formation of six anti-flak and six rocket-firing TF Xs to the Gulf of Lyons. The crews had been briefed to attack any ships in the area irrespective of nationality ! They had found a ship of about 2,000 tons carrying international markings, near Cape l'Espiguette, and attacked. Following heavy attacks with rockets and cannon the vessel appeared to have survived and indeed their was some return fire, and a Beaufighter flown by Flt. Sgt. Arther L. Hewitt was sent into a high-speed stall finally crashing into the sea. Both Hewitt and his navigator Flt. Sgt. Jack F. Garnett, were killed.

In the afternoon on the same day a further strike force of four 39 Squadron airplanes and four of No. 272 Squadron encountered a ship off Cap Cerbère and attacked it. The Spanish vessel *Jose Illueca* of 648 tons was listing badly to starboard and sank later with the death of two of the crew. On 22 April, another Canadian, Flt Lt. T. G. Pearse, led a strike force of twelve Beaufighters, six from each squadron to a position west of Sète in southern France, where they located a vessel of about 2,000 tons with "Switzerland" clearly displayed amidships. Having been issued instructions to sink-on-sight, the strike planes attacked the *Chasseral* of 3,129 tons leaving her on fire to steam for shore. By this time there were very few large enemy ships left in the region to attack and the strike wing began to assume different tasks. On 1 May, two No. 39 Squadron Beaufighters set out on a fighter patrol. Flying Officer Dennis A. Derby flying his first operational patrol in Beaufighter serial LZ154 chased off a Junkers Ju 88D-1 at low-level over the Spanish coast over Gerona. After an exchange of fire with the German planes rear gunner, the Beaufighters crew saw one of the Ju 88s engines begin to emit smoke. A little later the plane hit the ground at Borrassa, near the town of Figueres, and blew up.

The last ASV attack by the combined squadrons of the Strike Wing took place of the 6 May, 1944, when Squadron Leader Curlee led six of his own squadron's Beaufighters and six No. 272 Squadron airplanes against a merchant vessel escorted by two flak ships, at the entrance to Sète harbour. The strike planes were met by a barrage of flak from the ships and the shore, but none the less scored a number of hits on the merchantman which was the Spanish vessel *Cristina* of 2,192 tons. Its cargo comprised food and cigarettes for Allied PoWs. One crewman was killed in the attack and four others injured, including the Swiss Red Cross representative aboard. The vessel was later beached to avoid its complete loss. All the twelve Beaufighters returned to base safely.

A loss did occur on the 11 May, when Flt Sgt. Raymond Powell of No. 272 Squadron and his navigator Flt Sgt. Roy Satchell, failed to return from an evening patrol. For the rest of the month both squadrons were tasked with destroying German radar stations along the south coast of France, in preparation for the the D-Day landings. Four such attacks were made hitting installations at Cap Mele, Cap Camaret and Cap d' Antibes. On each occasion the strike force comprised of four No. 39 Squadron airplanes and six No. 272 Squadron. No. 39 Squadron airplanes were equipped with double rockets, the modification embodied by the units engineering officer Flt Lt. W. Bennett. Two rockets with 25-lb warheads were fitted under each rail, held together by brackets, producing a deadly double rocket projectile. In addition four of No. 272 Squadrons airplanes carried four 250 lb bombs each. The attacks proved extremely effective all the radar stations were set on fire and put out of action. No strike wing Beaufighters were lost.

At the beginning of June, the combined operations of the two squadrons ended. The crews were re-tasked to night patrols over the Italian coastline, looking for ships and to carry out some inland raids. On 5 June, two tank landing craft were destroyed by No. 39 Squadron. While No. 272 squadron continued operating from Catania in Sicily or Borgo in Corsica, carrying bombs to attack roads and bridges. Following D-Day as the war in southern Europe continued No. 39 Squadron began to incur heavy losses as it was flying both day and night sorties. But the unit was nearing the end of its maritime strike career and on 13 July, it completed a move to Biferno on the Italian Adriatic coast, where it became part of the newly formed Balkan Air Force. Meanwhile No. 272 Squadron equipped it cannon-firing airplanes for rocket-firing as it continued night flying operations.

The invasion of southern France, Operation *Dragoon* on the night of the 14/15 August met little opposition and within days the whole of the area was under Allied control. The remaining Luftwaffe units had withdrawn and the Beaufighter strike plane Sea War operations in the western Mediterranean came to an end.

Meanwhile, in May 1945, in the UK, the main action by aircraft of the strike wing comprising Nos. 236 and 254 Squadrons sank five U-boats in two days. On 3 May, at 17.20 hrs in the Baltic, thirteen Beaufighters of No. 236 Squadron and seventeen from No. 254 Squadron led by Wg Cdr. E. P. Hutton DFC attacked and sank *U-2503* and *U-2524*. The following day, the strike wing struck again when twelve aircraft of No. 236 Squadron and ten from No. 254 Squadron attacked and sank *U-236, U-393* and *U-2338*.

Bristol   Beaufighter X   - fitted with rocket projectile racks

BOEING B-17
FORTRESS I, II, IIA, III

In January 1942, the UK element of No. 90 Squadron's Boeing Fortress Is (B-17C) were transferred to No. 220 Squadron at Nutts Corner in Northern Ireland, for maritime reconnaissance duties until June 1942, when the unit became fully equipped with Fortress II, IIA forty-five of which were delivered to Coastal Command in 1942. Later, some of the eighty-five Fortress III (B-17G) delivered to the RAF, also served with Coastal Command the first entering service with No. 220 Squadron in late 1944. Fortress IIIs usually had their side nose guns removed, and the centimetric radar scanner replaced the ventral ball turret, and its offensive weapons could consist of 12 x 181 kg (400 lb) bombs or 16 x 113 kg (250 lb) depth-charges.

The Fortress II was the British version of the USAAF's B-17E which made its first flight in September, 1941. The Mk II and IIA variants all entered service with Coastal Command, working alongside the VLR Liberators to close the mid-Atlantic Gap, which shorter-range, airplanes, were unable to reach. The first Mk IIs entered service with No. 220 Squadron at Ballykelly, Northern Ireland, in July, 1942. Other Coastal Command Fortress units operated from Chivenor, North Devon, Benbecula, Iceland, and the Azores. Fortress IIA variants were delivered to No. 59 Squadron at Thorney Island, in December 1942, with the first patrol flown on 23 January, 1943. One Mk IIA (serial FK185) delivered, had been fitted with a 40mm Vickers 'S' gun, for the specific purpose to attack enemy submarines on the surface.

Fortress I AN537 'NR-L' of 220 Squadron, Nutt's Corner, Northern Ireland.

Plan view (camouflaged) Boeing B-17 Fortress II

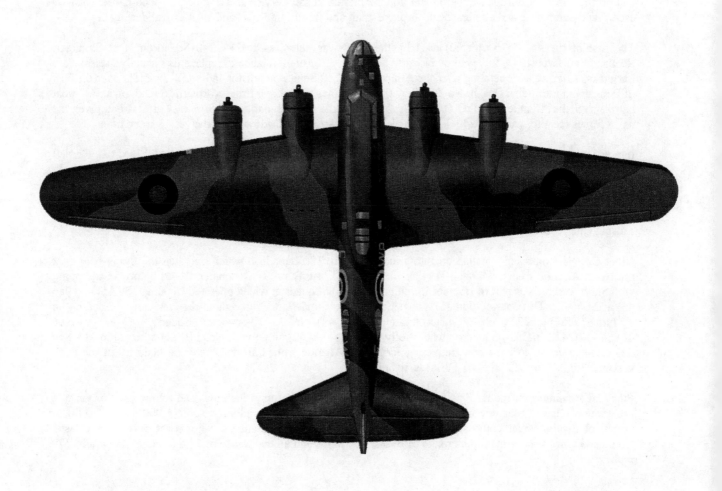

CONSOLIDATED
CATALINA

The Consolidated PBY Catalina flying-boat was widely used by the Allied air forces in the Pacific, Atlantic and off the coasts of Europe and North and South America. It saw service as a bomber, torpedo-carrier, convoy escort, anti-submarine and air-sea-rescue airplane, mail and freight transport and even as a glider tug.

The first of the 460 (576 ordered) used by the RAF was delivered to No. 240 Squadron at at Stranraer, Scotland, in March 1941, followed by No. 209 Squadron at Castle Archdale to replace its virtually useless Saro Lerwicks. After a year operating over the Atlantic, No. 240 Squadron left for India to fly patrols over the Bay of Bengal and the Indian Ocean. No. 209 flew their Catalinas from Loch Erne, Northern Ireland, on anti-U-boat patrols over the Atlantic with P/O D. A. Briggs spotting the German battleship *Bismarck* after it had given the naval forces the slip, with No. 240 Squadron also taking part in the shadowing of the vessel at the time.

Interestingly, two of Coastal Commands four WW II VCs were awarded to Catalina pilots, Flt Lt. D. E. Hornell of No.162 (RCAF) Squadron and F/O J. A. Cruikshank of No.210 Squadron (see details in appendix). In addition the final U-boat sunk by direct action in WW II was *U-320*, attacked at 04.45 hrs on 7 May 1945, in the Norwegian Sea, west of Bergen, by a Catalina 'X' of No. 210 Squadron flown by Flt Lt. K. M. Murray. Flt. Lt. Murray had spotted the boats periscope and snorkel and dropped four depth-charges, severely damaging it causing Oberleutnant Heinz Emmerich to scuttle her off the Norwegian coast.

Other Coastal Command Catalina operators included, No. 190 Squadron which operated the flying-boat over the North Atlantic from 1 March 1943 until it disbanded briefly on 31 December, 1943, before re-equipping with Short Stirling's as part of Bomber Command. No. 202 Squadron which operated Catalina 1b (Apr 41 - Jan 45) and Catalina IV (Oct 44 - Jun 45) alongside its Short Sunderlands throughout the war until disbanding on 12 June, 1945. No. 330 (Polish) Squadron (Jun 42 - Jan 43), No. 333 (Norwegian) Squadron (May 43 - Nov 45) and No. 422 (RCAF) Squadron who briefly (Jul 42 - Nov 42) along with No. 119 Squadron (Jun 41 - Sep 42) supplied crews to ferry new deliveries across the Atlantic from Canada where the majority of the RAF variants (170 Mk Ibs and 211 Mk IVBs) were built.

Standard armament for the RAF planes were one, 303-in machine gun in the bows and two in each of the side observation blisters, plus one in the ventral position aft of the step. In addition some 1,000 kg (2,200 lb) of bombs or depth-charges could be carried. With a crew of 5-6 the Catalina's major asset over other Coastal Command types was its maximum range of over 3,000 miles and an endurance of 17.6 hours at 281 km/h (179 mph) cruising.

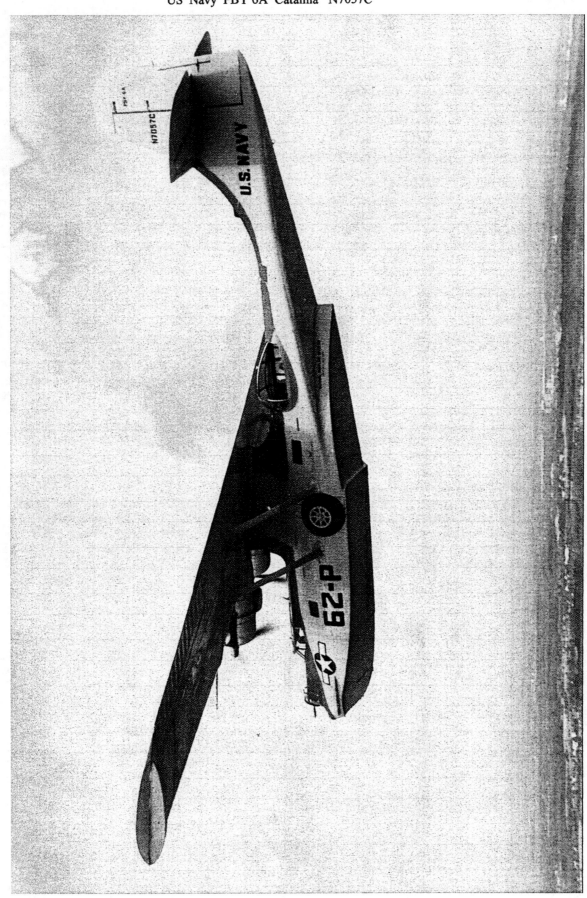

CONSOLIDATED
LIBERATOR

From 1941 until 1945 the American Consolidated Liberator proved to be one of Coastal Command's most effective weapons against the U-boat menace. Intended primarily as a heavy bomber, a severe shortage of long-range airplanes and its obvious potential as a "Very Long Range" (VLR) U-boat hunter, saw a small number of Liberator Is, with four 20mm Hispano cannon mounted in a pannier under the forward bomb-bay, enter service with No. 120 Squadron Coastal Command in 2 June, 1941. The three delivered were actually armed LB-30Bs (AM913, 914 and 922) to be used as training planes. The first true Liberator I (AM928) - with ASV radar and 20mm cannon, installed by Scottish Aviation at Prestwick, was tested by No. 120 Squadrons C.O. Wing Commander W. N. Cumming DFC at Prestwick on 6 August, 1941. The first operational Liberator sortie was flown by Flt Lt. S. J. Harrison (later to become C.O.) in AM924 'D' on 20 September, 1941, and from this time on, No. 120 Squadron was in continuous action against the U-boat menace for almost the whole of the war. The same airplane was in action again, this time flown by Flying Officer T. H. A. Llewellyn - on 4 October, escorting convoy OG75. It was engaged by a Fw 200 Condor and an intense aerial battle ensued with both airplanes sustaining damage, with the Liberator eventually succeeding in driving the German plane away from the ships. There were further encounters with enemy airplanes and while No. 120 Squadron struggled to meet its commitments with only a handful of Liberators, the patrols extended far out into the Atlantic, and to Arctic and Norwegian waters. The aircraft often operating from diverse bases around the UK, including Tiree, Predannack, Ballykely and St Eval.

Of major concern at this time was the atrocious weather and the amount of flak being put up by the German warships, as demonstrated on 13 December 1941, when Flt Lt Bulloch's (later Sqn Ldr.) Liberator serial AM928 'A' patrolling the Bay of Biscay, was hit wounding one of the crew, this, the squadron's first WW II casualty. In early 1942, No 120 Squadron began to receive a number of Liberator IIs, although only the Mk Is were suitable for VLR operations. But in May, 1942, the first Liberator IIIs began to arrive along with a number for co-located No. 160 Squadron to "learn the trade" before leaving for the Far East at the end of the year. On 21 July, No. 120 Squadron itself moved from Nutts Corner to Ballykelly, from which base Squadron Leader Bulloch, flying AM917 'F' made the units first U-boat attack — while escorting convoy OS37 — when he dropped six depth-charges on *U-89* as it submerged. On this occasion the U-boat was badly damaged and forced to return to port, although a year later she was sunk by depth-charges dropped by RN destroyers after she had been sighted by a Fairey Swordfish from NAS 811. In demonstration of the intensity of patrols, Squadron Leader Bulloch continued his watch after the raid and returned to base just after 02.00 hours on 22 July, some fifteen hours after taking off from Ballykelly. On 4 September, 1942, the squadron sent a detachment to Reykjavik, Iceland, for a year, on occasions using the USAAF base, at Meek Field (Camp Geck !). Here, having been joined by the main body of the squadron, it battled as much against the weather as it did against the enemy, although it did play an essential part in closing the 'Atlantic Gap' until it left to return to Ballykelly again in March, 1944. Where it remained until the wars end and disbandment on 4 June, 1945, having operated the Mk III, the longer-range G.R.5 with ASV III radar which it received in August 1943, and the GR.8 with improved ASV radar which it received in December, 1944.

The second Coastal Command Liberator unit to form in the UK was No. 160 Squadron at Thurleigh, Bedfordshire, on 16 January, 1942 as a heavy bomber unit intended for the Middle East. However, the situation in the area with the Japanese fleet threatening invasion of Ceylon, No. 160 Squadrons role changed, and on 7 May, a detachment was sent to Northern Ireland at Nutts Corner, so that crews could gain experience in maritime patrol and ASV duties for a month. Although the detachment rejoined the main body and on 7 June the unit began to fly out to Palestine to begin night bombing raids to stem Rommel's advance towards Egypt. This element of No. 160 Squadron remained in theatre until 14/15 January, 1943, when it was absorbed by No. 178 Squadron. But in the UK it was not the end of the matter. On 1 October, 1942, (in effect retrospective from 16 September) the Air Ministry defined No. 160 Squadron as the Middle East Detachment — with a new No. 160 Squadron to form - as a maritime patrol unit under the command of Wing Commander C. A. Butler. The new 160 Squadron began working up at Thorney Island with No. 86 Squadron in October, 1942, with Liberator IIIs. Finally in November, Liberator GR.5s began arriving at Thorney Island, and it was with these aircraft that No. 160 Squadron began to leave for overseas again immediately after Christmas arriving at Ratmalana, Ceylon, in January, 1943. The first ASW missions over the Indian Ocean flown by two of the squadrons airplanes (FL929 'W' and FL939 'M'), on 6 February.

As No. 160 Squadron's sister unit No. 86 Squadron at Thorney Island left for Aldergrove, Northern Ireland, in March 1943, what remained of No. 160 Squadron moved to Beaulieu to continue its training, where it was joined by Liberator Flight No. 1 (Coastal) Operational Training Unit and soon along with No. 301 Ferry Training Unit from RAF Lyneham, all transited to the Far East to develop the long-range ASW operations over the Bay of Bengal and assume a new task of photographic reconnaissance over Sumatra and the Nicobars, as well as mine-laying operations. The unit remained in this theatre until June 1946, when it returned to the UK, where it aircraft compliment was reduced to six for general reconnaissance and air-sea-rescue duties, pending delivery of Avro Lancaster GR. 3 in August, and re-numbering to No. 120 Squadron in September.

The third UK Liberator unit was No. 224 Squadron at Tiree, that began to receive the type in July, 1942. It had been planned the squadron should receive Liberators IIs to replace its Lockheed Hudsons in February, 1942, but events such as the attack on Pearl Harbour on 7 December, 1941, severely affected deliveries of airplanes from the United States and re-equipment was postponed. Eventually three Liberator IIIs (FK218, FK223 and FL910) were delivered on 18 July, and the unit began to work up on type while maintaining operations on Hudsons. On 9 September, 1942, the squadron moved to Beaulieu, and began Liberator operations, sinking its first U-boat *U-216* on the 20 October in the Atlantic, west of Ushant. Liberator FL910 'H' flown by Flying Officer D. M. Sleep dropped six depth-charges from a height of 30 feet, which hit the U-boat and it exploded on impact with debris flying into the air damaging the tail surfaces of the Liberator. The damage meant the aircrafts control surfaces had to be tied forward with all the crew in the forward part of the aircraft to keep the tail up to make a crash landing at Predannack, with only one member of the crew injured.

In April, 1943, No. 224 Squadron moved to St Eval, Cornwall, and began using rocket projectiles and the new American Mk 24 Acoustic Homing Torpedo. In September 1944, the squadron moved to Milltown, by this time its airplanes were using the Leigh Light mounted under the starboard wing to supplement its new weapons. One of the squadron's most notable U-boat "kills" occurred on 8 June, 1944, when Flt Lt. K. O. Moore (RCAF) flying Liberator 'G' sank *U-629* and *U-373* in the English Channel south-west of Ushant, within thirty minutes of each other. *U-629* was sunk at 02.15 hrs following a radar contact, the attack carried out in moonlight with six depth-charges. A second radar contact at 02.40 hrs revealed *U-373* at 2.5 miles range and attacking from a height of 50 feet, with a further six depth-charges a second U-boat was sunk. This was the first and only time two U-boats had been sunk in a single sortie, a feat for which Flt Lt. Moore received the DSO.

The fourth Liberator unit, No. 59 Squadron in August 1942, must have been the shortest operational life of the type with any unit, as throughout December the squadron was already receiving Boeing Fortress IIA replacements. The squadron received two Mk IIIA Liberators from the 'Battle of the Atlantic' batch released by the USAAF (LV342 and LV343) received while it was still based at RAF North Coates and these were followed by ten new Mk IIIs once the squadron had relocated to Thorney Island. With conversion training in full swing, in October an additional three Liberators arrived, but suddenly in spite of the fact the squadron had already started operations on type, the Liberators were withdrawn and the squadron received Boeing Fortresses (B-17s) instead, throughout December 1942 and January 1943, and within the month were flying operations with their new mount. Throughout February and March, 1943 a number of ASW patrols and convoy escorts were flown, with the squadron on occasions encountering the formidable FW 200 Condors, until again, it was informed it was to receive new aircraft. In March, 1943, Consolidated Liberator GR.5s began to arrive, with long-range tanks and centimetric ASV radar and once more No. 59 Squadron became a Liberator operator, this time until the wars end. Based at Ballykelly, Northern Ireland, the squadron now provided cover for the convoys heading for Liverpool and Clyde harbour areas. The squadron's Liberators ranged far and wide, including Norwegian waters and the Bay of Biscay, as well as long patrols over the North Atlantic. Its first U-boat raid occurred on 29 May 1943, when Flying Officer H. A. Moran flying FL984 'S' on escort duty with military convoy AT45 which included the *Queen Mary*, attacked *U-552*, which although it fired back was forced to submerge. The squadron then went on to have a number of successes both in the Atlantic and other waters.

The fifth Liberator unit was No. 86 Squadron which had reformed as a Coastal Command unit, on 6 December 1940, at Gosport, with Bristol Blenheim IV beginning convoy escort duties off the East Anglian coast on 28 March, 1941. In June, it re-equipped with Bristol Beaufort's for mine-laying duties which started on 15 July, as well as flying reconnaissance and ASR missions until the crews passed through a torpedo training course and anti-shipping strikes began on 11 November with the first torpedo bomber operation taking place on 12 December. Following a detachment to St Eval, Cornwall, on 13 December, which was joined by the main body of the squadron in January 1942, anti-shipping patrols were flown off the French coast until March, when the squadron moved to northern Scotland. Patrols and strikes off the Norwegian coast then continued until July, when its aircraft were sent to the Middle East and its personnel moved to Thorney Island where it reduced t o a cadre. Its first Liberator arrived on 5 October, followed by one of the 'Battle of the Atlantic' ex-USAAF Mk IIIA airplanes (LV346), along with fresh aircrews for conversion training. Operations began in February, 1943, and the following month the squadron moved to Aldergrove in Northern Ireland, there to begin a highly successful Coastal Command career. On 6 April, it sank its first U-boat when Flt Lt. C. W. Burcher piloting FL930 'R' sighted a surfaced U-boat while on patrol in the Atlantic south-west of Iceland 18 miles from convoy HX231. Burcher carried out two attacks, dropping five depth-charges to sink the submarine, *U-632*.

On 12 May, 1943, the squadron scored the first hit with the newly delivered American-designed acoustic homing torpedo ('Mk 24 Mine'). Flt Lt. J. Wright flying Liberator 'B', attacked *U-456* which was about to submerge near to convoy HX 237 in the Atlantic. The U-boat dived immediately on spotting Wright's Liberator but the torpedo functioned perfectly, hitting the U-boat which then surfaced. By now, Wright was forced to leave the scene, but before so doing he advised the convoy's SOE, of the situation who despatched a destroyer to the area, only to find on arrival the submarine had disappeared, either sunk as a result of Wright's attack or having been scuttled by the crew. Having moved to Ballykelly on 3 September, 1943, on 25 March, 1944, No. 86 Squadron moved to Reykjavik, Iceland, to relieve No. 120 Squadron and then to Tain in the western Highlands on 1 July, where it remained to fly patrols out to and up the Norwegian coast for the rest of the war.

No. 53 Squadron began its Coastal Command career in February, 1941, when it moved its Bristol Blenheim IVs to St Eval, for patrols and anti-shipping operations off the French coast and in July it converted to Lockheed Hudson.s. Anti-U-boat patrols were the main order of the day but shipping strikes were flown from North Coates, Lincolnshire in the spring of 1942,until early July when it was sent to America to assist our Allies ward off the U-boat menace, that Admiral Doenitz had transferred to the almost undefended Eastern seaboard. Anti-U-boat patrols began from Rhode Island on 23 July, and following a move to Trinidad, in the Caribbean, in August the unit started to return to the UK on 23 November, to reform at Davidstowe Moor on 31 December. With its Hudsons returned to the UK, rather unexpectedly in February, 1943, the squadron re-equipped with obsolete A.W. Whitley VIIs but on moving to Thorney Island, on 28 April, conversion to Liberators began, the first two GR.5 aircraft taken on charge on 11 May. By June, the squadron had received twelve GR.5s and two second-hand Mk IIIs for crew training. Operations commenced over the Bay of Biscay in July, with the squadron moving successively to Beaulieu in September 1943,and to St Eval in January, 1944. New equipment in the shape of the GR.6 began arriving in May 1944, and by September, when it moved to Reykjavik in Iceland for flying patrols over the North Atlantic for the rest of the war, it was fully equipped with the GR.6 variant. Later in January 1945, receiving the GR.8 variant.

No 311 (Czech) Squadron began its operational life in September 1940, as a Vickers Wellington bomber unit with No. 3 Group Bomber Command, transferring to Coastal Command in April, 1942. Moving to Aldergrove, Northern Ireland on 28 April to fly patrols with its Wellingtons, over the Atlantic until it moved to Wales in June. On moving to Beaulieu in May, 1943, it received its first Liberator GR.5 serial BZ743, on 5 June. As more Mk 5s arrived training and familiarisation commenced on these rocket-carrying airplanes. Four rocket-projectiles could be carried on racks on each side of the forward fuselage. By the end of July No. 311 had received fifteen Liberators and were ready to start operations on 21 August. Unfortunately this was a somewhat inauspicious occasion as the airplane flown by the squadrons C. O. Wing Commander J. Breitcetl, failed to return from patrol. However, operations continued and at 13.45 hrs, on 10 November 1943, Flt. Sgt. Zanta flying Liberator 'D' attacked U-966 with rocket-projectiles, after it had already been badly damaged by two Liberators of the US Navy and Vickers Wellington 'B' of No. 612 Squadron flown by W/O I. D. Gunn. Flt Sgt. Zanta's action dealing the final blown, with the badly damaged U-boat blown up by her crew in 53 metres of water, two miles off the Spanish coast south-east of Punta de la Estaca de Bares at about 16.00 hrs the same day. Later on 27 December while flying anti-shipping strikes a No. 311 Squadron airplane found the German blockade-running ship *Alsterufer* trying to reach Bordeaux and bombed it to such an extent the crew were forced to abandon ship and the vessel was later sunk by a No. 86 Squadron Liberator. No. 311 Squadron began to convert to Liberator GR.6 in February 1944, but for some reason this was abandoned and the squadron moved to Predannack towards the end of February with Mark 5 variants for patrols over the Bay of Biscay. Moving to Tain, northern Scotland, in August, for patrols off the Norwegian coast where again conversion to GR.6 commenced in early 1945, and this time was completed with the type flown until the end of the war.

Although most of the German U-boat campaign was centred in the Atlantic and the Bay of Biscay the sinking of many Allied merchant vessels off the coast of West Africa led to the deployment of No.200 Squadron with Liberator GR.5 in 1943, until transferred to India in April, 1944. Having relinquished its Mark 5s to No. 160 Squadron in Ceylon, No. 200 Squadron converted to the GR.6 variant, for ASW, ASV and other operations including meteorological sorties and ASR patrols until transferred in April 1945, to special duties, mainly involving supply-dropping missions, and the delivery of clandestine forces into enemy-occupied territory, in Burma. Another prominent overseas Liberator unit was No. 354 Squadron initially based at Drigh Road, Karachi and later Minneriya, Ceylon for convoy escort duties, ASW and ASV patrols over the Bay of Bengal.

Chronologically in the UK the next squadron to receive Liberators, was No. 547 Squadron, with the first aircraft received at Davidstowe Moor in September, 1943, with deliveries for operational training commencing in November, at Thorney Island, Sussex, when GR.5 serial FL961 arrived on charge. Following work up on type, the unit moved to St Eval, Cornwall, to join Nos. 53 and 224 (also later No. 206) Squadrons to form a Liberator Wing. Operations over the Bay of Biscay began early in 1944, continuing until September, when the squadron sent a detachment to Tain,in Scotland, where patrols were mixed with anti-shipping strikes off the Dutch and Norwegian coasts. Meanwhile, in April 1944, the squadron began to receive the GR.6 variant the first, serial EV897 received on 22 April, but by the end of June only eight aircraft had been received and the unit continued to operate both types, flying cover for the Allied invasion fleet landing in Normandy on D-Day.

By September, 1944, No. 547 Squadron had fully converted to Liberator GR.6 and relocated to Leuchars, Scotland, to fly ASW patrols in the areas around Iceland, the Faeroes, Shetland and Norway - with at this time many of the U-boats having left the French Atlantic ports, heading through this area. Towards the end of the year the squadron operated mainly at night, utilising Leigh Light to search for U-boats. It then took part in a series of low-level Coastal Command attacks in strength under the code name *Chilli*. The first being a raid by No. 547 in conjunction with No. 206 Squadron into the Baltic, where they sighted and attacked four U-boats and other vessels. Additional *Chilli* attacks saw No. 547 Squadron sinking the cable ship *Budjadingen* off Bornholm on 24 March, and on 5 May, Flt Lt. G. W. Hill flying a new Liberator GR.8 KK299 'E' attacked *U-534* in the Kattegatt, north of Helsinger. The U-boat, normally used for weather-reporting duties was on her last voyage to take urgently needed spare parts and supplies to the U-boat flotillas now concentrated in Norwegian ports. Having been sighted in company with two other boats, Flt Lt. Hill attacked, but was hit by heavy return fire from the boats and crashed into the sea. Liberator 'G' of No 86 Squadron flown by W/O J. D. Nicol, then made two attacks through heavy flak to drop ten depth-charges, to sink the U-boat. On the same day another of the squadrons airplanes flown by Fg Off. A. A. Bruneau, Liberator 'K' sank *U-2521* following a depth-charge attack through heavy enemy flak, in the Baltic, south-east of Aarhus. One of the squadron's last mission's of the war was to escort the surrendered cruisers *Prinz Eugen* and *Nurnberg* into captivity on 25 May, 1945.

One of the Command's longest serving units was No. 206 Squadron which following a spell in the Azores with Boeing Fortresses in 1943, returned to the UK at Davidstowe Moor at the end of March, 1944 to convert to Liberator GR.6. The first three airplanes (EV871, 873 and 874) taken on charge on 20 April, 1944, by this time the squadron having relocated to St Eval. Operations began in early May, with ASW patrols in the Bay of Biscay area and as D-Day approached (6 June), the unit flew *Stopper* patrols against enemy submarines and surface vessels threatening the Allied invasion fleet. On 10 June, a patrolling 206 Squadron Liberator 'K' flown by Flt Lt. A. D. S. Saunders, flew in support of a U-boat attack by four D. H. Mosquitoes of No. 248 Squadron led by Flt Lt. S. G. Nunn to make two depth-charge attacks to sink *U-821* in the English Channel, north of Ushant. The next day, the 11 June the squadron relocated north to RAF Leuchars, Scotland, where it remained for the rest of the war, to fly Leigh Light patrols off the Norwegian and Dutch coasts. The unit starting to receive Liberator GR.8s with new centimetric ASV radar in February, 1945, with which to continue operations until the war's end.

Another long serving unit with a similar wartime history, was No. 220 Squadron who re-equipped with Liberator GR.6s in 1944, with a total of seven received on 10 October; serials EW318, KG865, 866, 903, 904, 905 and 906, all taken on charge from the Coastal Command GR Aircraft Pool at Haverfordwest. With more aircraft received from the Preparation Pool at St David's the squadron began operations from St Eval on 4 December. With re-equipment complete (the unit had previously operated Fortress III in the Azores), the unit returned to Lagens, with its new mounts to fly ASW patrols over the South Atlantic until the wars end. Briefly returning to St Davids, at the end of May, 1945, to re-equip with the improved GR.8 variants.

In the final year of the war a number of maritime squadrons in the Far East received Liberators, including No. 203 Squadron at Madura, in southern India, receiving GR.6s in November 1944, the unit having the dubious honour to suffer the last RAF operational Liberator loss of the war : on the 14 August 1945, when Fg Off Law's Liberator 'M' *Marmaduke* was shot down not far from the Island of Krakotoa, having set out with a second squadron Liberator piloted by Fg Off Tetlock to attack a Japanese merchantman sailing in the Sunda Straits, between Sumatra and Java. Unfortunately all but two of Fg Off Law's crew were lost with hostilities in the Far East ceasing the very next day...

Four other overseas RAF Liberator units at this time included Nos 320 and 321 Squadrons established with personnel from the Royal Netherlands Naval Air Service. No. 321 had taken Liberator GR.6s on strength to supplement its Catalina flying-boats in December, 1944 in the Cocos Islands, to operate alongside a Flight of No. 203 Squadron Liberators. No. 292 (ASR) Squadron that had operated over the Bay of Bengal since February, 1944 on air-sea-rescue duties moved to Agartala, in February, 1945 to be closer to operations as the front-line moved eastwards towards Burma, until disbanding on 14 June, 1945. Its duties taken over by Nos 1347, 1348 and 1349 Liberator Flights. Briefly No. 8 Squadron in Aden in early 1945, re-equipped with Liberators for ASR duties until disbanding on the 1 May. But, two weeks later at Jessore in India, No. 200 Squadron with Liberator GR.6s was re-numbered No. 8 Squadron, moving its airplanes to Ceylon for special duty flights flying supplies to guerilla forces in Malaya until the Japanese surrender and disbandment at Minneriya, on 15 November, 1945.

The last RAF squadron to use the Liberator was No. 228 Squadron, which had formed at St Eval, Cornwall, from No 224 'Y' Squadron after the war on 1 June, 1946. Using its GR.6 and GR.8s to transfer freight and passengers to Iceland, Gibraltar, the Azores and North Africa, with detached crews carrying out general reconnaissance, air-sea-rescue amd meteorological operations with the airplanes, until disbanding on 30 September, 1946.

In total between 1941 and 1945, the RAF had received around 2,000 Liberator B-24/C-87 variants and 27 PB4Y-2s Liberator C.IX transports, most supplied Lend-Lease. Around 42% of these were supplied to Coastal Command and overseas maritime units, as well as their associated training, ASR and special duties units (see appendix). From 1941, the Liberator became an indispensable tool in the RAF's war at sea. It sank and damaged more U-boats than any other type of aircraft. Although it was not an easy airplane to fly and at times a tradesman's nightmare, it was respected and remembered with affection by all who operated it. It was unique, in that it was the first 'heavy' to use a nose-wheel landing gear, and although fitted with a number of complex systems to test the ground crews patience, (in particular the electrics and fuel management systems), its Pratt & Whitney Twin Wasp radial engines were the most reliable of all P&W's design ever to see operational service. It is of interest that long after the war at sea had subsided that the Indian Air Force (IAF) resurrected thirty-six Liberators the RAF had left in a dump at Chakeri, Cawnpore, and put them back into service as general reconnaissance and anti-submarine airplanes and used them until the end of 1968... In fact one IAF crew flew the same airplane throughout the whole of their service careers, all retiring at the same time the type was finally withdrawn from use.

Main RAF Maritime (Coastal Command) Liberator variants: (B-24 = American military designation)

LB-30B - (Ex - B-24A), with engines and airscrews as LB-30A - P&W Twin Wasp R-1830-33 14-cylinder air-cooled radials and Hamilton Hydromatic airscrews. (6 delivered, 1 crashed soon after arrival)

Mk I - (B-24A) VLR variant with 2,400 mile range. Armed LB-30B with four 20mm Hispano cannon mounted under the forward bomb-bay. ASV antenna's fitted in the nose, outer wings and dorsal positions. (19 delivered, two loaned to BOAC. AM918 and AM920 as G-AGDR, G-AHYB) One (AM927) for special duties as C-87. AM910 used for various experimental work (ASV radar)

Mk II - (B-24C) Armed LB-30 with two power-operated Boulton Paul gun turrets. One fitted in the dorsal position aft of the wings and one in the extreme tail, increasing the airplanes overall length from 63 feet 4 in. to 66 feet. (137 delivered) One Mk II (AL504) with armament removed became Prime Minister Winston Churchill's personal transport. Named *Commando*.

Mk III - (B-24D) modified to British requirements. P&W Twin Wasp R-1830-43 engines with turbo-superchargers. Coastal Command VLR variant with additional fuel tanks and certain equipment removed. Most had Martin tail turret replaced by a Boulton Paul turret with .303 in machine guns Some fitted with ASV radar after delivery to Coastal Command. Deliveries commenced April, 1942.   (366 delivered)

Mk IIIA - (B-24Ds) Designation for Mk IIIs supplied Lend-Lease which differed from the contract Mk IIIs Later was used to define those airplanes converted to ASV-equipped Mk IIIs. Then was; UK Designation applied to airplane released at the request of British Prime Minister - under the special "Battle of the Atlantic" requirement, 1942. These 11 ex-USAAF airplanes (LV336-346) were non-standard to the RAF and were delivered between March and August, 1942.

GR. 5 - A developed (B-24/ Mk III) long-range variant for Coastal Command with centimetric ASV radar — a scanner was either mounted under the nose in a 'Dumbo' fairing, or in a rotating retractable unit under the fuselage, aft of the bomb-bays. Deliveries of this variant began in November, 1942. Some used as VLR airplanes with Leigh Light fitted.

B/GR. 6 - Convair B-24J, with nose, top, tail, and 'ball' (ventral) turrets and: B-24L Ford, Willow Run Plant, Detroit - built airplanes. In the GR.6 for Coastal Command the ball turret was replaced by a centimetric ASV radar scanner, similar to that of the GR.5. (1,157 delivered)

GR. 8   Similar to GR.6 for Coastal Command but to higher detailed modification standard and improved ASV radar.

Consolidated B-24 Liberator Development

In January 1939 Consolidated approached the USAAC with the proposal to produce a long range bomber superior to the Boeing B-17. On 29 December 1939 the XB-24 made its first flight at San Diego. This lead to 18 431 more aircraft, the largest production of any American combat type and the highest number of a bomber aircraft ever....

With so large production run, inevitably there were a host of modifications which changed designations.

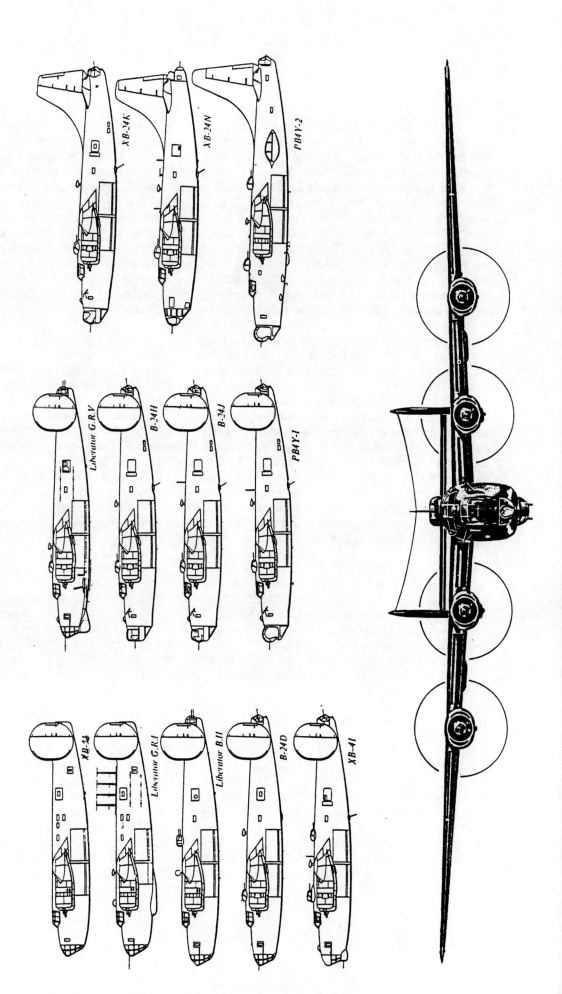

XB-24K

XB-24N

PB4Y-2

Liberator G.R.V

B-24H

B-24J

PB4Y-1

XB-24

Liberator G.R.I

Liberator B.II

B-24D

XB-41

D. H.
MOSQUITO

The D. H. Mosquito was originally conceived in 1938, as a small bomber primarily of wooden construction to conserve vital metals and ease production. It would rely for its safety on speed rather than defensive armament. The main variant deployed by Coastal Command, from September 1944, was the Fighter-Bomber VI which did excellent work with the Banff Strike Wing; comprising Nos. 235, 248 and 333 Squadrons. In 1944, provision was made to supplement its standard offensive armament with four rocket projectiles under each wing in place of its two 50 gallon drop tanks or wing bombs. Most Coastal Command Mosquitoes carried eight 60-lb rockets in addition to their front guns, the rocket projectiles when fired in salvo packed enough firepower to topple a 10,000 ton cruiser. Some Mk XVIII Mosquitoes carried a 57 mm Molins gun (equivalent to an army 6 pounder field gun) firing 6-lb shells. These airplanes which entered service with No. 248 Squadron in October 1943, were originally named Tse-Tse after the African insect not unlike the mosquito. Although not always capable of sinking a U-boat on their own, as with the Beaufighters operating in 'strike wing' echelons they were used to great success to locate the U-boats and other enemy shipping negotiating the notorious Bay of Biscay while entering and leaving port and while skirting the coasts of France and Norway.

Another Mosquito squadron to carry the automatic loading 57 mm Molins gun was No. 618 Squadron who by the autumn of 1943, had formed a Special Detachment with their Mk VIs originally intended to carry a variation of the 'Highball' dambusting bomb to attack the Tirptiz. The idea eventually abandoned. Instead the Special Detachment joined No. 248 Squadron's Bristol Beaufighters on operations at Predannack, Cornwall. The detachment was deployed on a trial basis to assess how effective the gun would be against U-boats and whether the D. H. Mosquito was a suitable platform for it. The powers that be decided in order to properly assess its potential at least four attacks on U-boats should be made. The detachment was ready to commence operations by October 1943, and the unit soon found and damaged its first U-boat, although unfortunately the mission was aborted when the gun jammed. The detachment crews comprising: F/O A. J. L. Bonnet and his navigator F/O A. M. Nichol, together with Flying Officers D. J. Turner, D. Curtiss, A. H. Hilliard and W/O J. B. Hoyle began flying almost daily sorties either alone or in pairs, or sometimes escorted by Beaufighters of No. 248 Squadron. A number of other crews also flew the 'Tsetse's' at this time with the unit having accompanied No. 248 Squadron to Portreath, on 16 February 1944, with No.248 Squadron itself now fully equipped with Mosquito Mk VI and XVIII Coastal Command variants.

The next U-boat encounter by the trials detachment occurred on 25 March 1944, when two Mosquito XVIIIs, 'L' crewed by Flying Officers Turner and Curtiss and 'I' with F/O Hilliard and W/O Hoyle on board escorted by four ('C', 'G', 'M' and 'X') Mosquitos of No. 248 Squadron led by Flt Lt. L. S. Dobson in 'G', attacked and sank *U-976* in the Bay of Biscay, west of St Nazaire. The 'strike' echelon having been dispatched at the behest of H. Q. No. 15 Group, Plymouth, sighted a U-boat off La Pallice escorted by a destroyer and two mine-sweepers. F/O Turner made four and F/O Hilliard one attack with their Tsetse gun. The 57 mm 6-lb shells pierced the Type VIIC U-boats thin pressure hull causing her to flood and fill with Chlorine gas, causing the crew to abandon ship. The survivors were fortunate to be picked up by the accompanying destroyer and mine-sweepers.

A further extremely important raid off Lorient, was undertaken by No. 248 squadron almost a month later on 23 April, 1944. A strike echelon, comprising two Mk VIIIs; 'O' piloted by Squadron Leader Atkinson DSO DFC with navigator F/O V. C. Upton and 'E' crewed F/O Hilliard and W/O Hoyle accompanied by four Mk VIs ('K', 'R' 'W' and 'P') flown by pilot/navigator crews, Flt Lt. Cobbledick - F/O W. R. M. Belcher; F/O K. Norrie - Flt. Sgt. B. J. Bland; Flt. Lt. L. S. Dobson - F/O C. Hardy and Flt Sgt. L. C. Doughty - Flt Sgt. R. Grime respectively attacked *U-155*. Commissioned on the 23 August 1941, *U-155* was a successful boat for the *Kreigesmarine* having completed nine patrols sinking a total of 25 ships amounting to 139,537 tons, one of them being HMS *Avenger* at 13,785 tons. Even then, following the attack, although severely damaged *U-155* managed to limp back into port only to take to sea again in September 1944, surviving the war to surrender on 4 May, 1945 in Fredericia, Denmark. For his part in the attack Flt Sgt Doughty in Mosquito 'P', who, under intense fire pressed home a relentless attack almost single-handed, releasing two depth-charges and scoring many hits with cannon fire, was awarded the DFC.

On 18 September 1944, six more No. 248 Squadron Mosquitoes, one Mk XVIII 'O' and five Mk VIs 'B', 'E1', 'J', 'U' and 'V', on patrol off the Norwegian coast led by Wing Commander G. D. Sise, badly damaged *U-867*, and left it listing about 10-15 degrees to port. The majority of the damage done by Mosquito 'B' crewed by W/O H. A. Corbin CGM and Flt. Sgt. M. J. Webb DFM. The next day the U-boat was picked up on radar by Liberator 'Q' of No. 224 Squadron piloted by Flt Lt. H. J. Rayner, who seven minutes after the radar contact sighted the stricken vessel which none the less put up a heavy flak barrage while Rayner dropped six depth-charges compounding the damage already done, causing Kapitan Arved von Muhlendahl to scuttle the boat, with about fifty men left floating in a massive pool of oil. But even though the engagement had taken place not far off the Norwegian coast there were no survivors...

D. H. Mosquito FB VI - Illustration

The D.H. Mosquito F.B. VI Fighter-Bomber with Rocket Projectile equipment

FAIREY
SWORDFISH III

While it is common knowledge that the antiquated-looking Fairey Swordfish biplane was primarily intended for use by the Royal Navy to operate from Fleet Air Arm carriers as a torpedo-bomber, many are not aware the type served for several months in 1945, as the primary equipment of No.119 Squadron RAF. On 29 October, 1944, No. 119 Squadron equipped with Fairey Albacore Is moved to Belgium at forward operating base B.83 Knocke/Le Zoute near Zeebrugge on the Belgium coast, becoming the only Coastal Command squadron to operate from mainland Europe during WW II.

In January 1945, the enemy began deploying midget submarines of the Seehund, Molch and Biber class in the shallow waters off Belgium and Holland, with the potential they could cause serious disruption to shipping operating in the English Channel. No. 119 Squadron under C.O. Squadron Leader Norman Wilkinson was ordered to counter these small and difficult targets - while at the same time converting to the ASV X radar - equipped Fairey Swordfish considered the idea platform for the very difficult night inshore patrols, possessing excellent endurance and armed with a variety of bombs and flares. The ASV radar fitted between the undercarriage precluding the carriage of a torpedo. Crew conversion was undertaken at the units former UK base at Bircham Newton in Norfolk, where the Station Flight had a number of Swordfish IIIs on inventory. Meanwhile the squadron began operations with its elderly Albacores and the first sighting was made on 23 January, but by the end of the month it was fully equipped with Swordfish. While training continued at Bircham Newton for the loss of two Swordfish (NF342) and (NF413) written off in accidents on the 2 and 3 February, respectively, the rather uncomfortable three-hour patrols continued uneventfully.

However, the situation changed dramatically on the night of 9/10 March, when NF307 'NH-G' was lost, believed shot down with the loss of the crew Flt Lt. F. Sutton and Fg Off Radford. Ironically Flt Lt Sutton's death was an ironic tragedy as this was the only squadron Swordfish lost in the brief period it operated the type and Sutton had been one of the first to fly the type as a Sgt Pilot when it entered service in 1935. Two nights later the unit scored its first "kill" when the crew of NF377 'NH-R' attacked and sank a "Seehund" early on in its evening patrol. The following night the same crew in the same airplane sank a "Biber", only an hour after the crew of NF344 'NH-L' had sunk another Biber off the entrance to the port of Rotterdam. The following night another Biber "kill" was claimed. The squadron continued its patrols to VE Day, but no further "kills" were made.

The squadrons final patrol was made by Squadron Leader Wilkinson on the evening of the 8 May, with the official surrender due to take effect at midnight. At 21.00 hrs Wilkinson attacked a Biber off Schouen Island, which was in fact the last air attack of any kind during the war in Europe. Thereby, the Fairey Swordfish biplane creating its own niche in the history of aerial warfare. On the 22 May, all the surviving 119 Squadron Swordfish led by Squadron Leader Wilkinson left Knocke in formation for Bircham Newton, which was maintained over No.16 Group Coastal Command H.Q. at Chatham. The Swordfish brief five month career with Coastal Command ended when the squadron finally disbanded on 25 May, at Bircham.

HAWKER
SEA HURRICANE (FAA)

The Sea Hurricane with R-R Merlin II or III engine, appeared in three versions: the Mk. IA 'Catafighter' in 1941, fitted with catapult spools, slinging gear and naval radio for use from CAM ships (CAtapult-equipped Merchantmen) which were introduced in the Spring of 1941 for the air protection of convoys at sea before the advent of escort carriers ; the Mk. IB (1941) fitted both catapult spools and deck arrester gear for aircraft carrier use ; and the Mk. IC (1942), with the same airframe as the Mk. IB but with Hurricane Mk II fighter four-cannon wings. All Sea Hurricane variants were conversions from existing Hurricane land-fighters and as such there were no new build Sea Hurricanes.

Although the catapult Sea Hurricanes were successful in reducing the number of enemy bombing raids on Allied convoys, the major disadvantage with the scheme, was of course the Catafighter could not return to the launch ship, and if, as was often the case they were not within flying distance of a shore base, the pilot was forced to bail out into the sea in the hope of being rescued by a passing Allied vessel. The situation was improved slightly by the fitment of two 45 Imp gallon auxiliary tanks beneath the wings during the later stages of the scheme

Later with about 40 escort carriers supplied to the RN by the Americans the Sea Hurricanes operated alongside FAA Fairey Swordfish from these vessels, in particular providing valuable cover for the Allied convoys bound for Russia. Following the diaster of convoy PQ. 17 (see appendix) convoy PQ.18 which sailed from Loch Ewe for North Russia on 2 September 1942, was afforded Swordfish and Hurricane air cover from the escort carrier *Avenger*. When the inevitable happened and PQ. 18 was attacked, Sea Hurricanes of Nos. 802 and 883 Squadrons FAA together shot down five enemy aircraft and damaged seventeen others. Four Hurricanes were lost in the action but fortunately three pilots survived.

One of the Sea Hurricanes greatest successes was in the Mediterranean in August 1942, when some 70 FAA Sea Hurricanes, Fulmars and Marlets operating from the carriers *Victorious, Indomitable* and *Eagle* were engaged in three days of air fighting against a force of 500 German and Italian bombers, torpedo carriers and escort fighters. Sea Hurricanes, aided by the Fulmars and Martletts, shot down 39 enemy airplanes and damaged many others for the loss of only eight of their own. Many times they drove off attacking Italian Cant Z. 1007 and Junkers Ju 88s and one pilot alone Lt. R. J. Cork DSC shot down three German and three Italian airplanes in his Sea Hurricane.

One of the last major actions in which the carrier-based Sea Hurricanes were involved was the Malta convoy of August 1942. From November 1942, the Supermarine Seafire took its place on the large Royal Navy aircraft carriers, although the Sea Hurricane continued to serve in the escort carriers until mid-1944, with the last of the front-line FAA Sea Hurricane units to serve afloat being No. 835 NAS in *Nairana* in September 1944.

Photo

FAA Hawker Sea Hurricane

101

HANDLEY PAGE
HALIFAX G.R. II, GR V

The prototype H. P. Halifax bomber took to the air for the first time on 25 October, 1939, and the first series production Halifax almost a year later. Service introduction of the seven-seat, four-engined, heavy-bomber followed in November 1940, and the first operational mission was flown by No.35 (Bomber) Squadron on the night of the 11/12 March, 1941.

By the end of 1942, Halifax II Series I and IA aircraft were also serving with Coastal Command, under the designation Halifax GR II; all were armed with a 0.5-in (12.7 mm) machine gun in the nose, in place of Bomber Command airplanes 0.303-in (7.7 mm) calibre weapons. Some airplanes were fitted with four-blade propellers. Some of the first deliveries went to No. 58 Squadron at Holmesley South, in December 1942, for anti-submarine patrols over the Western Approaches. The first U-boat "kill" for the squadron fell to Halifax 'M' piloted by Wing Commander W. E. Oulton who sank *U-266* with a depth charge attack on 15 May 1943, in the Atlantic, North of the Azores. A number of other No. 58 Squadron successes in 1943; included *U-463*, sunk on the same day by Halifax 'R' flown by Flying Officer A. Birch, in the Western Approaches south-west of the Isles of Scilly.

The Halifax G.R. II was followed into Coastal Command service by the G.R. V variant, which was a forced development of the Series IA due to a shortage of Messier undercarriage assemblies. The G.R. V fitted with a Dowty undercarriage in its place, with the addition of a 0.5-in machine gun fitted in the ventral position when a radar was not fitted. The most prolific Coastal Command operators of the G.R. V variant were the five squadrons employed on meteorological duties, Nos. 517, 518, 519, 520 and 521, with some G.R. Vs delivered to No. 608 Squadron for operation in the Mediterranean. No. 608 Squadron gaining notoriety, being the first RAF unit to score a U-boat "kill" *(U-755)* using rocket projectiles.

In addition to anti-U-boat patrols, No. 502 Squadron in the UK used its Halifaxes to attack enemy shipping off the French coast until September 1944, when it moved to Stornoway, Scotland, for attacks on enemy shipping off Norway, until disbanding on 25 May, 1945.

LOCKHEED
HUDSON

The Lockheed Hudson was originally built for the British Government against an order by the British Purchasing Commission, the aircraft being the military variant of the Lockheed Type 14 Super Electra transport plane. They were in production from 1939 to June 1943 and were the first American aircraft to be delivered by air to Britain. The Hudson has a number of notable first's with Coastal Command; the Hudson III was the first to carry the British developed Mk IA airborne lifeboat, first used operationally by a Hudson-equipped squadron in May, 1943, to rescue the crew of an RAF bomber forced down in the North Sea, 50 miles off the British coast ; on the 8 October 1939, a Hudson of No. 224 Sqaudron Coastal Command, piloted by Flt Lt. Womersly shot down the first enemy aircraft of the war, a Dornier Do 18 flying boat during a patrol over Jutland, and on 31 January, 1940 fourteen Hudsons became the first Coastal Command airplanes to be fitted with ASV radar, which later in conjunction with the Leigh Light proved so effective in detecting surfaced U-boats at night or in poor visibilty; on 28 May 1943, a Hudson of No. 608 Squadron Coastal Command operating from Bilda in North Africa, was the first RAF aircraft to sink a U-boat by means of rocket projectiles fired from beneath the wings.

After the collapse of France in 1940, two Hudson squadrons operated from Northern Ireland to strengthen the anti-U-boat force and some of these airplanes were involved in the hunt for the *Bismarck* in April, 1941. Another Hudson squadron, No. 269, operated over the Western Approaches from its base in Iceland.

It is of interest, that with only a 500 kg (1,000-lb) bomb-load or four depth-charges, Hudsons on anti-shipping patrols, were involved in the destruction or surrender of no less than twenty-four U-boats from 27 August 1941 to 5 October 1943. Including: *U-77 ; U-83 ; U-97 ; U-167 ; U-259 ; U-273 ; U-331 ; U-336 ; U-403 ; U-411 ; U-442 ; U-447 ; U-563 ; U-570 ;U-573 ; U-594 ; U-595 ; U-605 ; U-619 ; U-646 ; U-755.* The main honours were shared fairly evenly between, Nos. 233, 269 and 500 Squadrons each with five "kills", followed by Nos. 48 (3), 608 (2), 58 (1) and 459 (RAAF) (1).

Having re-equipped with Hudson I at RAF Leuchars, Scotland, No. 233 Squadron began anti-shipping patrols after the Germans invaded Norway, in April 1940, continuing until December that year. Following a spell in Northern Ireland the squadron moved to Cornwall to fly patrols over the Bay of Biscay and in December 1941, a detachment was sent to Gibraltar, with all but two of the squadrons U-boat "kills" achieved in the Mediterannean. Adding to the Lockheed Hudson's unique list of Coastal Command first's, on 27 August, 1941, a No. 269 Squadron Hudson 'S', on patrol in the North Atlantic, flown by Squadron Leader J. H. Thompson executed the first capture of a U-boat by the RAF. Following a depth-charge attack by the Hudson, Kapitanleutnant Hans Joachim Rahmlow, affixed a white-backed chart to the periscope. The Hudson then circled *U-570* until relieved by a Catalina flying-boat of No. 209 Squadron, until the trawler *Northern Chief* arrived at 22.50 hrs. The next day a destroyer and a trawler tried to take the vessel in tow but it was not until the trawler *Kingston Agate,*which was specially fitted for towing arrived, that it was possible to get a line aboard. None the less by 18.00 hrs on 28 August all the crew had been taken off by the destroyer *Niagara* and the U-boat was under tow to Thorlakshafn, Iceland, where it arrived on 29th. She returned to Britain at Barrow-in-Furness on 21 September 1941 to be overhauled and re-commisisoned as HMS *Graph*. Britain deployed the *Graph* mainly on experimental duties, although she did undertake some operational patrols until she ran aground at Islay on 20 March, 1944, on her way to the breakers yard. An interesting aside, was, when the U-boat crew arrived at the PoW Camp at Grizedale Hall, Rahmlow and his officers, against regulations forbiddng 'kangaroo courts', whereby PoW's court's martialed each other,an 'Honour Court' was held under the jurisdiction of Korvettenkapitan Otto Kretschmer of *U-99*. Two of the officers were acquitted but Rahmlow and the 1 WO were found 'guilty'. Rahmlow was sentenced to virtual isolation for the rest of the war while 1 WO Leutnant zur See Bernhard Berndt,was offered the opportunity to make amends by infiltrating the Barrow shipyards to sink the submarine.
He managed to escape from the camp but was apprehended and arrested by a Home Guard unit,who's intention was t o return him, but fearful of what reception he might receive at the camp,in a further attempt to escape his captors he was shot.

U-619 was sunk on 5 October 1942, by Hudson 'N' of No. 269 Squadron flown by F/O J. Markham who had been escorting convoy ONS 136 in the North Atlantic. F/O Markham had sighted the U-boat at five miles from an altitude of 4,000 feet and dived to just 20 feet to strafe the boat with its .303in guns and drop its four Mk XI depth-charges. On circling the area Markham and his crew observed oil and wreckage on the surface with Hudson 'W' also from No. 269 Squadron who overflew the area thirty minutes later confirming oil and debris still coming to the surface.

Lockheed Hudson - No. 224 Squadron

SARO
LERWICK

The Saro Lerwick flying-boat was the third in the trio of the airplanes on which the fledgling Coastal Command decided to build its foundations at the end of the 1930s. Unfortunately as with the Botha and Blenheim it failed to meet expectations and indeed in some quarters it was highly critiscised for its poor performance and handling. It was the second of the new monoplane flying-boats ordered by the RAF, the first being the Short Sunderland. The Lerwick was produced to meet AM Spec. R.1/36, which called for a twin-engined flying-boat of 25,000 lb all up weight and top speed of 235 mph, a crew of six, three power-operated defensive turrets and a bomb load of 2,000 lb. An initial order for ten was placed in April 1937, as the Saro S. 36 Lerwick, to include three prototypes.

The S.36 was all-metal with a very single-step planing hull; control surfaces were fabric covered and all carried trim tabs. The high-set cantilevered wing carried two 1,375 hp Bristol Hercules II or IV sleeve valve radial engines. The tail was a standard single fin rudder configuration. Originally intended to be operated by a crew of nine, normally a crew of six or seven was used. Defensive armament comprised an FN4 bow turret mounting a Vickers 'K' gun, dorsal twin .303 Browning-equipped FN8 and quadruple .303 Brownings in the tail FN4A, and provision for a 2,000 lb bomb or depth-charge load.

The first prototype (L7248) took to the air during November, 1938 from Cowes, Isle of Wight, in the south of England, flown by test pilots Leslie Ash and Frank Courtenay. Almost immediately it was revealed not all was well with the design. The flying-boat was found unstable in roll and yaw while cruising, hands-off flight was impossible and the elevators were over-balanced. In addition poor handling on water indicated problems with the planing hull design. The second prototype L7249, joined L7248 in early 1939, and company trials continued until L7248 was delivered to the Maritime Aircraft Experimental Establishment (MAEE) at Felixstowe for full type trials on 14 March. MAEE comfirmed the company test pilots findings and the flying-boat was returned to Cowes for modification, where it was fitted with an extended chord rudder together with extended fins. Meanwhile L7249 which had taken the place of the first prototype at the MAEE, sank on 1 September 1939, after it endeavoured to take-off with the camera-gun hatch open. The airframe later recovered and used for static testing.

During January 1940, L7248 was fitted with twin end-fins and rudders in an attempt to improve its flying characteristics, but later these were abandoned in favour of the more conventional 'fix' of enlarging the fin leading edge and extending the rudder chord, which did in fact improve directional control. At the same time the hydrodynamic problems were being investigated at RAE Farnborough and by the end of the year Short Bros Ltd., had been invited to help resolve the problem. RAE proposed solutions which involved moving the step aft and deepening the planing bottom; Shorts proposed fitment of a Sunderland style rear fuselage, a revised tailplane, altering the step depth and a complete Sunderland planing bottom. Subsequently a comprise solution evolved, which entailed moving a deeper step slightly aft of the original position and lowering the planing bottom. Albeit this reduced, but did not cure the instability. At the same time it was realised the required maximum speed was unattainable, with only 214 mph possible and that take-off runs were exceptionally long, and that with the Bristol Hercules on it limits, engine overheating was occurring. An attempt to reduce the flying-boats maximum take-off weight failed to acheive any improvement in its performance.

As a result of all these ensuing problems in the autumn of 1939, AVM Sholto Douglas put the Lerwick under severe scrutiny, writing to Air Chief Marshal Sir W. R. Freeman, informing him of the complaints made by the pilots that had tested the new flying-boat at the same time detailing the outstanding problems with the aircraft. On 24 October 1939, series production was terminated, but was partially re-instated in November and by February, 1940, due to the shortage of operational flying-boats had been completely reinstated, with an agreed limit of 21 to be delivered. Series airplane's were delivered with an increased wing incidence from 3.5° to 5.5°, and this did help reduce the roll and yaw problems. Finally in December 1939, in spite of continued protestations from the MAEE and others, the Lerwick entered service with No. 209 Squadron, based at Oban, Scotland, for patrols over the Atlantic. Serial L7255 making its first operational patrol on Christmas Day.

As operations intensified more faults and problems emerged. In early 1940, it was found that the bomb doors were likely to fall open in flight due to poor hydraulics, and a locking device was installed. By May, a corrosion trap in the area of the rear turret had been identified and by September, it was agreed single-engine flight was not possible, with the pilot unable to maintain altitude and direction against the torque of the single engine operating at higher revs...

Unfortunately returning from an aborted patrol on 17 February 1940, the ill-fated Lerwick claimed the lives of four of its crew when after stalling on approach to land, it struck the water heavily and collasped its starboard wing float, as a result L7253 turned over and sank, only two of its six crew surviving the incident. During May, 1940 as No. 209 Squadron received more new builds on charge, serviceability peaked at 81% but the following month this dropped by more than half, mainly due to problems with the Bristol Hercules engines. On 16 June, L7261 arrived at Oban from Pembroke Dock but was lost thirteen days later while taxying, when heavy crosswinds caused a float to collapse again and the flying-boat overturned, fortunately without loss of life this time. On 16 June, 1940, the squadron relocated to Pembroke Dock and in August all Lerwicks were grounded for rudder trim tab alterations and modifications to the floats. Following, the squadron returned north to Stranraer to resume maritime patrols but in a very short time four Lerwicks were lost.

On 21 November 1940, L7251 sank at its moorings on Loch Ryan after the front turret and entrance hatches were not secured properly. On 6 December, L7255 also sank while moored at Loch Ryan, a collapse of the starboard float due to poor workmanship associated with the earlier modification work was suspected. On 7 January 1941, L7262 was holed during an unusually long take-off run and sank with the loss of two lives; on 22 February L7263 was reported missing, mysteriously in fine weather, and was never seen again. Against the Commands better judgement the grave shortage of aircraft forced No. 209 Squadron to continue to operate the Lerwick throughout 1940, with servicability problems continuing to escalate. Faults included collapse of throttle levers (one airplane whilst on the water), leaking hydraulics, turret ring problems, defective ASI aand leaking fuel tanks.

During the Spring of 1941, it was intended No. 209 Squadron should return to Oban, but eventually it transferred to Northern Ireland, at Lough Erne, County Fermanagh. Subsequently, L7252 was lost in rough seas off Milford Haven, luckily without loss of life, while operating temporarily from Pembroke Dock. In March, 1941, during rountine inspection at the MAEE, Felixstowe, L7248 was found to have a problem with the wing, revealed by the discovery of buckling in the upper surface wing skinning, indicating severe upward deflection of the wing, later thought to have occurred during a landing in very heavy seas, or following side-slip and leaf tests at the MAEE. In the summer of 1941, a number of modifcations were made to the remaining airplanes fitted with the more powerful Hercules IV engines, but with the arrival of the first Consolidated Catalina (AH542) in April, 1941, the Lerwick was gradually withdrawn from use. The final No. 209 Squadron operational sortie on type underaken on 29 April when L7267 provided escort for SS *Arden Vohr*.

In the meantime the surviving airplanes had joined No. 4 (Coastal) OTU at Stranraer, with nine delivered by the end of May, 1941. During operations with No. 4 OTU three further Lerwicks were lost. On 14 October, L7268 was destroyed when the port engine failed and the flying-boat crashed into the sea killing nine of those aboard and injuring three, the extra personnel having flown without permission. L7257 sank at its moorings during a gale at Invergorden, on 11 November and finally L7265 crashed at Invergorden during a heavy-landing on 21 December. An inquiry set up after the loss of L7265 produced the following statement "the Lerwick is unstable in all three planes and pilots must be prepared to retrim the aircraft at any time, particularly during the approach and landing." Pilots Note's stated. "On take-off torque effect would cause a swing to starboard, corrected by rudder and advancing the starboard engine ahead of the port." Landing notes were particularly precise, specifying a speed of 117 mph at 500 feet and touch-down at 93 mph, using rumble approach with full flap.

The numerous accidents and servicability problems inevitably curtailed the Lerwicks operational activities and engagements with the enemy were somewhat limited. However, those of note, occurred on 25 March, 1940 when L7256 while still with No. 209 Squadron bombed a submerged U-boat, but without success. During July, L7262 took part in the search for a lost Fokker T. 8W of No. 320 Squadron. Although, mostly poor aircraft availability and other circumstances pemitted only mainly routine patrol duties in which No. 209 Squadron was involved until it received Catalinas, in April 1941, to commence ASW patrols over the Atlantic.

On 2 April, 1942, one Lerwick was transferred to No. 422 Squadron (RCAF) at Lough Erne to supplement the three Catalina flying-boats that arrived later in July, and by August the squadron had seven Lerwicks on strength. As might be expected with operational stresses on the Lerwick again it continued as before and it was during this period that L7267 was destroyed when, alighting in a moderate sea and gusting wind, the flying-boat hit the water, bounced and skidded, then lost its tail entire tail section. It was believed this accident was the fault of an inexperienced pilot not observing the vagaries of the Lerwick as defined previously in the Pilots Notes. The final accident occurred to the original surviving prototype L7248 on 21 October while undergoing calibrations near Dumbarton, when according to eyewitness, quite inexplicably the starboard wing dropped and the airplane dived into a hill killing all seven on board. A board of enquiry served to support the firmly held belief the Lerwick was a complete lemon from start to finish when it concluded that the airplane had suffered a partial engine failure and further stated "the handling characteristics have never been satisfactory when flying on one engine" ! But already on the 12 October the type had been withdrawn from operational service use for good, and by the end of the month, most had been sold to Scottish Aviation or sent to Greenock to be broken up.

Illustration - Saro Lerwick

SHORT
SUNDERLAND

Of the many types of airplanes used by the RAF in WW II it was the Short Sunderland flying-boat that was synonymous with Coastal Command. The flying-boat saw 21 years of uninterrupted service as a maritime patrol plane serving throughout the war and beyond. Its comprehensive defensive armament prompted the Germans to nickname it the "Flying Porcupine". Most of the famous flying-boats career was dedicated to important anti-submarine and convoy escort duties, in the Atlantic, North Sea, the Mediterranean and the Indian Ocean.

Project S.25, had got under way in late 1934, and the prototype (K4774) took to the air on 16 October 1937, even so when WW II broke out in September 1939, there were no more than twenty-three in service. The Sunderland I was a large, central-hull flying-boat of all-metal construction powered by four 1,010 hp Bristol Pegasus XXII radial engines, which drove three-blade metal airscrews with variable pitch. Maximum speed was 338 km/h (210 mph) at 2,000 m (6,500 ft), with a cruising speed of 289 km/h (180 mph) at 1,752 m (5,750 ft). The original defensive armament (increased later) consisted of seven machine guns : one at the nose, four in a tail turret, and two, hand-operated in the rear fuselage. It could carry up to 907 kg (2,000-lb) of bombs or depth-charges. Eight depth-charges were carried inside the fuselage in a bomb room and were slid out sideways through a door along two tracks below the wings. The crew consisted of eleven men, including: captain (pilot), 1st pilot, 2nd pilot, navigator, engineer, wireless operator and three gunners, fitter, rigger, plus reliefs.

The first series airplane flew on 21 April, 1938, and all twenty-one of the first two batches were completed by the end of the year, although one had been lost in a night landing accident. In the summer of 1938, deliveries to Pembroke Dock began where No. 210 Squadron began to work up on type. Later long delivery flights of the aircraft, were made to Singapore where the type entered service with No. 230 Squadron at Seletar, replacing their Singapore IIIs. In November 1938, the second Pembroke Dock unit, No. 228 Squadron received its aircraft and in June, 1939, No. 204 Squadron at Mount Batten, Plymouth, received its first aircraft by now forsaking its bright silver livery for camouflage. At the time war was declared No. 228 Squadron was 'on tour' in the Mediterranean looking for suitable bases from which to operate the 'boat', but returned to "Pee Dee" a week after hostilities broke out. All three squadrons immediately began operational flying with No. 204 Squadron covering the South-West approaches, and Nos. 210 and 228 Squadrons covering the North Atlantic approaches.

As already mentioned the types first notable incident of what would be an impressive wartime career occurred on 18 September, 1939, when No. 204 and 228 Squadron aircraft were involved in dramatic rescue of merchant seamen from the British tramp steamer *Kensington Court*, which had been torpedoed 70 miles off the Scilly Isles. The Sunderlands had picked up the ships distress signals, and the first airplane reached the ship 10 minutes before she sank. Landing on rough seas the first flying-boat from No. 228 took on board 20 of the 34 survivors from an overcrowded lifeboat. Shortly afterwards the second aircraft from No. 204 Squadron captained by Flt Lt. Barrett, arrived to rescue the remaining seamen and within an hour all the survivors were back in the UK. In the following months both Nos. 204 and 210 Squadrons managed to find and attack enemy U-boats, but without results as the 100-lb anti-submarine weapons they were using at the time were virtually useless, against such a sturdy foe. Nevertheless the mere presence of the Sunderland in the U-boats operational areas served to act as a "Scarecrow" helping to keep them submerged. At the same time it was realised cover was needed to the north of the British Isles and No. 210 Squadron was dispersed to a number of locations in Scotland including; Woodhaven, Sullom Voe, Invergordon, Stranraer and Oban. Towards the end of the year a fourth unit joined the Coastal Command battle order, No. 10 Squadron RAAF whose personnel had arrived at Mount Batten for familiarisation on type before returning 'down under'. But instead, the unit was assimilated into Coastal Command and became operational early in 1940, with nine Mk Is, flying Atlantic patrols.

As 1940 unfolded, it was clear the Sunderlands were being deployed mostly on anti-U-boat patrols rather than its intended task of general reconnaissance of German surface vessels. The detachments at Sullom Voe in the Shetlands played a vital role in detecting surface and submarine traffic passing out into the Atlantic between Scotland and Norway. In April, 1940, the Sunderland fleet was boosted when No. 201 Squadron replaced its Saro Londons with the type. This was fortuitous as with the German invasion and subsequent occupation of Norway the Sunderlands were hard pressed in this area maintaining patrols up the Norwegian coast into the Arctic Circle, often making 14 hour flights in atrocious weather. During the Norwegian campaign it was a Sunderland of No. 204 Squadron that was the first RAF aircraft to report the movements of the German invasion fleet. Later, it was the Sunderlands that transported senior officers to Norway, often in the face of attack by enemy aircraft. One of its VIP passengers was Major-General Carton de Wiart, V C., who commanded Allied Forces in Central Norway. During this period the Sunderlands encountered heavy enemy air opposition, in the form of Junkers Ju 88s and sometimes when near the coast, Messerschmitt Me 109s. Though some flying-boats were lost, the airplanes often fought back to drive off their attackers, with one crew having been attacked by no less than six Ju 88s downing two before retreating. Another Sunderland survived an attack by four Me 109s and although badly damaged, downed one.

Meanwhile, Short Bros endeavoured to 'beef up' the flying-boat by fitting 815 hp Bristol Pegasus XVIII engines with two-speed superchargers, as well as fitting a rear FN4A tail turret in place of the two mid-upper hatches; and a Frazer Nash FN7 two-gun dorsal turret was also fitted. The most significant enhancement being the addition of ASV II radar giving rise to the four 'goal post' antenna on top of the rear fuselage and the Yagi aerials under each wing-tip. Equipped with ASV the flying-boat was now able to take on a more offensive role as for example on 3 July 1940, when a No. 10 Squadron RAAF airplane found a surfaced U-boat south-west of Bishop's Rock and sunk it, the first outright Sunderland "kill", *U-26*.

In 1941, the first Sunderland Mk IIs began to enter service and a detachment of three Sunderland Is of No. 210 Squadron at Oban were used to form No. 95 Squadron which within a month had left for Gibraltar en-route for its new base at Freetown, Sierra Leone to begin ASW patrols over the Central/South Atlantic and convoy protection down the West Coast of Africa, in particular to keep an eye on Vichy French ships operating out of French West Africa. At the same time the type became extremely active in the Mediterranean involved in the fighting and subsequent evacuations in Greece and Crete, airlifting some 800 people to safety, with the flights undertaken at night to avoid interception, with one airplane carrying as many as 84 people on one flight.

As the Germans redirected their attention to the South Atlantic, No. 95 Squadron was joined by No. 204 who left the Shetlands to provide reinforcements. Also at this time American Consolidated Catalina flying-boats began to enter RAF service, and with their greater range and endurance served to complement the veritable Sunderland. Although the Sunderlands were concentrated in the Mediterranean and the mid-Atlantic where the U-boat offensive was inflicting horrific losses. Although it often meant hours of routine patrols indispersed with occasional moments of high drama and actions stations, as when Flt Lt. Lindsey's crew of No. 201 Squadron was attacked by a Focke Wulf Fw 200 Condor when following a prolonged engagement the German plane was forced to ditch into the sea. A number of 210 Squadrons Sunderlands were also engaged by Fw 200s although this was compensated for in January 1941, when Flt Lt. Baker's airplane engaged and sank the Italian submarine *Marcella*, the unit by now equipped with the superior Torpex depth-charge.

During 1941, Short Bros and the Marine Aircraft Experimental Establishment carried out a considerable amount of work to improve the flying-boats aerodynamics and eventually the Mk III incorporating a number of structural modifications to the hull was introduced. Giving increased speed and range capability, the first Mk III entering service in December, 1941. This version was to become the standard WW II type, having a twin Browning nose turret later supplemented by a Vickers K gun mountings fireable from the waist hatches.

As operations continued into 1942, the workload on the Sunderland units continued to escalate and Coastal Command already in 1941, had returned No. 228 Squadron to the UK and it was Nos. 10 (RAAF), 201, 210 and 228 Sunderland squadrons supplemented by a growing number of Catalina equipped units that were to implement the new Coastal Command strategy on the U-boat Battle in the Atlantic. The new strategy was to provide regular and more stringent patrols in the areas near the U-boat bases on the Atlantic coast of France to catch them on the way out and when returning. It was not long before this began to show dividends and by the summer of 1942, there was a distinct rise in the number of U-boat sinkings. Albeit the Germans countered by providing the U-boats with long-range fighter cover and once again the Sunderlands found themselves in running battles with the Ju 88s, Messerschmitts and a number of other enemy types. A number of Sunderlands having been engaged by either enemy airplanes or having been fired on by the U-boats or their flak boats even if they returned to base, were so badly damaged they sank on landing.

In June 1942, a number of Sunderland IIIs augmented No. 202 Squadrons Mk IIs, and Catalinas at Gibraltar, as part as the Commands intensification of operations on the U-boat front. At the same time a number of new Sunderland squadrons were formed; number No. 423 Squadron (RCAF) on the 18 May, at Oban, receiving its first Mk IIs in July, with operations beginning on 23 August; a second RAAF unit, No. 461 Squadron formed from a nucleus supplied by No. 10 Squadron becoming operational on 1 July, to begin patrols over the Western Approaches and the Bay of Biscay. An early success for No. 461 (RAAF) Squadron occurred on 30 July when Sunderland 'U' flown by Flt Lt. D. Marrows sunk *U-461*. Marrows raid followed concerted attacks on three U-boats sailing together in the Atlantic (*U-461, 462 and 504*), by a number of airplanes including a 53rd Squadron American Air Force Liberator, two RAF Halifaxes and a Catalina, with *U-462* scuttled following an attack by a H. P. Halifax of No. 502 Squadron, and *U-504* claimed by the Royal Navy.

On 5 August No. 246 Squadron reformed at Bowmore, receiving Sunderlands in October, beginning ASW operations on 12 December but was disbanded on 30 April, 1943, with its airplanes distributed to Nos. 226, 330 and 422 Squadron (RCAF). No. 422 Squadron had relinquished it newly acquired Catalina flying-boats for Sunderland IIIs in November, 1942. Although No. 210 Squadron, one of the original Sunderland operators had converted to Catalinas the year before.

To counter the U-boat "stay on the surface and fight" policy the RAAF squadrons at Plymouth, tried various fixed gun installations in the nose of their Sunderlands and, after a number of different layouts, decided on four fixed .303-in Browning forward-firing machine guns, controlled by the pilot. These experiments had taken place in 1943, and subsequently it was decided it should become a series production modification - with the flying-boat now truly living up to it "Flying Porcupine" nickname, with no less than fourteen .303-in Brownings and two .303-in Vickers K guns. Also in 1943, No. 330 (Norwegian) Squadron based in Iceland, relinquished its last Northrop N3-PB seaplanes and Catalina for Sunderland IIIs at Oban, moving to Sullom Voe on 12 July to begin operations along the Norwegian coastline, much of it, routine maritime patrol flying. The Canadian and Australian squadrons on occasion did register the odd U-boat "kill" but in a similar vein many operational missions were mundane patrols in the most appalling weather.

Meanwhile, Shorts had continued development of the Sunderland and decided to fit Bristol Hercules engines as used in the Stirling bomber to the flying-boat. This in turn gave rise to a heavier structure and the new airplane with a larger and redesigned planing bottom was to designated the Mk IV. But with a number of other changes incorporated and the length of time it took to produce the new mark it, finally emerged as the Short Seaford. With a parallel development fitted with four 1,200 hp American Pratt & Whitney R-1830-90Twin Wasp engines entering service, with No. 228 Squadron as the Mk V in February, 1945. The other major improvement at this time was the installation of ASV Mk VIC radar with scanners fitted under the wing-tips replacing the massive drag-inducing ASV III antenna arrays. Some Mk III airplanes fitted with the Mk VIC radar were redesignated Mk IIIAs.

Operationally the work up for D-Day in June 1944, had seen patrols in the Western Approaches increase in intensity to keep the English Channel free of U-boats. But with the success of Operation *Overload*, and the Atlantic U-boat bases along the French coast lost to the Germans, and the accent on the Pacific War gaining momentum, the German surrender in May, 1945, brought a rapid change in deployment for the Sunderland squadrons. No. 95 Squadron that had been so vital flying ASW patrols from West Africa for so long, ended its days flying yellow fever serum to the Cape Verde Islands, until disbanding in June, 1945. No. 119 Squadron that had only operated the Sunderland for six months from September, 1942 until April 1943, was already redeployed on night coastal E-boat and R-boat (midget submarines) patrols from Belgium. No. 201 Squadron still remained operational in the UK with Coastal Command. No. 204 Squadron and No. 228 Squadrons dis banded at "Pee Dee", in June, 1945. No. 230 Squadron had already moved to Ceylon, in February 1944, continuing its war against the Japanese, initially. Subsequently becoming involved in casevac operations operating with the 3rd Indian Division. In May 1945, it moved to Akyab to fly ASV missions over the Gulf of Siam and in July, 1945, it was joined by Sunderlands of No. 240 Squadron although this unit was engaged primarily on meteorological, ferry and transport duties. Eventually in April 1946, following a brief spell in Singapore, No. 230 Squadron returned to "Pee Dee", to take its place in the peacetime battle order with its Sunderland Vs. No. 240 finally disbanding at Koggala, Ceylon on 31 March, 1946. The Canadian and Australian squadrons had either disbanded or returned home after VE Day.

With the official cessation of hostilities in Europe on the 8 May, 1945, and Admiral Doenitz instructions to the German U-boat fleet to surrender to the nearest port. Coastal Command maintained precautionary anti-U-boat patrols for another four weeks, and the last of these sorties was made by a Sunderland of No. 201 Squadron flying from Lough Erne in Northern Ireland, on 3/4 June, 1945. Nevertheless the Sundeland had an impressive post-war career, taking part in the Berlin Airlift operating from the lakes near Berlin, carrying some 4,847 tons of freight, and also saw service in the Korean War, in particular in the ASR role, being the only RAF aircraft to fly operationally in the conflict. However, by the mid-1950s the flying-boat had in reality become outmoded for war, instead being replaced by long-range maritime patrol landplanes. The last home-based RAF squadrons, (Nos. 201 and 230) stood down at Pembroke Dock in January, 1957. Leaving only Nos. 205 and 209 Squadrons in the Far East. The final operational RAF flight made by two Sunderlands of No. 205 Squadron from RAF Seletar, Singapore was made on 15 May, 1959. In recognition of the long and sterling service afforded the flying-boat units of the RAF throughout a 21 year career, a Mk III variant serial ML824 is preserved at the RAF Museum Hendon, north London.

A Short *Sunderland* flying-boat on patrol over the North Atlantic.   Two squadrons were still on first-line duties
with Coastal Command seventeen years after entering service in 1938, the longest period of any aircraft in its
original operational role.

Extract from an original painting by Gp Capt Norman Hoad AFC

VICKERS TYPE 642
(ASR) WARWICK I/II

Originally intended as a Vickers Wellington bomber replacement, delays of the types entry into operational service precluded this, and most served in the general reconnaissance or air-sea-rescue roles with Coastal Command. A shortage of Bristol Centaurus engines meant the Warwick did not enter series production until July 1942, with P&W Double Wasp Is, by which time its deployment as a heavy bomber had been overtaken by the introduction of other more capable bomber designs. Nevertheless it carried an armament of eight .303 in machine guns in three turrets, two in the nose turret, two in a mid-upper turret and four in a tail turret. The bomb-bay could accommodate up to 2,000 lb of bombs, mines or depth-charges. In January 1943, it was decided to develop the bomber for air-sea-rescue duties with Coastal Command, capable of carrying an under-fuselage slung airborne lifeboat. The ASR. I was similar to the GR. I with slight mofications to the bomb-bay to permit carriage of the Uffa Fox Mk. IA airborne lifeboat containing engines, rocket gear and parachutes. Weighing 772 kg (1,700 lb), the lifeboat, was 7.17 m (23 ft 6 in) long and 1.67 m (5 ft 6 in) wide, it was carried under the fuselage by way of a single central attachment, which picked up the ordinary bomb-bay lugs in the aircrafts bomb-bay. The normal bomb sight and bomb release were used for aiming and releasing the lifeboat. It was dropped on six 9.76 m (32 ft) diamater parachutes which were pulled out by a pilot chute attached to the airplane by a static line.

Powered by two Pratt & Whitney Double Wasp R-2800 radial engines the A.S.R. I entered service with No. 280 Squadron at Langham, Norfok, in August, 1943, to undertake long patrols over the North Sea. ASR squadrons wartime sorties mostly involved long patrols, often in excess of 7.5 hours over predetermined search areas, often to drop survival gear and aluminium sea markers and smoke floats so as to guide any nearby vessels to the scene to execute a pick up. Sometimes the Warwicks remained in the vicinity for hours flying ahead of the vessel in large orbits to guide it to the scene.

In the summer of 1944, the Warwick's trailed Coastal Command's Beaufighter's on 'Strike Wing' operation's out over the North Sea staying close to the action, with Lindholme survival gear and sometimes an airborne lifeboat aboard should an unfortunate Beaufighter be downed. A brief look at No. 280 Squadron's activities at the time affords the reader a 'snapshot' of Warwick ASR operations. On 29 July, Warwick 'E' took off from Langham, Norfolk at 09.10, piloted by Flying Officer Harvey and set a course for Heligoland Bight adjacent to the designated search area. Eventually a 'K' Type dinghy was found although unfortunately the pilot occupant had already succumbed to the rigours of the elements. Six hours later the rather saddened crew landed back at base. The following day Warwick 'V' took off at 14.00 hrs on an ASR sortie but was recalled to Langham due to poor visibility in the search area. Later, at 17.15 hrs the search was resumed but again, after an hours flying in less than idea conditions the mission was aborted.

The squadrons next Heligoland assignment occurred on 7 August with Warwick 'L' taking off at 11.30 hrs. At 13.00 hrs a low flying Luftwaffe Junkers Ju 88 appeared on the starboard bow, flying towards the Warwick. It flew directly underneath with about 30m (100 ft) clearance,too fast for the Warwicks gunners to give it a burst from the two .303 in nose guns. Fortunately it was reported the same Ju 88 was shot down a short time later by two patrolling North American P-51 Mustang fighters, which were in the area. A month later on 9 September, the squadron was detailed for Beaufighter duties again, accompanyiny the 'Strike Wing' on a sweep. One Beaufighter was seen to be heading back to Langham obviously in some sort of trouble. As the Warwicks themselves returned to Langham at 11.30 hrs, the burnt-out remains of a downed 'Beau' was noted just off the end of the runway. Later at the squadron debrief the full details of the crash were revealed:

The troubled No. 455 Squadron Beaufighter had made a very rough landing before catching fire as it came to rest. No. 455 Squadrons C.O. Wing Commander Jack Davenport DSO DFC who was in the watch tower, saw the crash and raced to the scene in his car. The navigator had managed to get clear but the pilot had his feet trapped. Despite exploding ammunition Wg Cdr. Davenport dived into the flames, mounted the fuselage to heave his fellow Australian out of his flying boots, on to the wing, and carried him to the awaiting ambulance. A feat for which he received the George Medal.

WW II Coastal Command Warwick ASR operators and bases are detailed below:

No. 269 Squadron	Azores	Oct 1944 — Mar 1946
No. 276 Squadron	Portreath (det Cherbourg)	Apr 1944 — Nov 1944
No. 277 Squadron	Portreath	Nov 1944 — Feb 1945
No. 278 Squadron	Bradwell Bay	Nov 1944 — Feb 1945
No. 279 Squadron	Thornaby	Nov 1944 — Sep 1945
No. 280 Squadron	Thornaby	Oct 1943 — Jun 1946
No. 281 Squadron	Thornaby	Nov 1943 — Oct 1945
No. 282 Squadron	Davidstowe Moor	Feb 1944 — Jul 1945

Occasionally the squadron was called upon, in addition to its normal ASR duties, to fly 'X-Patrols'. These involved night patrols of the North Sea or English Channel, locating ship movements, intercepting transmisisons and possibly acting as a relay station, monitoring the distress frequency and being available for any emergency operations. In spite of the perceived excitment of clandestine operations, some X-Patrols could, be quite boring. As for that made on 4 February 1945, when Warwick 'Z' took off from Beccles, Suffolk at 17.45 hrs with Flying Officer Harvey at the controls for an eight hour flight, in which time absolutely nothing of note occurred, with the crew glad to return to base and a late meal. In contrast on the previous day Warwick 'O' that took off at 12.30 hrs on an ASR sortie had an action packed afternoon and evening. The Warwick located two dinghies, dropping Lindholmes to the occupants and later were instrumental in getting them picked up by a high-speed rescue launch. Later seven aircrew were found floundering in the sea and they were saved by a Consolidated Catalina flying-boat which landed and took them on board, following location details signalled from the Warwick, which returned to base with a very satisfied crew after a 7.5 hour sortie.

An even more exciting 'X-Patrol' was flown on 23/24 February when Warwick 'A' captained by Squadron Leader Hillditch took off at 18.45 hours to patrol the English Channel. With the aircraft flying at 600 m (2,000 ft) (normal search height being 500 ft) it was a bright moonlit night, with only slight scattered cloud. The Warwick had been airborne for several hours flying relatively long legs south-west to north-west from the Isle of Wight to the Brest Peninsula. About halfway on the south-west leg nine German E-boats were seen on the port quarter, there shilouettes clear in the moonlight. As the airplane drew abeam a salvo of flak greeted them, the tracers uncomfortably close to the port wing.

After taking evasive action, the E-boats were tracked at a safer distance with information and position reports signalled to mission control back at base. It was not long before rocket-firing Beaufighters appeared on the scene, an excited 'Aussie' voice was heard on the intercom "There they are the B.....ds !". Although the Warwick being close to its patrol duration limit was forced to leave the scene, without ever discovering the outcome of the engagement, as another X-Patrol plane joined the action...

Later, Nos. 179 and 251 Squadrons received the G.R.5 variant with two Bristol Centaurus IV engines. The GR.5 was basically similar to the GR.1 except for armament. The nose and mid-upper turrets were removed and replaced by three manually operated 0.5 in guns one in the nose and one in each side of the fuselage midway between the wing and the tail. The four-gun tail-turret was retained. It carried the Leigh Light and the normal offensive weapons load of bombs, mines or depth-charges.

Authors Note: The foregoing operational account is based on an article entitled *"We Shall Be There"* by former Flt Lt. John Lewery (RAF). Published in Flypast May 2002.

Vickers Warwick ASR Mk I with Mk IA lifeboat under fuselahe
and   ASV II Radar attenna array   (ASV II radar displt)

The Vickers-Armstrongs Warwick A.S.R. Mk. I with the Mk. IA airborne lifeboat under the fuselage.

ASV Mk II radar screen

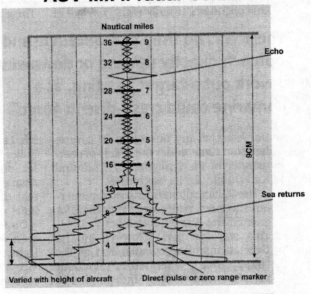

VICKERS
WELLINGTON

Shortage of airplanes led to the Vickers Wellington bomber being adapted for Coastal Command and by 1942, five squadrons were operating the GR.VIII variant. No.172 Squadron's Mk VIII's to be the first Coastal Command aircraft to be fitted with the Leigh Light. These were followed by the GR.11 the Coastal Comand version of the Mk X and the GR 12, 13 and 14 with uprated engines. The GR.11 and GR.12 were both fitted with Bristol Hercules VI or XVI engines, and carried no above fuselage "goal post" radar masts as the centimetric ASV III antenna was carried in a chin radome beneath the nose. Retractable Leigh lights were installed and their was provision for two 18-in torpedoes.

In August 1942, seven Wellington VIIIs were detached to Wick, in north-east Scotland, for patrols over the North Sea and later these airplanes were used to form No.179 Squadron on 1 September. Meanwhile No. 172 Squadron continued with Leigh Light patrols over th Western Approaches and the Bay of Biscay with a number of sightings and in March 1943, the squadrons airplanes were fitted with ASV III to supplement the Leigh Light. This soon brought results with the squadron averaging one sighting for every four sorties. On 20 March 1943,Wellington 'G' attacked *U-448* which unfortunately escaped unscathed. But later a modicum of success was achieved by Wellington 'Q' of No. 172 Squadron piloted by F/O W. H. T. Jennings who on 24 July, made a radar contact on *U-459*, in the Atlantic, NW of Cape Ortegal, although unfortunately on the attack the Wellington was hit by concentrated flak fired from the U-boat and crashed into its target with only one survivor, Sgt. A. A. Turner. *U-459* actually survived this attack to be sunk later by a No. 549 Squadron Wellington which attacked with depth charges. Forty survivors of the 59 man crew and Sgt Turner were later picked by the Polish destroyer ORP *Orkan*. Later between October 1943 and April 1944, the squadron had detachments operating from Gibraltar and the Azores.

A prominent operator of the Wellington was No. 304 (Polish) Squadron, that had formed as a light-bomber unit with Fairey Battle Is in August 1940. But following conversion to Wellington bombers after a year with Bomber Command, it transferred to Coastal Command in May 1942, to fly general reconnaissance patrols over the Bay of Biscay. From April to June 1943, the squadron was based in East Anglia flying anti-E-boat patrols over the North Sea. Specialised GR.8s were received in July 1943, for anti-U-boat patrols with a move to Davidstowe Moor seeing a return to the Biscay area with Wellington GR.14s received in September, 1943. The following year brought a move to Benbecula, Scotland, for patrols over the the North Atlantic, until returning to Cornwall in March, 1945.

No. 407 Squadron (RCAF) also was a prolific user of the Wellington GR variant beginning with the GR. 10 to fly anti-U-boat patrols from various locations around the UK operating successive marks including the GR.11, GR.12 and GR. 14 until April 1945, when detachments were sent to operate from Langham to fly searches for midget submarines off the Dutch coast until the disbandment of the squadron on 24 June, 1945.

No. 415 Squadron (RCAF) commenced operations as a torpedo-bomber unit with Bristol Beauforts in September, 1941. Throughout 1942, a mix of Bristol Blenheim IV and H. P. Hampden I were flown on anti-submarine patrols until relinguishing the Blenheims to begin anti-shipping patrols at night with the Hampdens with bombs and from August 1942, with torpedoes after undergonig a training course. After moving to Scotland ASV duties continued until November 1942, when the squadron moved back south to Bircham Newton having already detached airplanes to St Eval, Cornwall, for operations off Brittany. The Hampdens normally operated at night but were obsolete for torpedo-bombing duties and in September 1943, conversion to Wellington GR.12 and GR.13 began. The units new task was to use its Leigh Light Wellingtons to locate midget submarines while its ex-RN Fairey Albacore Is attacked them with bombs. As well as a number of E-boats the squadron also added a number of merchant vessels and naval craft to its list of enemy ships sunk or damaged. By May 1944, the squadron had ten Wellington GR. 13s and twenty-two Albacores on strength but in July 1944, the Albacores were passed to No. 119 Squadron ahead of them receiving ASV-equipped Swordfish IIIs. At the same time its general reconnaissance Wellingtons were superceded with H. P. Halifaxes and the squadron joined Bomber Command for the remainder of the war as part of No.6 (Canadian) Group.

No. 524 Squadron reformed on 7 April 1944, at Davidstowe Moor with Wellington GR. 13 for patrols against E-boats off the French coast.

Summary Coastal Command Vickers Wellington variants.
DWI (Direct Wireless Installation) Wellington I
As magnetic mines could not be swept by normal means the Admiralty and the Royal Aircraft Establishment devised a way to explode them. A small number (5-6) Vickers Wellington airplanes were fitted with a circular 48 feet underfuselage magnetic loop to create a large magnetic field in the vicinity of magnetic mines laid in the sea lanes by the Germans, in order to cause them to explode. The current to supply the magnetic loop was supplied from generators mounted in the bomb-bay driven by Ford V 8 automotive engines bolted to the floor in the Wellington's rear fuselage. It was invented, developed and put in service in 3 months. It is all credit to the crews that flew these handful of converted Wellingtons, that often ignoring recommended safety procedures, flying as low as 25-40 feet in just a few months (Jan 40 - May 40) they helped remove the danger to Allied shipping from enemy magnetic mines. The Command's DWI Wellington's accounting for at least one-eighth of all the magnetic mines swept or detonated between November 1939 and May 1940.

Mk VIII
Fitted with two 1,000 hp Bristol Pegasus Mk XVIII air-cooled radial engines. The Mark VIII was a conversion of the Mk IC for service as a General Reconnaissance bomber with Coastal Command. The Mk VIII carried the same armament as the Mk IC, six .303 machine guns and up to 1,500 lb of bombs or depth-charges, as well as mines or teo 18 in torpedoes and later the Leigh Light.

GR. 11
Fitted with two Bristol Hercules VI or XVI engines. General Reconnaissance and Torpedo-bomber version of Mk X bomber. Armament as Mk VIII but capable of carrying up to 4,500 lbs of depth-charges, mines or two 18 in torpedos. Also fitted with Leigh Light.

GR. 12
Fitted with two Bristol Hercules VI engines. Coastal Reconnaissance bomber with reduced range, capable of carrying up to 5,100 lbs of bombs, depth-charges or mines. Also fitted with Leigh Light. Armament 6 x .303 in machine guns.

GR. 13
Fitted with two Bristol Hercules XVII engines, General Reconnaissance bomber for Coastal Command. Armament as for Mk VIII, capable of carrying up to 5,000 lb of bombs, mines, or depth-charges.

GR. 14
Fitted with two Bristol Hercules XVII engines, General Reconnaissance bomber. nose nose turret as fitted with ASV Mk X radar in under-chin radome. Armament still consisted six .303 in machine guns, four in tail-turret and two in beam positions. Retractable Leigh Light in rear of bomb-bay. Same offensive load as for G.R. 13.

DWI Wellington with Leigh Light installation

The Leight Light
installation in a turret to be
fitted to a DWI Wellington.

Wellington mounted with magnetic coil to detonate magnetic sea mines.

Performance and Offensive Capability Coastal Command Airplanes WW II.

Aircraft & Mark	Cruising Speed	Endurance (hours)	Bombs, Torpedoes	Guns
Avro Anson 1	158 mph	5.5	360 lb	2 x .303 m.g. Note: Early in the war some No. 500 Sqn aircraft had 2 additional mgs and C.O.s a/c 1 hand-operated 20 mm gun in bottom fuselage.
A. W. Whitley V	185 mph	9	up to 7,000 lb bombs	4 x .303 in powered tail-turret 1 x .303 in mg in nose turret
Blackburn Botha	209 mph		up to 2,000 lb	3 x .303 m.g.
Bristol Beaufort I	200 mph	6	1,500 lb or one 18-in 1,605 lb torpedo semi-enclosed	2 x .303 guns in nose and dorsal turret. Some with .303 gun in blister below nose and two beam guns.
Bristol Blenheim IV	200 mph	6	1,000 lb internally	1 x fixed .303 gun forward and twin .303 in guns in dorsal turret
Beaufighter I C	321 mph (max)	5	—	4 x 20 mm cannon. 6 x .303 machine guns
Beaufighter T.F. X	303 mph (max)	5	1 x 1,650 lb or 2,127 lb torpedo or eight rockets plus 2 x 250 lb bombs	4 x 20 mm cannon in nose 1 x .303 in mg in rear
Boeing Fortress	317 mph (max)	Range 3,000 miles	12,800 lb bomb-load	10-13 x 0.50 in mg
Catalina Ib	179 mph	17.6	2,000 lb	4 x .303 in mg
Liberator G.R III	303 mph (max)	Range 2,800 miles	8,800 lb bombs or 8 depth-charges	10 x 0.5 in machine guns
D. H. Mosquito VI	380 mph (max)	Range 1,205 miles	2 x 500 lb bombs or rocket projectiles under wings	4 x 20 mm cannon and 4 x .303 machine guns forward.
Fairey Swordfish III	104 mph	350 nautical miles	3 x Mk VII depth-charges or eight 60 lb RPs below the wings	1 x Fixed Browning .303 forward 1 x Lewis or Vickers 'k' gun aft.
Halifax II Series IA	217 mph	Range 1,860 miles	5,800 lb	1 x Vickere gun in nose. 4 x .303 in
Lockheed Hudson I	190 mph	6	750 lb	Brownings in dorsal & rear turrets
Saro Lerwick I	165 mph	Range 1,540 miles	2,000 lb	1 x Vickers gun in nose turret Twin Brownings in dorsal turret Four Brownings in tail turret
Saro London II	129 mph	5.2	2,000 lb	3 x .303 in Lewis guns
Short Sunderland I	210 mph (max)	12	2,000 lb	7 x .303 in mg
Supermarine Stranraer	105 mph	7.2	1,000 lb	3 x .303 in Lewis guns
Wellington IC	200 mph	10.6	1,500 lb	6 x .303 in mg
Warwick ASR I	224 mph (max)	Range 2,300 miles	—	8 x .303 in mg

Notes: Operational Flying

i. Maximum speed was possible for only an extremely limited period. Except for tactical manoeuvring, bomber and fighter planes mostly flew at speeds between 'most economical cruising' and 'maximum continuous cruising'. This of course varied with the different types of airplanes, but usually average 'cruise' speeds fell respectively between 55-80% and 80-90% of the maximum speed.

ii. Range and associated bomb-load gives some idea of the relative performances of various types operated. The figures shown refer to early marks of airplanes flying at 'most economical cruising' speed at the specified height at which the greatest ranges could be obtained. Allowance is made for take-off but not for landing, the range quoted being the maximum distance the airplane could cover in still air 'flying to dry tanks'. In addition in planning of operations a reduction in range by 25% was usually made to allow for navigation errors, tactical manoeuvring, weather conditions and numerous other factors.

iii. Endurance, is the time an airplane can continue flying under given conditions without refuelling. This being a vital factor of Coastal Command over-water operations, operating at an 'economical cruising speed, consistent with maximum safe endurance as determined under normal operational circumstances (i.e. not including possible long engagements with the enemy).

APPENDIX I : Summary of Coastal Command U-boat Sinkings WW II

(Note :- A total of 784 U-boats were sunk or destroyed in WW II this list includes only those losses either directly or indirectly attributed to RAF Coastal Command operations).

Sep 1939 - 1941 (raids/sinkings by aircraft - 6)

U-boat	& Type	Date of Attack	Aircraft	Squadron	Pilot	Remarks
U-26	1A	3 July 1940	Sunderland I RB-H	No.10 (RAAF) Sqn		First Sunderland flying-boat "kill"
U-31	VIIA	11 March 1940	Blenheim IV UX-O	No. 82 Sqn	Sqn Ldr. M.V. Delap	Salvaged 19/3/40 Re-commissioned 3/7/40. Sunk by RN 2/11/40
U-55	VIIB	30 January 1940	Sunderland I DQ-Y	No. 228 Sqn		Scuttled. Shared attack included RN convoy escorts
U-206	VIIC	30 Nov 1941	Whitley V YG-B	No. 502 Sqn	F/O R. W. G. Holdsworth	First Coastal Command ASV radar atttack
U-452	VIIC	25 August 1941	Catalina Ib WQ-J	No. 209 Sqn	F/O E. A. Jewiss	
U-570	VIIC	27 August 1941	Hudson II UA-S	No. 269 Sqn	Sqn Ldr. J. H. Thompson	U-Boat was captured by Britain. *Graph*

1942 (raids/sinkings by aircraft - 24)

U-boat & Type		Date of Attack	Aircraft	Squadron	Pilot	Remarks
No. Unknown		18 February 1942	Whitley			Attacked U-boat on surface
U-74	VIIB	2 May 1942	Catalina Ib TQ-C	No. 202 Sqdn	Flt Lt. R. Y. Powell	Joint RN/Coastal Command Operation
U-89	VIIC	16 August	Liberator OH-	No. 120 Sqdn	Sqn Ldr. T. M. Bulloch	Sighted not attacked (see text)
U-653	VIIC	18 August	Liberator	No. 120 Sqdn	Sqn Ldr T. M. Bulloch	Severely damaged
U-132	VIIC	5 November	Liberator OH-	No. 120 Sqdn	Sqn Ldr. T. M. Bulloch	RN / RAF
U-216	VIID	20 October	Liberator III XB-H	No. 224 Sqdn	F/O D. M. Sleep	
U-259	VIIC	15 November	Hudson III MK-S	No. 500 Sqdn	F/O M.A.Ensor DFC	
U-261	VIIC	15 September	Whitley V GE-B	No. 58 Sqdn	Sgt. B. F. Snell	
U-331	VIIC	17 November	Hudson 'Z' 'L' 'C'	No. 500 Sqdn		Also FAA Albacore
U-372	VIIC	4 August	Wellington	No. 203 Sqdn		Joint RN/RAF attack ASV-equipped aircraft.
U-411	VIIC	13 November	Hudson MK-D	No. 500 Sqdn	Sqn Ldr J. B. Ensor	
U-412	VIIC	22 October	Wellington VIII 'B'	No. 179 Sqdn	Flt Sgt. A. D. Martin	No. 179 Squadron Leigh Light aircraft
U-502	IXC/40	6 July	Wellington VIII 'H'	No. 172 Sqdn	P/O W. B. Howell an American volunteer	Ist attack by Wellington and Leigh Light
U-559	VIIC	30 October	Wellesley I KU-H	No. 47 Sqdn		RN / RAF
U-573	VIIC	1 May	Hudson ZS-M	No. 233 Sqn		Escaped to Spain.
U-578	VIIC	10 August	Wellington I KX-H	No. 311 (Czech) Sqn	F/O Josef Nyvlt	
U-595	VIIC	14 November	Hudson 'C' 'D'	No. 608 Sqdn		Hudsons F, J, K , X and W No.500 Sqn
			Hudson F, J, K, X,W	No. 500 Sqdn		
U-597	VIIC	12 October	Liberator III 'H'	No. 120 Sqdn	Sqn Ldr. T. M. Bulloch DFC	
U-599	VIIC	24 October	Liberator XB-G	No. 224 Sqdn	P/O B. P. Liddington	Joint RN/RAF
U-605	VIIC	14 November	Hudson ZS-B	No. 233 Sqdn		
U-611	VIIC	8 December	Liberator 'B'	No. 120 Sqdn	Sqn Ldr. D. J. Isted	
U-619	VIIC	5 October	Hudson UA-N	No. 269 Sqdn	F/O J. Markham	
U-627	VIIC	27 October	Fortress II	No. 206 Sqdn	P/O R. L. Cowey	Joint RN/ RAF
U-705	VIIC	3 September	Whitley V KN-P	No. 77 Sqdn	Flt Sgt.A.A MacInnes	
U-751	VIIC	17 July	Whitley VII TG-H	No. 502 Sqdn		Plus Lancaster 'F' of No. 61 (Bomber) Sqn on loan to Coastal Command

1943   (raids/sinkings by aircraft - 82)

U-boat & Type		Date of Attack	Aircraft		Squadron	Pilot	Remarks
U-77	VIIC	28 March	Hudsons	'L' & 'L'	Nos 48 & 233 Sqns		1st attack
		29 March	Hudson	OY-V	No. 48 Sqdn		2nd atack
U-83	VIIB	4 March	Hudson	MK-V	No. 500 Sqdn	Sgt. G. Jacimov	
U-97	VIIC	16 June	Hudson	'T	No. 459 (RAAF)	F/Sgt. D. T. Barnard	
U-106	IXC	2 August	Sunderland	DQ-N	No. 228 Sqdn	F/O R. D. Hanbury	U-106 intially damaged by No. 407 RCAF aircraft
			Sunderland	UT-M	No. 461 (RAAF)	Flt Lt. I. A. Clark	
U-109	IXB	7 May	Liberator III	'P'	No. 86 Sqdn	P/O J. C. Green	
U-126	IXC	3 July	Wellington XII	'R'	No. 172 Sqdn	Flt Sgt. A. Coumbis	
U-134	VIIC	24 August	Wellington VIII	'J'	No. 179 Sqdn		
U-167	IXC	6 April	Hudson	ZS-W	No. 233 Sqdn	Flt Sgt. K. R. Dalton	
			Hudson	ZS-L		Flt Lt. W. E. Willets	
U-169	IXC	27 March	Fortress I	VX-L	No. 206 Sqdn	F/O A. Samuel	
U-197	IXD2	20 August	Catalina Ib	'C'	No. 259 Sqdn	F/L L.O. Bennett	
			Catalina Ib	'N'	No. 265 Sqdn	F/O C. E. Robin	RCAF
U-200	IXD2	24 June	Liberator III	'H'	No. 120 Sqdn	Flt Lt. A.W. Fraser	
U-211	VIIC	19 November	Wellington XIV	'F'	No. 179 Sqdn	F/O D. M. McRae	DFC RCAF
U-221	VIIC	27 September	Halifax II	BY-B	No. 58 Sqdn	F/O E. L. Hartley	
U-225	VIIC	15 February	Liberator III	'S'	No. 120 Sqdn	F/O R. T. Turner	
U-227	VIIC	30 April	Hampden I	UB-	No. 455 (RAAF)	Flt Sgt. J. S. Freeth	
U-258	VIIC	20 May	Liberator III	'P'	No. 120 Sqdn	Sqn Ldr. J. R. E. Proctor	
U-265	VIIC	3 February	Fortress II	'N'	No. 220 Sqdn	P/O K. Ramsden	
U-266	VIIC	15 May	Halifax	BY-M	No. 58 Sqdn	Wg Cdr W.E. Oulton	
U-268	VIIC	19 February	Wellington	'B'	No. 172 Sqdn	P/O G. D. Lundon	ASV - Leigh Light
U-273	VIIC	19 May	Hudson	UA-M	No. 269 Sqdn	F/O J. N. Bell	
U-274	VIIC	23 October	Liberator	XB-Z	No. 224 Sqdn	Sqn Ldr E. J. Wicht	Joint RN/ RAF Wicht was Swiss national
U-280	VIIC	16 November	Liberator	BX-M	No. 86 Sqdn	F/O J. H. Brookless	

U-boat & Type		Date of Attack	Aircraft	Squadron	Pilot	Remarks
U-304	VIIC	28 May	Liberator III 'E'	No. 120 Sqdn		
U-332	VIIC	29 April	Liberator XB-D	No. 224 Sqdn		Operation *Derange*.
U-336	VIIC	4 October	Hudson UA-F	No. 269 Sqdn	Flt Sgt. G. C. Allsop	
U-337	VIIC	16 January	Fortress I VX-G	No. 206 Sqdn	P/O L. G. Clark	Joint RAF/RN
U-338	VIIC	20 September	Liberator 'F'	No. 120 Sqdn		Joint RN/RAF
U-340	VIIC	2 November	Wellington 'R' 'W'	No. 179 Sqdn		
U-341	VIIC	19 September	Liberator RB-A	No. 10 (RAAF)	Flt Lt. R. F. Fisher	
U-376	VIIC	10 April	Wellington 'C'	No. 172 Sqdn	P/O G. H. Whitley	ASV - Leigh Light
U-383	VIIC	1 August	Sunderland III DQ-V	No. 228 Sqdn	Flt Lt. S. White	
U-384	VIIC	20 March	Fortress II 'B'	No. 206 Sqdn	P/O L. G. Clark	
U-389	VIIC	5 October	Liberator 'X'	No. 120 Sqdn	Flt Lt. W. McEwen	
U-391	VIIC	13 December	Liberator FH-B	No. 53 Sqdn	Sqn Ldr. G.	
U-403	VIIC	17 August	Hudson 'O'	No. 200 Sqdn	Crawford	
			Wellington 'HZ'	Free French AF	F/O P. R. Horbat	Joint 479 AS Group/RAF
U-404	VIIC	28 July	Liberator XB-W	No. 224 Sqdn		
U-417	VIIC	11 June	Fortress II 'R'	No. 206 Sqdn	F/O R. Sweeny	
U-418	VIIC	1 June	Beaufighter VI ND-B	No. 236 Sqdn		Lt Cdr. F.J. Brookes RN
					F/O M. C. Bateman	
U-419	VIIC	8 October	Liberator 'R'	No. 86 Sqdn	Flt Lt. J. Wright DFC	
U-420	VIIC	26 October	Liberator III RB-A	No. 10 (RAAF)		
U-435	VIIC	9 July	Wellington 'R'	No. 179 Sqdn	P/O E. J. Fisher	
U-440	VIIC	31 May	Sunderland III NS-R	No. 201 Sqdn	Flt Lt. D.M. Gall	
U-442	VIIC	12 February	Hudson VI 'F'	No. 48 Sqdn	F/O G. R. Mayhew	
U-447	VIIC	7 May	Hudson 'X'	No. 233 Sqdn	Sgt. J. V. Holland	
U-454	VIIC	1 August	Sunderland RB-B	No. 10 (RAAF)	Flt Lt. K. Fry	Aircraft shot down both pilots killed. 6 crew survived
U-456	VIIC	13 May	Liberator 'B'	No. 86 Sqdn	Flt Lt. J. Wright	Joint RAF/RCAF & Canadian Navy.
			Sunderland II AB-G	No. 423 (RCAF)		
U-459	XIV	24 July	Wellington 'Q'	No. 172 Sqdn	F/O W. H. Jennings	
U-463	XIV	15 May	Halifax II BY-R	No. 58 Sqdn	F/O A. Birch	
U-465	VIIC	2 May	Sunderland III UT-M	No. 461 (RAAF)	Flt Lt E. C. Smith	
U-468	VIIC	11 August	Liberator V 'D'	No. 200 Sqdn	F/O L. Trigg DFC	The aircraft crashed with all lost F/O Trigg awarded VC
U-469	VIIC	25 March	Fortress II 'L'	No. 206 Sqdn		
U-470	VIIC	16 October	Sunderland III 2-S	No. 422 (RCAF)		Shot down.
			Liberator 'E'	No. 120 Sqdn	F/Lt H. Kerrigan	First time sonobouys used by RAF - Liberator 'Z'
			Liberator 'Z'	No. 120 Sqdn	Flt Lt. B. Peck	But not until U-boat sunk.
			Liberator 'C'	No. 59 Sqdn	P/O W.G. Loney	
U-489	XIV	4 August	Sunderland 'G'	No. 423 (RCAF)	F/O A. A. Bishop	Joint RAF/RCAF crew. Atlantic, SE of Iceland
U-504	IXC/40	30 July	Halifax II V9-U	No. 502 Sqdn		Joint RN / American Coastal Command
			Sunderland III UT-U	No. 461 Sqdn		
			Liberator 'O'	US 53rd Sqdn		
U-514	IXC/40	8 July	Liberator XB-R	No. 224 Sqdn	Sqn Ldr. T.M. Bulloch DSO DFC	Liberator 'R' trials aircraft modified to carry rockets.
U-519	IXC/40	10 February	Liberator 'T' *Tidewater Tillie*	2nd Sqn 480th Group	1 Lt. W. L. Sandford	USAAF unit attached to Coastal Command. Joint RN/RAF
U-528	IXC/40	11 May	Halifax 'D'	No. 58 Sqdn	P/O J. B. Stark	Also USN Catalina & RN
U-533	IXC/40	16 October	Bisley (Blenheim V)	No. 244 Sqdn		
U-528	IXC/40	11 May	Halifax II BY-D	No. 58 Sqdn		
U-529	IXC/40	15 February		No. 120 Sqdn		
U-535	IXC/40	5 July	Liberator FH-G	No. 53 Sqdn	P/O J. B. Stark	(U-529 - not conclusive)
U-540	IXC/40	16 October	Liberator 'S'	No. 59 Sqdn		
		17 October	Liberator 'D'	No. 59 Sqdn	F/L. E. Knowles DFM	Initial attack RNZAF
			Liberator 'H'	No. 120 Sqdn		DFM
U-542	IXC/40	28 November	Wellington 'H'	No. 179 Sqdn	W/O B. W. Turnbull Flt Sgt. D. Cornish	

1943 continued

U-boat & Type		Date of Attack	Aircraft	Squadron	Pilot	Remarks
U-558	VIIC	20 July	Halifax II BY-E	No. 58 Sqdn		Initially 179 Sqn then 224 then 479th AS Group
U-562	VIIC	19 February	Wellington 'S'	No. 38 Sqdn	F/O I. B. Butler AFC	Joint RN/RAF
U-563	VIIC	31 May	Hudson BY-R	No. 58 Sqdn	W/C W. Oulton	U-563 demise involved three Coastal Command squadrons Nos.58, No. 10 (RAAF) and 228 The Sunderland was shot for the loss of all crew. Whitley sank U564 later But was forced to ditch in sea. Captured near Brest
			Sunderland III RB-E	No. 10 (RAAF)	Flt Lt.Mainprize	
			Sunderland I DQ-X	No. 228 Sqdn	F/O W.O.French	
U-564	VIIC	14 June	Sunderland I DQ-U	No. 228 Sqdn	F/O L. B. Lee	
			& Whitley V RK-G	No. 10 OTU	Sgt. A. J. Benson	
U-566	VIIC	24 October	Wellington 'A'	No. 179 Sqdn		
U-594	VIIC	4 June	Hudson VI 'F'	No. 48 Sqdn	F/O H.C.Bailey DFM	
U-607	VIIC	13 July	Sunderland I DQ-N	No. 228 Sqdn	F/O R. D. Hanbury	
U-610	VIIC	8 October	Sunderland III 3-J	No. 423 (RCAF)		
U-614	VIIC	29 July	Wellington 'G'	No. 172 Sqdn	Wg Cdr. R. Musson	
U-617	VIIC	12 September	Wellington 'P' 'J'	No. 179 Sqdn	S/Ldr D. Hodgkinson	RCAF
U-620	VIIC	13 February	Catalina Ib TQ-J	No. 202 Sqdn	P/O W. H. Brunini	ASV - Leigh Light attack Also Hudsons Nos. 48 & 233 & Swordfish 833 & 886
U-623	VIIC	21 February	Liberator III 'T'	No. 120 Sqdn	S/Ldr. D. Isted DFC	
U-624	VIIC	7 February	Fortress IIA	No. 220 Sqdn	P/O G. Robertson	
U-628	VIIC	3 July	Liberator XB-J	No. 224 Sqdn	S/Ldr. P. Cundy DFC	
U-632	VIIC	6 April	Liberator III 'R'	No. 86 Sqdn	Flt Lt. C.W. Burcher	
U-635	VIIC	5 April	Liberator III 'N'	No. 120 Sqdn	F/O G. Hatherly	
U-643	VIIC	8 October	Liberators 'R' 'Z'	No. 86 Sqdn	'Z' Flt Lt. C.W. Burcher DFC	Joint Nos. 86 and 120 Squadrons
			Liberator IIIs 'T' 'G' 'L'	No. 120 Sqdn	'T' Flt Lt. D.C. Webster DFC	
U-646	VIIC	17 May	Hudson UA-J	No. 269 Sqdn	Sgt. F. W. James	
U-663	VIIC	8 May	Sunderland III RB-W	No. 10 (RAAF)		Attacked by No.10 Sqdn then sunk in accident
U-665	VIIC	22 March	Whitley RK-V	No. 10 OTU	Sgt. J. A. Marsden	
U-669	VIIC	7 September	Wellington 1-W	No. 407 (RCAF)	P/O E.M. O'Donnell	Leigh Light attack
U-706	VIIC	2 August	Hampden I GX-A	No.415 (RCAF) Sqn	RAF/USAAF	Last USAAF - Coastal Command operation before US Navy assumed responsibility for ASW.
			Liberator 'T'	479th AS Group	Capt. Jospeh L. Hamilton	
U-707	VIIC	9 November	Fortress II 'J'	No. 220 Sqdn		
U-710	VIIC	24 April	Fortress II 'D'	No. 206 Sqdn	F/O R. Cowey	
U-753	VIIC	13 May	Sunderland II AB-G	No. 423 (RCAF) Sqn	Flt Lt. J. Musgrave	Joint Coastal Command HMCS
U-755	VIIC	28 May	Hudson V 'M'	No.608 (Aux) Sqdn		The first RAF U-boat "kill" using rockets
U-844	IXC	16 October	Liberator 'L'	No. 86 Sqdn	Flt Lt. E. A. Bland	Joint RN/RAF raid. Aircraft 'L' broke-up on ditching Bland plus 4 others survived
			Liberator V 1-S	No. 59 Sqdn	P/O W. J. Thomas	
U-964	VIIC	16 October	Liberator XQ-Y	No. 86 Sqdn	F/O G. D. Gamble DFC BEM	
U-966	VIIC	10 November	Wellington 'B'	No. 612 Sqdn	W/O L. D. Gunn	Also Libaerators USN 'E' VP103, 'E' VP110 & 'R' VP 105. Wellington 'T' Shot down by U-boat
			Wellington 1-T	No. 407 Sqdn		
			Liberator V 'D'	No. 311 (Czech) Sqn	Flt Sgt. Zanta	

1944 (raids/sinkings by aircraft - 52)

U-boat & Type		Date of Attack	Aircraft	Squadron	Pilot	Remarks
U-107	IXB	18 August	Sunderland III NS-W	No. 201 Sqdn	Flt Lt. L. Baveystock	DFC DFM
U-193	IXC	28 April	Wellington 'W'	No. 612 Sqdn	F/O G. C. Punter	
U-231	VIIC	13 January	Wellington 1-L	No. 172 Sqdn	P/O W.N.Armstrong	RCAF
U-240	VIIC	16 May	Sunderland 'V'	No. 300 (Nor) Sqdn	Sub-Lt. C. T. Johnsen	
U-241	VIIC	18 May	Catalina IV 'S'	No. 210 Sqdn	F/O B. Bastable	
U-243	VIIC	8 July	Sunderland V RB-H	No. 10 (RAAF) Sqn	F/O W. B. Willey	Also involved second 10 Sqn aircraft & VP-105 B-24
U-270	VIIC	13 August	Sunderland III UT-A	No. 461 (RAAF) Sqn	F/O D. A. Little	RAAF
U-283	VIIC	11 Februay	Wellington 2-D	No. 407 (RCAF) Sqn	F/O P.W. Heron	Wellington 'N' of No. 612 attacked 10/2. Shot down
U-292	VIIC	27 May	Liberator V 1-S	No. 59 Sqdn	Flt Lt. V. Camacho	RCAF
U-297	VIIC	6 December	Sunderland NS-Y	No. 201 Sqdn		
U-317	VIIC	26 June	Liberator IIIa BX-N	No. 86 Sqdn	Flt Lt. G.W. Parker	
U-319	VIIC	15 July	Liberator VI PQ-E	No. 206 Sqdn	F/O D. W. Thynne	
U-347	VIIC	17 July	Catalina IV 'Y'	No. 210 Sqdn	F/O J. A. Cruikshank awarded V.C.	Only Cruikshank and 2nd pilot F/S Garnett survived
U-355	VIIC	1 April	TBM Avenger	No. 826 NAS FAA		Arctic, West of North Cape
U-361	VIIC	17 July	Liberator IIIa BX-U	No. 86 Sqdn	P/O M. G. Mosely	
U-364	VIIC	30 January	Wellington 1-K	No. 172 Sqdn	Flt Sgt.L.D.Richards	Aircraft lost hit by flak Crew lost
U-373	VIIC	8 June	Liberator XB-G	No. 224 Sqdn	Flt Lt. K. O. Moore DSO & US Silver Star	RCAF Also sank U-629 on same sortie (2 in 30 mins)
U-385	VIIC	11 August	Sunderland III UT-P	No. 461 (RAAF) Sqn	P/O I. Southall	
U-423	VIIC	17 June	Catalina 'D'	No. 333 (Nor) Sqdn	Lt. C. F. Krafft	
U-426	VIIC	8 January	Sunderland III RB-U	No. 10 (RAAF)		
U-476	VIIC	24 May	Catalina IV 'V'	No. 210 Sqdn	Capt.	SAAF
U-477	VIIC	3 June	Canso (Catalina) 'T'	No. 162 (RCAF)	F.W.L.Maxwell F/L.R. E. MacBridge	RCAF
U-478	VIIC	30 June	Liberator IIIa BX-E	No. 86 Sqdn	F/O N. E. Smith	
U-545	IXC	10 February	Wellington 'O'	No. 612 Sqdn	P/O M. Painter	RAAF
U-571	VIIC	28 January	Sunderland III UT-D	No. 461 (RAAF)	Flt Lt. R. D. Lucas	RAAF
U-601	VIIC	25 February	Catalina IV 'M'	No. 210 Sqdn		
U-608	VIIC	10 August	Liberator FH-C	No. 53 Sqdn	Wg Cdr.R.Gates AFC	
U-618	VIIC	14/15 August	Liberator FH-G	No. 53 Sqdn	Flt Lt. G. Potier DFC	ASV - Leigh Light attack
U-625	VIIC	10 March	Sunderland III 2-U	No. 422 (RCAF)	W/O W.F. Morton	Attack flown by Flt Lt. S. W. Butler (RAF)
U-629	VIIC	8 June	Liberator XB-G	No. 224 Sqdn	Flt Lt. K. O. Moore DSO & US Silver Star	RCAF

1944 continued

U-boat & Type		Date of Attack	Aircraft	Squadron	Pilot	Remarks
U-675	VIIC	24 May	Sunderland 'R'	No. 4 (C) OTU	F/O T. P. Frizell	RAAF
U-715	VIIC	13 June	Canso 'T'	No. 162 (RCAF) Sqn	Wg Cdr. Chapman	RCAF
U-740	VIIC	9 June	Liberator V 'F'	No. 120 Sqdn	Flt Lt.A.K Sherwood	
U-742	VIIC	18 July	Catalina IV 'Z'	No. 210 Sqdn	F/O R. W. Vaughan	
U-761	VIIC	24 February	Catalina 1b TQ-G	No. 202 Sqdn		Joint USN/RN/RAF attack
U-772	VIIC	30 December	Wellington 'L'	No.407 (RCAF) Sqn	ASV - Leigh Light	
U-821	VIIC	10 June	Mosquitos 'T' 'S' 'V' 'W' Liberator 'K'	No. 248 Sqdn No. 206 Sqdn	led by Flt Lt. S. G. Nunn Flt Lt. D. S. Saunders	Joint attack. Later No. 228 lost Mosquito. to VP boat
U-846	IXC	4 May	Wellington 'M'	No. 407 (RCAF) Sqn	Flt Lt. I. J. Bateman	
U-852	IXD2	2 May	Wellington VIII 'G'	No. 8 Sqdn	F/O J. R. Forrester	& Wellingtons of No.621 inc. 'E' (F/O H.R. Mitchell)
U-867	IXC	19 September	Liberator XB-Q	No. 224 Sqdn	Flt Lt. H. J. Rayner	Initial attack by Sunderland of No. 248 Squadron
U-871	IXD2	24 September	Fortress IIA 'P'	No. 220 Sqdn	Flt Lt A. F. Wallace	
U-955	VIIC	7 June	Sunderland NS-S	No. 201 Sqdn	Flt Lt. L. Baveystock	DFC DFM
U-970	VIIC	8 June	Sunderland III 'R'	No. 228 Sqdn	Flt Lt. C.G.	DFC
U-976	VIIC	25 March	D. H. Mosquito 'I' D. H. Mosquito 'L'	No. 618 Sqdn No. 618 Sqdn	F/O A. H. Hilliard F/O D. J. Turner	Trials aircraft. Escorted by 4 Mosquitos of No.248 Sqn led by Flt Lt. L.S. Dobson
U-980	VIIC	11 June	Canso A GK-B	No.162 (RCAF) Sqn	F/O L. Sherman	
U-981	VIIC	12 August	Halifax II V9-F	No.502 (Aux) Sqn		ASV Mk II radar. 600-lb anti-submarinebomb
U-988	VIIC	15 June	Wellington XIV 2-A	No. 304 (Polish) Sqn		Not confirmed.
U-990	VIIC	25 May	Liberator V 'S'	No. 59 Sqdn	Sqn Ldr. B. Sisson	
U-998	VIIC	16 June	D. H. Mosquito 'H'	No. 333 (Nor) Sqdn	Lt E. Johansen	Assisted by two other No. 333 Sqn Mosquitos
U-1060	VIIF	27 October	Liberators 'Y' 'H' Halifaxes 'D' 'T' V9-	No. 311 (Czech) Sqdn No. 502 (Aux) Sqdn		Initial attack by 1771 NAS Fairey Firefly I
U-1191	VIIC/41	25 June	Wellington 2-A	No.304 (Polish) Sqn	Flt Lt. L.	
U-1222	IXC/40	11 July	Sunderland NS-P	No. 201 Sqdn	Flt Lt. B.F. Waters	DFC
U-1225	IXC/40	24 June	Canso A GK-P	No.162 (RCAF) Sqn	Flt Lt. D. Hornell	Hornell forced to ditch died awarded P/H VC

1945 (raids/sinkings by aircraft - 31)

U-boat & Type		Date of Attack	Aircraft	Squadron	Pilot	Remarks
U-246	VIIC	29 March	Sunderland NS-H	No. 201 Sqdn		RN Ships *Hesperus* and *Havelock* plus RAF
U-251	VIIC	19 April	22 aircraft D.H. Mosquito anti-sub sweep	Banff Strike Wing Nos. 143 235, 248 and 333 Sqdns	led by Wg Cdr. A. H. Simmonds	
U-320	VIIC	7 May	Catalina IV 'X'	No. 210 Sqdn	Flt Lt K. M. Murray	Last U-boat sunk by direct action in WW II
U-321	VIIC	2 April	Wellington 2-Y	No. 304 (Polish) Sqn	W/O R. Marczak	
U-396	VIIC	23 April	Liberator BX-V	No. 86 Sqdn	Flt Lt. J.T. Lawrence	Unconfirmed
U-534	IXC	5 May	Liberator BX-G	No. 86 Sqdn	W/O J. D. Nicol	Initial attack Liberator 'E' No. 547 Squadron
U-579	VIIC	5 May	Liberator 2V-K	No. 547 Sqdn	F/O A. Bruneau	
U-843	IXC	9 April	Mosquito VI LA-A	No. 235 Sqdn	F/O A. J. Randall	Branff Strike Wing
U-905	VIIC	20 March	Liberator BX-B	No. 86 Sqdn		
U-927	VIIC	24 February	Warwick V OZ-K	No. 179 Sqdn	Flt Lt.A.G.Brownhill	ASV Leigh Light
U-1007	VIIC	2 May	Typhoon Ib MR-	No. 245 Sqdn		
U-1008	VIIC	6 May	Liberator BX-K	No. 86 Sqdn		
U-1017	VIIC	26 April	Liberator 'Q'	No. 120 Sqdn	F/O H. J. Oliver	
U-1065	VIIC	9 April	D. H. Mosquitos	Banff Strike Wing Nos. 143, 235, 248 Sqns	Led by Sqn Ldr H. H. Gunnis DFC	4 Mossies damaged. 3 landed & interned Sweden 1 crashed in sea (Film Unit)
U-1106	VIIC/41	29 March	Liberator XB-O	No. 224 Sqdn	Flt Lt. M.A. Graham	
U-1210* (see 3032)	VIIC/41	3 May	Typhoon Strike Wing			
U-1276	VIIC/41	3 April	Liberator XB-U	No. 224 Sqdn		Joint RN/RAF
U-236	VIIC	4 May	22 aircraft of Beaufighter Strike Wing	No. 236 Sqdn (12) No. 254 Sqdn (10)		
U-393	VIIC	4 May				
U-2338	XXIII	4 May				
U-2359	XXIII	2 May	35 Mosquitos Banff SW	No. 143 Squadron and No. 235 Squadron		Also aircraft from Nos. 248, 333 & 404 Sqns
U-2503	XXI	3 May	30 aircraft of Beaufighter Strike Wing	No. 236 Squad (13 a/c) No. 254 Squad (17 a/c)	Led by Wg Cdr. E. P. Hutton DFC	
U-2521	XXI	5 May	Liberator 2V-K	No. 547 Sqdn		
U-2524	XXI	3 May	30 aircraft of Beaufighter Strike Wing. Plus Mustang escorts	No. 236 Squad (13 a/c) No. 254 Squad (17 a/c) Nos. 65 and 118 Sqdns	Led by Wg Cdr. E. P. Hutton DFC	
U-2534	XXI	6 May	Liberator BX-K	No. 86 Sqdn		
U-2540* (see 3032)	XXI	3 May	Typhoon Strike Wing			
U-2635	XXIII	5 May	Liberator XB-S	No. 224 Sqdn	Flt Lt. J. C. Downey	
U-3030* (see 3032)	XXI	3 May	Typhoon Strike Wing			
U-3032*	XXI	3 May	Typhoon Strike Wing	Nos. 175, 184 and 245 Sqns		3 sunk and two damaged including *
U-3503	XXI	8 May	Liberator BX-K	No. 86 Sqdn		
U-3523	XXI	6 May	Liberator BX-G	No. 86 Sqdn	Flt Lt. T.H. Goldie	DFC

APPENDIX II.
Raids and sinkings of U-boats by US Aircraft & Units, 1942-45 in the Atlantic Sea War.

U-boat & Type		Date of Attack	Aircraft	Squadron	Pilot	Remarks
U-656	VIIC	1 March 1942	Catalina	USN VP-82		Sunk in Atlantic South of Cape Race
U-503	IXC	15 March 1942	Lockheed Hudson	USN VP-82		Sunk in Atlantic SW of Newfoundland
U-701	VIIC	7 July 1942	Liberator	USAAF 396th BS		Sunk in Atlantic West of Cape Hatteras
U-464	XIV	20 August 1942	Catalina 'R'	USN VP-73		Sunk in Atlantic SE of Iceland.
U-582	VIIC	5 October 1942	Catalina 'I'	USN VP-73		Sunk in Atlantic South of Iceland
U-408	VIIC	5 November 1942	Catalina 'H'	USN VP-84	Lt. Millard	Sunk in the Baltic off Hela
U-164	IXC	6 January 1943	Catalina	USN VP-83		Sunk in Atlantic NW of Pernambuco
U-524	IXC/40	22 March 1943	B-24 Liberator	1st Squadron 480th Bomb Group USAAF	Lt. W. L. Sandford	Atlantic South of Madeira
U-174	IXC	27 April 1943	Lockheed Ventura	USN VB-125	Lt. T. Kinaszczuk USNR	Atlantic South of Newfoundland
U-657	VIIC	14 May 1943	Catalina	USN VP-82		Atlantic SW of Iceland Mk 24 Mine
U-569	VIIC	22 May 1943	TBM Avenger (2)	VC-9 (USS Bogue)	Lt. W. F. Chamberlain Lt. H. S. Roberts	First U-boat sunk by USN aircraft from escort carrier
U-467	VIIC	25 May 1943	Catalina 'F'	USN VP-84	Lt R. C. Millard	Atlantic, W of Faeroe Islands
U-217	VIID	5 June 1943	Avenger & F4F	VC-9 (USS Bogue)	Lt McAuslan (Avenger)	North Atlantic
U-118	XB	12 June 1943	Avenger & F4F	VC-9 (USS Bogue)	Lt W. F. Chamberlain (Avenger)	Atlantic, West of Canary Islands
U-388	VIIC	20 June 1943	Catalina 'I'	USN VP-84	Lt. E. W. Wood USNR	Atlantic SE of Cape Farewell
U-194	IXC/40	24 June 1943	Catalina 'G'	USN VP-84	Lt. J. W. Beach	Atlantic South of Iceland
U-951	VIIC	7 July 1943	Liberator 'K'	1 st Squadron 480th Bomb Group USAAF	Lt. Walter S. McDonnell	North Atlantic
U-232	VIIC	8 July 1943	Liberator 'Q'	2nd Squadron 480th ASG USAAF	Lt. James H. Darden	Atlantic, SW of Cape Finisterre
U-506	IXC/40	12 July 1943	Liberator 'C'	480th Group USAAF	2 Lt. Ernest Salm	N. Atlantic, West of Vigo
U-487	XIV	13 July 1943	Avenger & F4F	VC-13 (USS Core)	Lt R. P. Williams (Avenger) Lt. Earl F. Steiger (F4F)	Mid-Atlantic South of Azores
U-160	IXC	14 July 1943	Avenger & F4F	VC-29 (USS Santee)	Lt. John H. Ballentine Lt. 'Brink' Bass	Atlantic, South of the Azores
U-509	IXC/40	15 July 1943	Avenger & F4F	VC-29 (USS Santee)	Lt. Claude N. Barton Ensign Jack D. Anderson	Atlantic, North-west of Madeira
U-67	IXB	16 July 1943		VC-13 (USS Core)	Lt. J. Wiliams	Atlantic, Sargasso Sea
U-513	IXC/40	19 July 1943	Martin Mariner	USN VP-74	Lt. R. S. Whitcombe	South Atlantic, SE of San Francisco
U-558	VIIC	20 July 1943	Liberator 'F'	19th Squadron 479th AS Group USAAF	1st Lt. Charles F. Gallmeier	Atlantic, NW Cape of Ortegal. (shared with RAF No. 58 Squadron)
U-662	VIIC	21 July 1943	Catalina	USN VP-94	Lt. R. H. Howland USNR	Atlantic
U-527	IXC/40	23 July 1943	TBM Avenger	VC-9 (USS Bogue)	Lt. Stearns	Atlantic, South of the Azores
U-598	VIIC	23 July 1943	Liberator	USN VB-107	Lt. William R. Ford	South Atlantic NE Cape of San Roque
U-622	VIIC	24 July 1943		8th Air Force		Norway, Trondheim
U-404	VIIC	28 July 1943	B-24 Liberator 'Y' B-24 Liberator 'N' Liberator 'W'	4th Squadron 479th ASG USAAF. No. 224 Squadron RAF	Maj. Stephen D. McElroy 1st Lt. Arthur J. Hammer Fg Off R. Sweeney	North Atlantic
U-43	IXA	30 July 1943	Avenger & F4F	VC-29 (USS Santee)	Lt. Richmond Lt. van Vranken	Atlantic, SW of the Azores

U-boat & Type		Date of Attack	Aircraft	Squadron	Pilot	Remarks
U-591	VIIC	30 July 1943	PV-1 Ventura	USN VB-127	Lt. Walter C. Young USNR	South Atlantic South-east of Recife
U-199	IXD2	31 July 1943	Martin Mariner Hudson Catalina	USN Brazilian Air Force	Lt. William F. Smith	South Atlantic East of Rio de Janeiro ("kill" accredited to Brazlian Air Force)
U-117	XB	7 August 1943	Avenger & Wildcat	VC-1 USS *Card*	Lt. Ashbury H. Sallenger	North Atlantic
U-664	VIIC	9 August 1943	Avenger (2) & F4F	VC -1 USS *Card*	Lt. C. G. Hogan USNR Lt. Forney Lt. Hodson (F4F)	Atlantic North-west of the Azores
U-525	IXC/40	11 August 1943	Avenger & Wildcat	VC- 1 USS *Card*	Lt. Charles G. Hewitt Ensign Jack H. Stewart	Atlantic NW of the Azores
U-604	VIIC	11 August 1943	PV-1 Ventura Liberator	USN VB-129 USN VB-107		South Atlantic
U-185	IXC/40	24 August 1943	Avenger & Wildcat	VC-13 USS *Core*	Lt. Robert P. Williams Lt Martin G. O'Neill	Atlantic
U-84	VIIB	24 August 1943	Avenger	VC-13 USS *Core*	Lt William A. Felter	North Atlantic
U-847	IXD2	27 August 1943	Avenger 2 x F4F Wildcat	VC-1 USS *Card*	Lt Ralph Long	Atlantic, Sargasso Sea
U-161	IXC	27 September 1943	Martin Mariner PBM-3C	USN VP-74	Lt. Harry G. Patterson	South Atlantic, North East of Bahia
U-279	VIIC	4 October 1943	PV-1 Ventura	USN VP-128	Cdr. C. L. Westhofen	North Atlantic
U-460	XIV	4 October 1943	Avenger	VC-9 USS *Card*	Lt. R. L. Stearns USNR	Atlantic, North of the Azores.
U-422	VIIC	4 October 1943	Grumman F4F Wildcat Avenger	VC-9 USS *Card*	Ensign Joseph D. Horn Lt. Stewart B. Holt	Atlantic, North of the Azores
U-402	VIIC	13 October 1943		USS *Card*	Lt-Cdr. Howard M. Avery Ensign Barton C. Sheelah	North Atlantic
U-378	VIIC	20 October 1943	Grummam F4F-4 Wildcat TBF Avanger	VC-13 USS *Core*	Cdr. Charles W. Brewster Lt R. W. Hayman USNR	North Atlantic, North of the Azores
U-220	XB	28 October 1943		VC-1 USS *Block Island*	Lt. Franklin M. Murray Ensign Harold L. Hanshuh	North Atlantic
U-584	VIIC	31 October 1943	3 x Avengers	VC-9 USS *Card*	Lt. Fowler Lt. Balliett + A. N. Other	Atlantic, North West of the Azores
U-848	IXD2	5 November 1943	4 x PB4Y Catalina 2 x NA Mitchell B-25	USN VP-107 1st Composite Sqn USAAF		Atlantic SW of Ascension Island. Attack lasted 5.5 hrs
U-849	IXD2	25 November 1943	Liberator	USN VB-107	Lt. M. V. Dawkins	South Atlantic, West of the Congo
U-86	VIIB	29 November 1943		USS *Bogue*	Lt. Bernard H. Volm	North Atlantic
U-172	IXC	12 December 1943		USS *Bogue*	Lt. E. C. Gaylord	Atlantic, West of Canary Islands
U-850	IXD2	20 December 1943	Grumman F4F Wildcat Grumman F4F Wildcat	VC-19 USS *Bogue*	Lt. Wallace A. LaFleur Ensign G. C. Goodwin Lt. H. G. Bradshaw	Atlantic, West of Maderia
U-345	VIIC	13 December 1943		USAAF		Baltic, Kiel
U-544	IXC/40	16 January 1944		USS *Guadalcanal*	Ensign Bert. J. Hudson Ensign William M. McLane	Atlantic, North West of the Azores.
U-271	VIIC	28 January 1944	Liberator 'E'	USN VB-103	Lt. C. A. Enloe	North Atlantic, West of Limerick.
U-177	IXD2	6 February 1944	Liberator	USN VB-107	Lt. C. I. Pinnell	South Atlantic, West of Ascension Island
U-761	VIIC	24 February 1944	Catalina '14' & '15' Catalina 'G' PV-1 Ventura	USN VP-63 No. 202 Sqn RAF USN VB-127		Plus HMS *Anthony* and HMS *Wishart* Strait of Gibraltar.
U-801	IXC/40	17 March 1944	Avengers	VC-6 *Block Island*	Lt. C. A. Wooddell Lt. Norman Dowty	Atlantic, South West of Cape Verde
U-1059	VIIF	19 March 1944	TBM Avenger Wildcat FM-2	VC-6 *Block Island*	Lt. Norman Dowty Lt. William H. Cole	Alantic, South West of Cape Verde

U-boat & Type		Date of Attack	Aircraft	Squadron	Pilot	Remarks
U-515	IXC	9 April 1944	TBF Avengers	USS *Guadacanal*		Atlantic, North of Madeira.
U-68	IXC	10 April 1944	2 x Avengers F4F Wildcat	USS *Guadacanal*		Atlantic, North West of Madeira
U-860	IXD2	15 June 1944	3 x Wildcats 2 x Avengers	VC-9 *CVE Solomons*	Lt. William F. Chamberlain Ensign George E. Edwards	South Atlantic, South of St Helena
U-543	IXC/40	2 July 1944	Avenger	VC-58 USS *Bogue*	Ensign Frederick L. Moore	Atlantic, Soth West of Tenerife
U-872	IXD2	29 July 1944		USAAF raid		Baltic, Bremen
U-890	IXC/40	29 July 1944		USAAF raid		Baltic, Bremen
U-891	IXC/40	29 July 1944		USAAF raid		Baltic, Bremen
U-892	IXC/40	29 July 1944		USAAF raid		Baltic, Bremen
U-1229	IXC	20 Auguast 1944	3 x TBM Avengers 2 x FM Avengers	VC-42 USS *Bogue*	Lt. A. X. Brokas'	Atlantic, South East of Newfoundland
U-863	IXD2	29 September 1944	Liberator	USN VB-107		Atlantic off Ascension Island
U-1062	VIIF	30 September 1944	Avengers	VC-36 Escort Carrier *Mission Bay*		This was the last U-boat "kill" by CVE Groups in the Atlantic until April 1945
U-906	VIIC	31 December 1944		USAAF raid also sank a number of boats under construction, including —	U-908, U-1011, U-1012 U-2530, U-2535, U-2537	North Sea, Hamburg.
U-3007	XXI	24 February 1944		USAAF raid		Baltic, Bremen
U-3036	XXI	3 March 1945	Boeing B-17	US 8th Air Force		Baltic, Bremen
U-3508	XXI	4 March 1945	B-24 Liberator	US 8th Air Force		North Sea, Wilhelmshaven
U-681	VIIC	11 March 1945	Liberator 'N'	USN VP-103	Lt. R. N. Field	English Channel
U-2515	XXI	11 March 1945		US 8th AF raid		North Sea, Hamburg
U-96	VIIC	30 March 1945	B-24 Liberator	US 8th AF raid		North Sea Wilhemshaven
U-329	VIIC	30 March 1945	Boeing B-17	US 8th AF raid		Baltic Bremen
U-429	VIIC	30 March 1945	B-24 Liberator	US 8th AF raid		North Sea Wilhemshaven
U-430	VIIC	30 March 1945	Boeing B-17	US 8th AF raid		Baltic, Bremen
U-870	IXC/40	30 March 1945	Boeing B-17	US 8th AF raid		Baltic, Bremen
U-884	IXD2	30 March 1945	Boeing B-17	US 8th AF raid		Baltic, Bremen
U-1167	VIIC/41	30 March 1945	Boeing B-17	US 8th AF raid		North Sea, Hamburg
U-2340	XXIII	30 March 1945	Boeing B-17	US 8th AF raid		North Sea, Hamburg
U-3042	XXI	30 March 1945	Boeing B-17	US 8th AF raid		Baltic, Bremen
U-3043	XXI	30 March 1945	Boeing B-17	US 8th AF raid		Baltic, Bremen
U-747	VIIC	1 April 1945		USAAF raid		North Sea, Hamburg
U-2542	XXI	3 April 1945		USAAF raid		Baltic, Kiel
U-3505	XXI	3 April 1945		USAAF raid		Baltic, Kiel
U-237	VIIC	4 April 1945		USAAF raid		Baltic, Kiel
U-749	VIIC	4 April 1945		USAAF raid		Baltic, Kiel
U-3003	XXI	4 April 1945		USAAF raid		Baltic, Kiel
U-982	VIIC	9 April 1945		USAAF raid		North Sea, Hamburg
U-4708	XXIII	9 April 1945		USAAF raid		Baltic, Kiel
U-326	VIIC	25 April 1945	Liberator 'K'	USN VP-103	Lt. Dwight D. Nott USNR	Atlantic, South West of Ushant
U-1107	VIIC/41	30 April 1945	Catalina 'R'	USN VP-63	Lt. F. G. Lake	Atlantic, West of Ushant

Photo   Martin PBM-3C Mariner

Photos - General Motors TBM Avenger

Grumman F4F-4 Wildcat

APPENDIX III.   Main German Operational U-boat Types, WW II.

Type VII
The Type VII was the largest class of submarine ever to be built by any country. They were built by a large number of different shipyards, therefore there was a large number of variations on the basic design. In addition a large number were modified giving rise to a number of new designations. As for example the Type VIID with mine shafts aft of the conning tower and the Type VIIF, which was intended as a transport vessel to carry torpedoes and mines for re-supply at sea.

Crew: *4 Officers, 40-56 men*
Displacement: surfaced 770 tonnes, submerged 1,040 tonnes
Dimensions :   Length: 66.5m ; Beam 6.2m ; Depth 4.7m
Performance : Max Speed: surfaced 17 knots, submerged 7.5 knots

Operational Radius : at high speed 3,300 sea miles
                        at cruise (10 knots) 8,500 sea miles (could be extended to 9,500)
                        submerged at 4 knots, 80 sea miles

Weapons :   Torpedo tubes: Bows 4 ; Stern 1 (some boats had the stern tubes welded shut)
Torpedos carried : 14 (later 12)
Guns :   1 x 88mm (250 rounds), 1 x 20mm anti-aircraft (4,400 rounds) - increased from 1942.

Total Builds :   Type VIIA (10) ; Type VIIB (24) ; Type VIIC (over 600) ; Type VIIC/41 included in VIIC
                     Type VIID (6) ; Type VIIF (4).

Type IX
The Type IX was a large ocean-going long-range patrol submarine, which when modified as IXDI and IXD2 became VLR, capable of covering up to 32,000 sea miles at 10 knots.

Crew: 4 Officers, 44-51 men
Displacement: surfaced 1,120 tonnes, submerged 1,430 tonnes
Dimensions :   Length: 76.5m ; Beam 6.8m ; Depth 4.7m
Performance : Max Speed: surfaced 18 knots, submerged 7.0 knots

Operational Radius : at high speed 5,000 sea miles
                        at cruise (10 knots) 13,500 sea miles
                        submerged at 4 knots, 65 sea miles

Weapons :   Torpedo tubes: Bows 4 ; Stern 2
Torpedos carried : 22
Guns :   1 x 105mm (200 rounds), 1 x 37mm anti-aircraft (575 rounds), 1 x AA 20mm (2,000 rds)

Total Builds :   Type IXA (8) ; Type IXB (14) ; Type IXC & IXC/41 (143)
                     Type IXD1 (2) ; Type IXD2 (30).

Type XB

The Type XB was a special mine-layer with free-flooding mine shafts in the bow and smaller shafts along both sides of the hull. The shafts along the sides held the torpedo mines while the free-flooding shafts accommodated the especially large submarine torpedoes. But by the time this new much larger type of boat became operational the task of approaching harbours to lay mines had become to risky due to the patrolling Coastal Command "strike wings", and most of these submarines were used instead, as supply boats.

Crew: 5 Officers, 47 men
Displacement: surfaced 1,763 tonnes, submerged 2,710 tonnes
Dimensions :   Length: 89.8m ; Beam 9.2m ; Depth 4.7m
Performance : Max Speed: surfaced 17 knots, submerged 7.0 knots

Operational Radius : at high speed 6,500 sea miles
                            at cruise (10 knots) 18,500 sea miles
                            submerged at 4 knots, 80 sea miles

Weapons :   Torpedo tubes: Bows 0 ; Stern 2
Guns :   1 x 105mm (200 rounds), 1 x 37mm anti-aircraft (2,500 rounds), 1x 20mm (2,000) AA

Total commissioned : (8)

Type XIV

The Type XIV was a purpose built supply boat capable of carrying some 650 tons of fuel. It had a range similar to the Type IXC and carried sufficent spare fuel to fill four Type VIIs. But by the time these boats became operational Bletchley Park was again on top of the U-boat W/T codes and although the *Kriegsmarine* went to great lengths to disguise the cruise distinations of these vunerable but essential refuellers, many were soon sunk.

Crew: 6 Officers, 47 men
Displacement: surfaced 1,688 tonnes, submerged 2,300 tonnes
Dimensions :   Length: 67.1m ; Beam 9.4m ; Depth 6.5m
Performance : Max Speed: surfaced 15 knots, submerged 7.0 knots

Operational Radius : at high speed (14 knots) 5,500 sea miles
                            at cruise (10 knots) 12,000 sea miles
                            submerged at 4 knots, 80 sea miles

Weapons :   Torpedo tubes: none
Guns :   1-2 x 37mm anti-aircraft (2,500 rounds), 1x 20mm (4,000) AA

Total commissioned : (10)

Type XXI
This was a new revolutionary design introduced towards the end of the war. Its hull was constructed in two roughly circular sections, with the lower section containing many batteries to give a high submerged speed. It was intended the Type XXI should replace all the Type VIIs and IXs that had survived the Atlantic Sea War so far, but only two saw operational service before the wars end.

Crew: *5 Officers, 52 men*
Displacement: surfaced 1,621 tonnes, submerged 2,100 tonnes
Dimensions :   Length: 76.7m ; Beam 8.0m ; Depth 6.3m
Performance : Max Speed: surfaced 15.6 knots, submerged 16.8 knots

Operational Radius : at high speed (15 knots) 5,100 sea miles
at cruise (10 knots) 15,500 sea miles
submerged at 10 knots, 110 sea miles

Weapons :   Torpedo tubes: Bows 6 ; Stern 0
Guns :   1 x 20mm twin anti-aircraft (16,000 rounds), with provision for heavier calibre guns.

Total commissioned : (120)

Type XXIII
These were also of revolutionary design, being small electro-boats with a large number of batteries for very fast underwater operation. They were very small and cramped. The torpedos had to be loaded from the outside and no spares could be carried. At one time it was thought some had been fitted with jet engines but this was later found to be untrue. It fact the high-underwater speeds were achieved by the diminished size and a high number of batteries powering conventional propellers.

Crew: *2 Officers, 12 men*
Displacement: surfaced 243 tonnes, submerged 275 tonnes
Dimensions :   Length: 34.5m ; Beam 3.0m ; Depth 3.7m
Performance : Max Speed: surfaced 10 knots, submerged 12.5 knots

Operational Radius : at high speed (8 knots) 2,600 sea miles
at cruise (6 knots) 4,450 sea miles
submerged at 10 knots, 35 sea miles or at 4 knots 194 sea miles

Weapons :   Torpedo tubes: Bows 2 ; Stern 0
Torpedoes carried : (2)
Guns :   none

Total commissioned : (60)

Only six sailed operationally before the wars end. U-2321, U-2322, U-2324, U-2326, U-2329 and U-2336.
Already with a number of successes ("kills), for one loss U-2324 to a mine on 26 December, 1944 in the Baltic,
North of Swindermünde.

APPENDIX IV. Losses of airplane deliveries at sea, en-route the UK from the United States.
It is common knowledge British and Allied merchant ships suffered terrible losses carrying vitally needed supplies across the Atlantic as deck cargo. By November 1942, the Germans had 200 U-boats on patrol with a further 170 in training, and Admiral Doenitz was in sight of his target of 300 U-boats operating in the Atlantic. Fortunately the tide turned in the Allies favour before this target was reached. By August 1942, aircraft fitted with ASV radar were making it almost impossible for the U-boats to surface and carry out their attacks on Allied merchantmen has they had done previously.

Probably the most disasterous of attacks befell the Russian convoy PQ-17, which sailed from Hvalfiordur, in Iceland, on 27 June 1942, when U-boat packs sank twenty-four out of the convoy's thirty-five merchant ships in the freezing Arctic waters. The loss to the Allies of essential Lend-Lease materials, included 4,246 lorries and gun carriers, 594 tanks and 297 airplanes. It was nothing less than a major disaster.

Summary of losses at sea of deliveries - British Purchasing Committee contracts and Lend-Lease.
Airacobra I Bell   (P-39D) Fighter   —   17 lost at sea en-route to Russia
Airacobra I Bell   (P-39D) Fighter   —   12
Argus I Fairchild Light transport   —   6

Baltimore Martin Light bombers   —   35
Boston III Douglas (DB-7A) bomber —   5

Kittyhawk Mk I/IA Curtiss Fighter-bomber   —   34 lost at sea en-route Australia, New Zealand, South Africa
Kittyhawk Mk II   Curtiss Fighter-bomber —   7
Kittyhawk Mk IV   —   6

Martlett I Grumman   Navy Fighter   —   10
Martlett II Grumman   —   11

Maryland Martin   Recce-bomber   —   5
Mohawk   Curtiss   Fighter   —   4
Mustang I North American   Fighter   —   21

Tomahawk IIB Curtiss G/attack fighter   —   31
Traveller Beechcraft   light transport   —   20 lost at sea SS *Agurmonte* 10 June 1943

Wildcat Grumman   Carrier fighter   —   5

When compared to the losses of convoy PQ-17, the foregoing appear relatively insignificant.

APPENDIX V. Four Coastal Command VCs were won in the war against the U-boats by :

Flying Officer Lloyd A. Trigg, VC, DFC, RNZAF No. 200 Squadron
Having won an earlier DFC for one certain, submarine "kill" and other 'probables' on 11 August, 1943, his Liberator 'D' was brought down over the Atlantic by accurate and heavy return fire after sinking *U-468*. The U-boat put up a barrage of flak which set the aircraft on fire before it began its attack. Trigg could have broken off, but instead held on and dropped six depth-charges with perfect accuracy : the U-boat sinking before the aircraft crashed with the loss of all its crew. U-boat survivors picked up later expressed their admiration for the coolness and courage displayed by the crew of the Liberator, which had pressed home their attack even though the airplane was heavily on fire before crashing into the sea at about 250 mph. It was this evidence that resulted in the posthumous award of the Victoria Cross. Fg Off Trigg being the first pilot awarded the VC engaged in ASW operations, and doubly unique in that the testimony of the survivors was partly instrumental in his securing the award.

Flight Lt. David E. Hornell, VC, RCAF No. 162 Squadron
Flt Lt. Hornell was a member of No. 162 (RCAF) Squadron that had arrived from Yarmouth, Nova Scotia to join Coastal Command in Iceland. On 24 June 1944, flying Canso 'P' (Catalina) serial 9754, Flt Lt. Hornell was returning to his detachment at Wick from patrol after ten hours in the air, when he sighted a surfaced U-boat. As the Canso flying-boat flew in to attack the U-boat (*U-1225*) responded with a barrage of flak which damaged the starboard engine so much, that Hornell had great difficulty in controlling the aircraft. Despite the damage he succeeded in defeating the last minute evasive action taken by the U-boat and dropped four depth-charges. However by now the "Cat" was so badly damaged the starboard engine had fallen off and the wing was on fire and Hornell was force to ditch. This was achieved successfully and the crew of eight with only one small dinghy between them then spent 21 hours in the water, four taking turns to sit in the dinghy, while the other four clung to the sides.

A Catalina of No. 333 (Norwegian) Squadron spotted the men on the 25 June at the same time as about 35 to 40 survivors about two miles away from the U-boat they had sunk. Eventually the German submarine crew succumbed to the cold and drowned as the day progressed. At 11.00 hrs the same day a patrolling Wellington aircraft dropped a lifeboat to the ill-fated Canso crew but they were too cold and exhausted to reach it. Eventually at 15.00 hrs an air-sea-rescue launch picked them up but by this time two had died in the dinghy and unfortunately Flt Lt. Hornell died shortly after rescue. He was awarded for pressing home his attack in the face of concentrated enemy fire, and for his courage and inspiration to the rest of the crew while in the dingy. Hornell was awarded a posthumous Victoria Cross, and one DSO, two DFCs and two DFMs went to the surviving members of the crew.

Flying Officer John A. Cruickshank, VC, RAFVR No 210 Squadron
Attacking *U-347* on 17 July, 1944, flying Catalina 'Y' of No. 210 Squadron, Flying officer Cruickshank, during the run in found he could not release the depth-charges, necessitating a second attack to sink the now alerted U-boat. The submarine now inflicted an enormous amount of damage on the flying-boat, releasing a considerable amount of flak which killed the navigator and four members of the crew. nevertheless Cruickshank pressed home his attack and dropped his depth-charges in a perfect straddle which sank the U-boat. The second pilot Flt. Sgt. Garnett, took over to fly the "Cat" back to Sullom Voe in the Shetlands.

Flt Lt. Cruickshank had refused morphia for his wounds and insisted on moving forward to the cockpit, where he assisted Garnett with the landing before he collapsed having lost so much blood from his 72 wounds being given an emergency transfusion in the aircraft before being removed to hospital.

For his gallantry in carrying out the attack and then refusing medication that would have prevented from landing the aircraft. Flt Lt. Cruickshank was awarded the Victoria Cross - the third awarded to a Coastal Command pilot, surviving the war, as the fourth Air VC of WW II.

Flying Officer K. Campbell VC RAFVR No. 22 Sqaudron
Flying Officer Campbell lost his life in a Beaufort torpedo-bomber attack on the German battlecruiser *Gneisenau* flying at mast height, in the heavily defended Brest harbour on 6 April 1941. Evidence for the citation was supplied by the French resistance.

APPENDIX VI. Government Code & Cypher School (GC & CS : Bletchley Park, Bucks.)

Between the wars, the RAF, for internal communications developed the Typex cypher machine and in 1928, rather ironically two cipher machines marketed by a German Company, *"Enigma Chiffriermaschinen"* *Aktiengesellschaft*, were purchased for examination by the Government's Code and Cypher School. The irony of course, that this was the now famous Enigma machine used by the Germans throughout the war to send out their encrypted messages to their armed forces in WW II.

The British Admiralty, having procured the machines appeared to show little interest in them as little mention is made of them until June, 1934, when Wing Commander O. G. W. G. Lywood, of Air Ministry Signals, became interested in the possibilities of Enigma and asked if he might borrow one of the machines. He received the following reply from the GC & CS :

25th June, 1934

Dear Lywood,

As regards the matter of the Enigma Cypher Machine, I have arranged that you may borrow this machine in order that it may serve as a model for your "engineers".

I feel, however, that I must point out that it is probable that this machine is covered by patents taken out in this country (they may have expired).

It may be advisable, therefore, that you should consult your patent experts before proceeding to make a direct copy of the machine.

Source PRO: AIR 2/2720 (the signature was missing from this original now historical document)

It was soon established that, indeed, the *"Enigma Chiffriermaschinen"* was covered by three British patents taken out by the German company, all of which were still valid. Lywood was advised by the Air Ministry Contracts Directorate:

In view of Section 29 of the Patents and Design Acts, the Air Ministry may by themselves, or by their contractors authorised in writing by them, make or use any patented invention for the service of the Crown, without any licence from the patenter. The department do not require the permission of the inventor to make his invention. (*not in the letter - he would be entitled to payment if an invention covered by a valid patent is used*) The terms for such making and using may be considered after the making or using of the invention. It is suggested that the question of infringement be referred to the branch in order that any payment due to the patentee may be considered, and put on record. Apparently no action to settle the matter could be taken while the apparatus is secret.

Note : the letter was signed "W. J. Pryce for Director of Contracts"; it was dated 2.6.34 — but this is thought to be in error as it is known it was not generated until late June, 1934.

It was on this basis that Wing Commander Lywood and his engineers commenced their work and by 1936, had was what was referred to as "the RAF Enigma". In March, that year the War office, displayed a very definite interest — and soon a Mr Sidney Hole was anxious to know, whether the "RAF Enigma" infringed Patent No. 207257 which he had taken out in February, 1924, for "Improvements in or relating to coding or decoding machines". Air Ministry Contracts was not sure, it admitted that if so, "the action to be taken will require careful consideration", adding:

At the moment the position is that two experimental sets incorporating the R.A.F. Enigma have been completed and are undergoing trial: no decision has yet been reached as regards adoption.

Air Ministry Contracts to the War Office, 24.3.36

Air Ministry Contracts admitted the possibility "of the RAF Enigma infringing patents obtained in the name of *Chiffriermaschinen Akt. Gesell.* "; it recommended War Office to send " a suitable non-committal reply" to Mr Hole. However, the next day Air Ministry Signals, informed Air Ministry Contracts :

The machine made for us was copied from the German "ENIGMA" with additions and alterations suggested by the Government Code and Cypher School.

This admission again raised the question with regards to the German patentees but with the deteriorating relations between Germany and the UK by 1937, the name "Type X" had replaced the "RAF Enigma" nomenclature. Twenty-nine machines had been built in the form described and permission was being sought to build 238 Mk II sets for distribution to lower formats (the War Office had requested 25 for trials). It was admitted *Chiffriermaschinen* Patent No. 267472 was being infringed, and:

"difficulty arises in remunerating the patentees, in the near future at any rate, since this would entail a suggestion that the department is using a cypher apparatus similar in some respects to that to which the patent relates". From this point the question of patent infringement is left in the air, with the conclusion the matter be deferred, "until such time as it is perishable to negotiate with them".

So, from 1939, Typex was in use at all RAF headquarters, providing an effective secure means of communication that remained in completely secure use throughout the war. The Army also used it for communications both at home and overseas, down to divisional level, again with no breach of security. It is all credit to Wg Cdr Lywood that he had the initiative and tenacity against all the odds to see his idea through...

With the outbreak of war it was soon realised something must be done with regards to monitoring German communications traffic, and in February, 1940, Flt Lt. (later Group Captain) Scott Farnie set up the first listening post at Hawkinge, in Kent. This was the invaluable "Y Service", which kept the Germans under constant radio surveillance, undetected throughout the war. Once established the ever increasing traffic demanded fluent German linguist and it was soon decided that women should be recruited for this work as well as men. one of the early recruits was Section Officer Aileen ("Mike") Morris MBE, who related later:

By the end of 1940, the Air Ministry Intelligence had an almost complete picture of the Luftwaffes Order of Battle, particularly in Western Europe. with all this knowledge added to the information that we were amassing at Kingsdown (West Kingsdown near Otford, near Sevenoaks, Kent) about the call signs and frequencies used by the various German squadrons to which we were listening, we were able for instance, to advise No. 11 Group Fighter Command, that the enemy raid that was approaching Beachy Head was probably made up of Me 109s of H/JG 51 based at St Omer. This would be most helpful for the Controllers, who would then be able to anticipate the probable route of the enemy aircraft. Later, when we had direction finding (D/F) facilities, we could pin-point the transmissions and thus knew the exact position of the enemy formation whose messages we were hearing. But even in those early days of the summer of 1940, we could almost certainly confirm the height at which the formations were approaching, and we might also be able to give some indication, from what we were hearing, of their intended action. On occasions it was possible that we would intercept the approaching Germans fighters R/T and it was particularly frustrating at this time there was no means of passing this information through to our own fighters...

At this time the monitoring of all German signals, "whether in low-grade or high-grade cypher, radio-telephony, or non-Morse transmissions, was the responsibility of the Y Service". And utterly dependent upon "Y" was "Station X", Bletchley Park, Bucks, the war station of GC & CS, with its dedicated team of genius that broke the German Enigma codes, thereby endowing the Allies with the priceless gift of Ultra. Indeed throughout the whole of the critical period - of the invasion threat and until the wars end, Ultra availed the British Government the means with which to determine the Germans intentions. Bletchley Park, even in the early days, played its part in the Battle of Britain, allowing Air Marshal Dowding to determine his tactics for the ensuing aerial engagements. Although at this time the amount of information available to BP was limited as with the Luftwaffe operating from closely linked bases in France, Belgium and Holland, the majority of its communications was made directly by land-line - impervious to Ultra. Ironically it was the Luftwaffe who became the most careless and insecure arm of the German Services in the use of the Enigma codes, and it was with the Luftwaffe communications that Bletchley cryptanalysts started their de-ciphers, penetration of enemy ciphers becoming an adjunct to operational effectiveness. At the time Ultra was not in evidence and Dowding was often sent his de-crypts from Bletchley by teleprinter through a Special Liaison Unit located in a sound-proof cubicle next to the Operations Room at Bentley Priory, Fighter Command headquarters in north London. At this time only Dowding and Air Vice-Marshal Keith Park, commanding No. 11 Group Fighter Command were aware of Ultra. But there is no record of what its precise usefulness to them was at this time, as the Command appeared to rely heavily on the Defence Teleprinter Network reserved for the services.

In the Sea War things were profoundly different especially when GC & CS began to read continuously and with little delay the wireless traffic (W/T) in the Home Water (*Heimisch*) setting of the German naval Enigma that were common, as yet, to the entire German surface navy in the Atlantic area and to the U-boats. GC & CS's first substantial break into these settings had come in the second half of March, 1941, when it read the traffic for February. By 10 May, it had read most of the traffic for April. The traffic for the month of May was read with a delay of between three and seven days. The most critical German ciphers, such as 'Hydra' were penetrated in June, 1941. It was at this time also that Bletchley Park had the good fortune to receive a German Enigma machine and code books captured from the surfaced submarine *U-110*, by an armed boarding party under the command of Sub-Lt. David Balme. The capture of the Enigma machine was pure chance, as it was only by chance, that one of the boarding party gathering the charts code-books and documents thinking it was just a typewriter, on pressing the keys and getting some strange results; he sent it up the hatch. When the U-boat *Kapitänleutnant* Jockel Hoppe realised what had happened it is believed he committed suicide... The Official War Office History, relates:

"yielded the short-signal code-books, which enabled GC &CS to read from May onwards the Kurzsignale, the short signals in which the U-boats transmitted their sighting reports and weather information. Captures (from other sources such as German trawlers etc) enabled GC & CS to read all the traffic for June and July, including "officer-only" signals. By the beginning of August it finally established its mastery over the Home Waters settings, a mastery which enabled it to read the whole traffic for the rest of the war except for occasional days in the second half of 1941, with little delay. The maximum delay was 72 hours and the normal was much less, often only a few hours.

The ultimate result of this new situation was that it "shifted the U-boat war into a new dimension. At last insight was possible into the whole life-cycle of a U-boat... Months, indeed years had to pass before the Tracking Room could claim with justice, to know more about U-boat deployments than Admiral Doenitz's own staff, but the summer of 1941, is the point Bletchley moved this process from the realm of guess-work into that of increasing authority.

Knowledge of U-boat movements and positions, derived from Ultra, enabled the Admiralty to re-route convoys from U-boat operational patrol areas. The realisation by British Intelligence of the importance of these developments in 1941 at Bletchley with regard to the Enigma codes, that from June, 1941, so as not to alert the Germans, that the code had been cracked, orders were given that no operations for the special purposes of capturing naval Engima material should be undertaken in case of alarming the enemy, should it compromise the fact that GC & CS had now mastered the code. Unfortunately not for long as on the 1 February, 1942, the U-boat Command added a fourth wheel to the Enigma machine for the communications of its Atlantic and Mediterranean U-boats, and this although devised for their own internal security, meant GC & CS were now unable except for occasional days to solve the U-boat settings, until the end of the year. It was this coupled to the fact that Admiral Doenitz now concentrated his U-boat fleet off the east coast of America that saw a massive rise in shipping losses in the first half of 1942. Which despite continuous improvements in Allied defences and resources saw no significant decline in U-boat successes until the beginning of 1943.

Just how bad the situation had become can be observed from the following figures :
In the first three months of 1942, total sinkings amounted to 834,164 tons with 537,980 attributed to U-boats (over 64%). The worst monthly total was in June, 1942, with 834,196 tons lost, 623,545 in the North Atlantic, and no less than 700,235 by U-boats (nearly 84%). But the largest contribution was in November : 729,160 tons out of a total of 807,754 (over 90%). Admiral Doenitz was well pleased at this juncture with his decision to concentrate his fleet on the American Atlantic coastline.

Fortunately in December, 1942, GC & CS reported it had broken the Enigma four-wheel key. The significance of which many historians believe was the explanation for the ultimate victory over the U-boat menace that was soon to follow. Obviously the Admiralty, at the time, was to say the least deeply relieved at the breakthrough; it knowing only too well the importance the decrypts of the German U-Boat Command communications was to Allied anti-U-boat operations.

APPENDIX VII.   Coastal Command WW II associated establishments and units.

Unit	Location & Date formed	Responsible for :-	Aircraft types used	Other details
Coastal Command Anti-Boat Devices School	Limavady 20 April 1945		Vickers Wellington VIII	Formed by redesignating Loran Training Unit. Disbanded 25 Aug 45
Coastal Command Communication Sqn/Flt. Coastal Command	1 May 1944 Northolt 7 April, 1945 Leavesden	Comms.	D.H Rapide, Master, Avro Anson Dominie, Oxford, Hudson	Disbanded at Leavesden 1 May, 1946.
Coastal Development Development Unit	30 December, 1940 Carew Cheriton	Air/Sea Warfare technical developments	Various	Disbanded 1 January 1945 at Angle. To Thorney Island as Air/sea Warfare
Coastal Command Fighter Affilation Training Unit	1 September, 1945 Langham		Vengeance IV, Martinet Queen Martinet Hurricane IIC	Disbanded 21 February 1946, Chivenor, Devon
Coastal Command Circus Fighter	15 March, 1944 Gosport		Spitfire	Disbanded 1 Sep 1945 at Thorney Island Became CCFATU
Coastal Command Flying Instructors School Coastal Command Instructors School	23 February 1945 St Angelo 29 October 1945		Master II, Martinet I Beaufort IIA, Mosquito III, Warwick II Wellington X Liberator VIII	Disbanded 1 April 1946. at Tain
Coastal Command Landplane Pilots Pool	1 November 1939 Silloth		Anson I, Hudson I, Beaufort I Wellington I	Disbanded 1 April 1940 Silloth. Became 1 OTU
Coastal Command Tactical Development Unit	22 October 1940 Carew Cheriton		Whitley V, Hudson I, Beaufort I, Wellington IA	Disbanded 30 December, 1940. Became Coastal Command Development
No. 1 (Coastal) OTU det Flight	Silloth 1 April 1940 Beaulieu Aldergrove Sept 1943		Various Liberator (10)	Disbanded 19 Oct 1943 Absorbed into No. 1674 HCU
No. 1674 Heavy Conversion Unit (HCU)	10 October, 1943 Longtown 19 Oct. 43	Training pilots and crews	All Marks of Coastal Command Liberators	Disbanded November 1945
1 (Coastal) Engine Control Demonstration Unit	19 October, 1943 Longtown		Vickers Wellington	Formed within 1674 HCU Disbanded 17 June 1944 at Angle became Engine
No. 111 (Coastal) OTU	20 August 1942 Oaks Field & Windsor Field, Nassau, Bahamas	Initially : Conversion training of crews from Commonwealth Air Training Plan	NA Mitchell I, II, III Liberator III, GR.5, 6, 8 Wellington XIV Halifax III. Also used Bermuda I, Gosling I Oxford I, Mosquito PR.35	From Feb 1943 trained GR Captains & crews for all RAF maritime patrol units world-wide Disbanded 21 May 1946 Lossiemouth, Scotland
No. 4 (Coastal) OTU	16 March 1941 Stranraer, Scotland formerly the Flying-Boat		Various	Disbanded 31 July 1947 at Pembroke Dock to become No.225 OCU

Bibliography :

Armitage Michael.	The Royal Air Force, Arms & Armour, London, 1995.
	Aviation Magazines & Periodicals. Various.
Meekcoms K. J.	The British Air Commission and Lend-Lease, Air Britain, London, 2000
Dancey Peter.	Personal Archives
Halley James.	The Squadrons of the Royal Air Force & Commonwealth, Air Britain, London, 1988.
Jane's	All The World's Aircraft 1945, Harper Collin's, London, Reprint 1996
Jak P. Mallmann Showell.	U-boat Commanders and Crews 1935-45. Crowood, Marlborough, Wilts, 1998
Kemp Paul.	U-boats Destroyed, Arms & Armour, London, 1999.
Lake Alan.	Flying Units of the RAF, Airlife, England, 1999
Lee Asher	Air Power, Duckworth, London, 1957
Lewis Peter. (Sqn Ldr)	Squadron Histories, Putnam, London, 1959.
	Public Record Office, London.
	RAF Golden Jubilee Souvenir Book, RAFBF Publishing, London, 1968.
Richards Denis	Royal Air Force 1939-45 Vol I. The Flight At Odds. HMSO. London, 1953
Robertson Bruce.	British Military Aircraft Serials, 1912 - 1966. Ian Allan, London, 1967
Robinson Anthony.	Dictionary of Aviation, Orbis Publishing Ltd., London, 1984
Terraine John.	The Right Of The Line, Sceptre, London, 1988
Thetford Owen.	Aircraft of the Royal Air Force since 1918, Putnam, London, 1988